S B
SIMPLIFIED BOOK-KEEPING
FOR SMALL BUSINESSES

Geoffrey Whitehead, B.Sc. (Econ.)

Formerly Senior Lecturer and
Head of Professional Studies Division
Thurrock Technical College
Essex

George Vyner Ltd.

By the same author

Published by George Vyner Ltd., Holmfirth, Huddersfield
The Class Teacher's Record Book
The Subject Teacher's Record Book
The Head of Department's Record Book
The Class Teacher's Lesson Preparation Book
The Subject Teacher's Lesson Preparation Book
Working for Yourself is *also* a Career
Choosing Options for Your Future in the World of Work
Self-employment *not* Unemployment

Published by John Murray Ltd., (Success Studybooks)
Success in Principles of Accounting
Success in Principles of Accounting (Answer Book)
Success in Business Calculations
Success in Accounting and Costing (with Answer Book)

Published by Heinemann Professional Publishing Ltd., (Made Simple Series)
Book-keeping Made Simple
Business and Enterprise Studies Made Simple
Commerce Made Simple
Economics Made Simple
Office Practice Made Simple
Secretarial Practice Made Simple
Business Law Made Simple
Elements of Banking Made Simple

Published by Shaw and Sons Ltd.,
Test yourself on the Highway Code
Professional Competence for Road Haulage Operators (with David Spurling)
Test Yourself on Road Haulage Operation (CPC) (with David Spurling)

Geoffrey Whitehead 1978

2nd Edition *(Revised and enlarged)* 1981
Reprinted and updated 1982, 1986 and 1987
3rd Edition *(Revised and enlarged)* 1991

PO 3485

ISBN 0 906628 05 9

Printed in Great Britain by Garnett Dickinson Print Limited, Rotherham and London

Some firms which supply useful information or services

For the Simplex System of Book-keeping:
  George Vyner Ltd. (Ref. S.B.S.B.)
  P.O. Box No. 1
  Holmfirth
  Huddersfield
  HD7 2RP

For: *Croner's Reference Book for Employers*
     Croner's Reference Book for the Self-Employed
  Croner Publications Ltd. (Ref. S.B.S.B.)
  Croner House
  173 Kingston Road
  New Malden
  Surrey KT3 3SS

For advice on Capital Transfer Tax mitigation schemes, through life assurance, and for Pension schemes and all financial planning:
  James Lemon FLIA
  23 Mulberry Close
  Cambridge
  CB4 2AS
  (0223) 358003

For the *'Money Which' Tax Savings Guide*
  Consumers Association
  14 Buckingham Street
  London WC2N 6DS

For advice on the formation of companies and the purchase of ready made companies:
  Natcom Services,
  46 St. Mary's Street,
  Ely,
  Cambs.,
  CB7 4EY
  (0353) 722460

For *Taxation Simplified* and *Smith's Taxation*
  Lofthouse Publications
  29 Ropergate,
  Pontefract,
  West Yorkshire,
  WF8 1LG
  (0977) 701315

Foreword

The owner of a small business has no time for elaborate systems of book-keeping, yet it is essential to keep clear, accurate accounts. We must be able to see easily whether the business is making a profit or loss so that future activities can be planned. We must also be able to produce, at any given time, the exact figures the law demands, especially for tax and VAT purposes.

The aim of this book is to give such business proprietors general basic guidance on the principles of book-keeping for their enterprise, and to offer them a specific system which can be adapted to any kind of business, whether trading, manufacturing or servicing.

George Vyner Ltd's Simplex System is the original simple system of book-keeping and has been refined over the years to meet the needs of all types of businesses. It is relatively inexpensive; is stocked by most leading bookshops and stationers and offers a free advice service to those who find difficulty in using the system. It is used by so many businessmen that regular reprints are necessary, so that changes in legal requirements etc, can be quickly taken into account.

In this book I have referred to a number of organisations and firms which offer services to the owners of small business. I have listed their addresses in the prelims at the front of the book, and would like to thank them for their cooperation at various stages. I would particularly like to thank Brian Senior of George Vyner Ltd. for his help and advice throughout the project.

Every effort has been made to check the accuracy of statements made in this book, but both the author and the publishers must make it clear that they cannot be held liable for possible misunderstandings or errors arising from the use of the book. We are not professional lawyers or accountants, who should always be consulted on complex matters.

Geoffrey Whitehead

Special Foreword to Teachers and College Lecturers

The Simplex System makes an ideal, practical exercise for pupils and students of all ages and all abilities. For those with a knowledge of double-entry book-keeping it shows how short-cuts may be taken with the double-entry system without destroying its underlying principles of sound record-keeping. The best time to present a module of Simplex book-keeping is the pre-Christmas and pre-Easter period when classes tend to be restless and seek something different, but which is also practical and educationally valuable. After such a module students return to their 'double-entry' with heightened interest and understanding. For those intending to take up a career in accountancy it is a useful introduction to a system many of them will spend their lives auditing.

For many pupils who show an independence of spirit, which leads teachers to conclude that they may themselves set up small businesses, the system is of great interest, while its very simplicity appeals to even the weakest of pupils, who only need to be able to add up money to keep perfect records.

While the exercises in this book may be enough for ordinary school or college purposes George Vyner Ltd. are prepared to send without charge exercises and working pages to teachers and lecturers wishing to present a Simplex Module. Please write to George Vyner Ltd., Freepost, Holmfirth, Huddersfield HD7 1BR, giving the number of students for whom working papers are required. A comprehensive 'Answers' section is also provided and students can check their own work.

Geoffrey Whitehead

Contents

Chapter One

The Accounting Requirements of the Small Business

1.1 Introduction

The owner of the small business requires a system of book-keeping which displays the following characteristics:

(a) It should be simple.
(b) It should require as few books as possible.
(c) It should not take up too much time.
(d) It should satisfy the tax inspector and the VAT officer without major help from a professional accountant.
(e) It should comply with the Companies Acts, where appropriate.
(f) It should enable the owner to judge the success of the business.

(a) Simplicity

The system adopted must be very simple, for the proprietor of a small business usually has to keep the books personally with little if any assistance from professional accountants. He/she may of course employ a book-keeper, but even that person does not want to keep a full set of books or follow a complete system of double-entry book-keeping. The system needs to be clear enough for the books to be kept properly even by a person who has no previous knowledge of accounting.

(b) As Few Books as Possible

Ideally only one book should be needed. However, it is usual in most systems to keep a separate Wages Book if there are employees, and there are advantages in having a separate book for Value Added Tax.

(c) The Time Required must be Small

Book-keeping records in most small businesses can only receive attention at odd moments when there are no more pressing problems to be dealt with. This means that the system should be based on separate entries, with as little as possible 'carried forward' from one day to the next, or one week to the next.

(d) Tax Requirements

The system should be sufficiently complete to satisfy the Income Tax authorities that it is a proper record, carefully and honestly kept. It should enable the proprietors to prepare their own Trading Account and Profit and Loss Account, without any real need to send the records to an accountant, though of course an accountant may be used if preferred. The proprietors must be able to answer any questions by the local inspector of taxes so that tax assessments can be agreed quickly and confidently. With regard to Value Added Tax, the book-keeping system must meet the requirements of the Customs & Excise authorities, and satisfy any inspection they may make to ensure that proper records are being kept.

(e) Compliance with the Companies Acts

If the firm is a company the book-keeping records must be adequate for the purposes of the Companies Acts 1985-89.

There are two kinds of company: the public company and the private company. The shares of important public companies may be bought and sold on the Stock Exchange. Public companies must keep a full set of book-keeping records, but their methods need not concern us in our study of small-business accounting. Private companies, of which there are over half a million in Britain, may not sell shares to the general public. Many of these companies are very small, with less than £1 000 of capital. Such private companies should find the simple systems of book-keeping described in this book quite adequate for their needs, but under the Acts they must have their books audited by a professional accountant.

(f) Judging the Efficiency of the Business

The astute businessperson will want to know how the business compares (i) this week with last week, (ii) this quarter with last quarter, (iii) this year with last year and (iv) with other investment possibilities. The owner of a shop or other small business who works sixteen hours a day for 362 days a year and is left with a profit smaller than he/she could earn as a bus conductor, a builder's labourer or a secretary is clearly wasting his/her time. Such people need to know this, and—with a little guidance from this textbook—the system used should enable them to judge their true business situation.

1.2 The Simplex System of Book-keeping

Many firms now offer simple systems of book-keeping for the small business. The system described in this book is known as the 'Simplex' system, and its copyright is held by George Vyner Ltd. This system has been selected because it is up to date, particularly easy to follow, and well suited to the needs of the small business.

The Simplex system consists of the Simplex D Account Book, with 52 weekly record pages, one for every week of the year. In addition, about ten further pages, which may be described as analysis pages, enable the proprietor to analyse receipts and expenses weekly, to add up useful quarterly totals and to obtain from these quarterly totals annual figures. A set of final accounts prepared from the annual figures reveal the profit for the year. These records may then be submitted to the tax inspector, and are adequate for tax purposes. Alternatively they may be submitted to an accountant, but the efficiency of the records will mean the accountant can readily check them and submit them without delay to the Inland Revenue Department.

Two further books—a Wages Book (if there are employees to be paid) and a VAT record book—are also available. An explanation of what is necessary to change over from an existing system of book-keeping to the Simplex system is given in Section 4.7.

Although the Simplex D (the D stands for Schedule D) Account Book is adequate for all types of businesses, George Vyner Ltd. have prepared special books for the Licensing trade (the Simplex Licensees' Account Book) and for farmers (the Simplex Everall Farm Account Book). These books are described in later chapters of this book.

1.3 Separating Business Accounts from Private Accounts

A problem which applies more to the small business than to the larger firm is that of distinguishing between business moneys and one's own private finances. Difficulties are bound to arise sooner or later unless two distinct sets of records are kept.

It is very desirable to have two separate bank accounts: one for personal cheques and one for business transactions. This may of course result in additional bank charges, but the extra cost is justified by the advantages.

1.4 Professional Accountancy Services

Although many proprietors successfully prepare their own final accounts using the Simplex System, and mention has been made that professional accountancy services are not required for routine book-keeping there are of course many matters for which specialist advice may be necessary. In particular the provision of pensions for the small businessman, and provision for Inheritance Tax, cannot be arranged without considering alternative schemes and seeking professional financial advice.

1.5 Exercises in Simplex Book-keeping

Business people wishing to get used to the Simplex System before starting up in business, and schools and colleges who wish to teach this simple type of accounting will find at the end of each chapter exercises to give practice in the use of the Simplex rulings. These may be entered in a Simplex D Account Book purchased especially for that purpose. For schools and colleges special arrangements are made. Please see the Foreword of the book.

Chapter Two
'Cash Flows' through the Small Business

2.1 What are 'Cash Flows'?

Before any business can operate successfully, cash must flow in; it may be in the form of capital contributions by the proprietor, or it may be borrowings made by the proprietor from a bank, building society, finance company or similar institution. Cash must flow out whenever stock is purchased or running expenses are met by the proprietor.

An accounting system, however simple, must record these 'cash flows', and enable the proprietor to compare the current cash flows with those of previous periods. Furthermore, the proprietor needs to see from these figures just how well the actual cash flows compared with the estimates he may have made when planning his present activities. A proprietor who 'budgets' ahead, and then compares actual costs and takings with the budgeted figures, is likely to discover adverse price movements (and perhaps pilfering or theft from the till) more quickly than the competitor who fails to make such estimates.

Cash flows may be divided into *(a)* cash inflows, *(b)* cash outflows and *(c)* turnover flows.

(a) Cash Inflows

This heading covers such items as:
- (i) capital contributions by the proprietor;
- (ii) bank loans;
- (iii) mortgages;
- (iv) loans from finance houses, money-lenders, etc.;
- (v) inflows from services rendered, e.g. rent received and commission received.

(b) Cash Outflows

The typical outflows of cash from a small business are:
- (i) payments for the purchase of capital assets;
- (ii) payments for the purchase of consumables, e.g. stationery and wrapping materials;
- (iii) running expenses, wages, rent, rates, petrol and oil, etc.;
- (iv) drawings by the proprietor (to support his/her personal household);
- (v) tax payments to the Inland Revenue and Customs & Excise authorities.

(c) Turnover Flows

Here we include:

(i) outflows as stock in trade is purchased for resale later;

(ii) inflows when goods are sold for cash;

(iii) inflows when customers, previously supplied with goods on credit, settle their debts;

(iv) where a business is a manufacturing business the arrangements are slightly different. Instead of outflows as stock-in-trade is purchased for resale later, we now have outflows for the purchase of raw materials and components which will be made up into our finished product for re-sale. We may also have outflows for factory overheads. We may regard these as all being turnover flows, since without them turnover would not be possible. We have to manufacture before we can sell!

Fig 2.1 illustrates these cash flows diagrammatically. Each type is considered in more detail in later chapters when we tackle the problem of recording the flows in the book-keeping records.

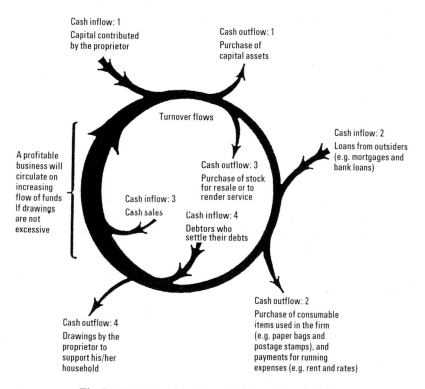

Fig. 2.1 *Cash flows in and out of the small business*

2.2 Adverse Effects on Cash Flows

An adverse effect on cash flows is anything that causes a cash flow *into* the business to be *reduced* for some reason, or a cash flow *out* of the business to be *increased* for some reason.

These adverse effects may be direct or indirect. A direct effect is one which operates on the cash itself. An indirect effect operates on the goods or assets of the business. The theft of goods is an example of an indirect effect: the end results is that the goods stolen cannot be sold, and hence cash inflows are reduced.

A business proprietor must always be alert to detect adverse effects on cash flows, and a preliminary list of the major items is given here to indicate areas requiring supervision.

(a) Adverse Effects which operate Directly on the Cash itself

   (i) Burglary, i.e. deliberate theft by outsiders.
  (ii) Theft of cash by the manager.
 (iii) Theft of cash by the staff.
 (iv) Incorrect change being given, either by accident or by design.
  (v) Payment of fraudulent invoices or statements.
 (vi) Payment of incorrect invoices or statements.
(vii) Making-up of wage packets for non-existent employees.

(b) Adverse Effects which operate Indirectly

   (i) Theft of assets.
  (ii) Theft of consumables.
 (iii) Theft of stock by staff.
 (iv) Passing-out of stock (to relatives and friends of staff).
  (v) Shop-lifting.
 (vi) Poor buying, e.g. wastage of perishable stock.
(vii) Excessive breakages, e.g. carelessness in the crockery department.
(viii) Excessive wear and tear on assets, e.g. use of company vehicles for private purposes.
 (ix) Destruction of stock by fire, etc.

At least some of these adverse effects should be discernible from a study of your book-keeping records. Some help in their detection is given later in this book (see pages 191-214), but it is very important to be alert at all times; to look for the assistant who is better dressed, or the manager who is more prosperous, than expected. If someone on the staff 'looks like a million dollars' it may well be *your* $1 000 000 he/she looks like.

2.3 Keeping control of Cash Flows

Besides understanding cash flows in and out of the business we need to have some sort of control system to budget for cash flows and anticipate when cash shortages are likely to develop and cash surpluses are likely to arise (so that they can be invested wisely). The Simplex D Book contains a double-page Cash Flow Forecast to help you keep control of your cash flows. (see Section 25.2)

2.4 Exercises on 'Cash Flows'

1. Explain the term 'cash flow' for the benefit of a young lady who proposes to set up in her local town as a florist. What sort of inflows and outflows of cash must she expect to meet during the first year of business life?
2. Asked by a school leaver what qualifications were needed in retail trade, the careers officer replied 'Honesty'. Why is honesty such an important qualification, and how would a dishonest employee affect 'cash flow' in any business that employed him/her.

Chapter Three
A Week's Accounting Records

3.1 The Simplex Page

Fig 3.1 shows a page from a Simplex account book. The individual parts of this page will be examined in detail later; here it is only intended that the reader should note the layout, and how it is used to record the cash flows discussed in Chapter 2. The illustration given in Fig. 3.1 is necessarily rather small. (The reader who is seriously considering adopting a Simplex system would be well advised to obtain a copy of the Simplex book and to study it in conjunction with the next few Chapters: understanding is much easier when the whole book is available full size.) There are 53 of these weekly pages in the Simplex Account book (since once every seven years we do get 53 weeks in the year).

3.2 Advantages of the Weekly Layout

The most important feature of the Simplex layout is the fact that figures do not need to be carried forward from one week to another, except in the 'Weekly Cash Report' and 'Weekly Bank Report'. Here of course a balance is usually in hand at the end of each week and must be carried forward.

It is a great advantage to have the work of each week kept separate from the work of every other week. It means that you need not carry forward totals of most items from week to week. 'Carrying forward' is a tedious and time-consuming process; moreover, it prevents the records of the current week from being kept until the records of the previous week have been recorded and carried to the current week. Provided that you add up the various columns on the page, check the cash in the till and carry it forward, and carry forward what appears to be the bank figure, no other carrying forward is necessary immediately. All other items, expenses and turnover are carried from the page direct to a final summary at the back of the book. This work can be postponed until an odd minute is available, and at busy times it can be left for several weeks if necessary without any real inconvenience. Readers who have used traditional book-keeping methods, which require records to be carried forward from week to week, will see at once the advantages inherent in the Simplex system.

3.3 A Brief Look at the Various Sections

Each section of the page records a particular activity for a period of one week. These activities may be distinguished as follows.

(a) The 'Receipts' Section

Here are recorded the daily takings for each day of the week, separated off into 'Daily Gross Takings' (cash), (cheques), (credit cards) and 'Other Receipts'.

RECEIPTS					Week No. Commencing:		PAID TO BANK			
Day/Date	Daily Gross Takings			Other Receipts Col 4	Particulars		Cash Col 5	Cheques Col 6	Credit Cards Col 7	TOTAL Col 8
	Cash Col 1	Cheques Col 2	Credit Cards Col 3							
Sun :										
Mon :										
Tues :										
Wed :										
Thur :										
Fri :										
Sat :										
Totals						Totals				

PAYMENTS FOR BUSINESS STOCK

Date or Chq. No.	To Whom Paid	Amount Paid	
		By Cash Col 9	By Cheque Col 10

PAYMENTS OTHER THAN FOR STOCK

Nature of Payment	Amount Paid	
	By Cash Col 11	By Cheque Col 12
Rent		
Rates		
Light and Heat		
Carriage		
Postages		
Paper		
Motor Expenses		
—do—		
Travelling		
Cleaning		
Printing & Stationery		
Repairs & Renewals		
Insurance (Business)		
Advertising		
Telephone		
Sundries		
Wages (Employees)		
Inland Revenue (PAYE + NI)		
Drawings of the Proprietor (see Note 4)		
Drawings – Partner 1		
Drawings – Partner 2		
Drawings – Partner 3		
Capital Items (see Note 3(1))		
—do—		
Totals		

WEEKLY CASH REPORT

	Cash in Hand (as counted) brought forward	
Add {	Gross Weekly Takings (Col 1 + Col 2 + Col 3)	
	Other Receipts (Col 4)	
	Cash Drawn from Bank	
	Total	
Deduct {	Stock Payments (cash)(Col 9)	
	Other Payments (cash)(Col 11)	
	Amount paid to Bank (Col 8)	
	Total	
	Cash Balance on books	
	Cash in hand (as counted) carr. fwd	
	Difference on books (+ or –)	

Totals

WEEKLY BANK REPORT

	Opening Balance brought forward	
Add {	Total Paid to Bank during week (Col 8)	
	Total	
Deduct {	Cash drawn from bank	
	Stock Payments (Col 10)	
	Other Payments (Col 12)	
	Standing Orders/Direct Debits	
	Bank and Interest Charges	
	Total	
	Closing Balance carried forward	

© GEORGE VYNER LTD
COPYRIGHT RESERVED REPRODUCTION OF THIS BOOK IN WHOLE OR IN PART STRICTLY FORBIDDEN.

Fig. 3.1 *Layout of a typical Simplex weekly page*

Week No. 14   **Commencing:** 2ND APRIL 19..

RECEIPTS

Day/Date	Daily Gross Takings Cash Col 1	Cheques Col 2	Credit Cards Col 3	Other Receipts Col 4	Particulars
Sun : 2/4	186 27				
Mon : 3/4	232 44	25 80	19 95	80 00	ENT. ALLOW.
Tues : 4/4	256 26			35 60	TAX REFUND
Wed : 5/4	112 27	12 64		5 48	DEBTOR. P. SMITH
Thur : 6/4	289 85	19 74	41 05		
Fri : 7/4	364 24	26 34			
Sat : 8/4	382 72	62 50	72 95		
Totals	1824 05	147 02	133 95	121 08	

PAID TO BANK

	Cash Col 5	Cheques Col 6	Credit Cards Col 7	TOTAL Col 8
			19 95	19 95
	420 00	66 88		486 88
	520 00	59 72	41 05	619 77
Totals	940 00	125 60	61 00	1126 60

PAYMENTS FOR BUSINESS STOCK

Date or Chq. No.	To Whom Paid	Amount Paid By Cash Col 9	By Cheque Col 10
3/4	J. CONLAN & SONS.	48 50	
3/4	J. BREWER & CO. LTD.		36 50
4/4	A. J. GOOD LTD.		136 85
5/4	J. BROWN & CO. LTD.	33 80	
7/4	F. LIVESEY & CO.	26 70	
7/4	A. NEWCOMBE		86 25
	Totals	109 00	259 60

PAYMENTS OTHER THAN FOR STOCK

Nature of Payment		Amount Paid By Cash Col 11	By Cheque Col 12
Rent		35 00	
Rates			
Light and Heat			63 50
Carriage		9 45	
Postages £1·70 24p. £2·38		4 32	
Paper			27 46
Motor Expenses	PETROL	16 12	
—do—	REPAIRS		86 50
Travelling		7 32	
Cleaning		5 00	
Printing & Stationery			23 20
Repairs & Renewals			15 78
Insurance (Business)			
Advertising			
Telephone			
Sundries		1 05	
Wages (Employees)		65 75	
Inland Revenue (PAYE + NI)			27 96
Drawings of the Proprietor (see Note 4)		95 00	
Drawings – Partner 1			
Drawings – Partner 2			
Drawings – Partner 3			
Capital Items (see Note 3(1))			
—do—			
Totals		229 01	244 40

WEEKLY BANK REPORT

	Opening Balance brought forward		1343 56
Add {	Total Paid to Bank during week (Col 8)		1126 60
	Total		2470 16
	Cash drawn from bank	— —	
	Stock Payments (Col 10)	259 60	
Deduct {	Other Payments (Col 12)	244 40	
	Standing Orders/Direct Debits	— —	
	Bank and Interest Charges	— —	
	Total		504 00
	Closing Balance carried forward		1966 16

WEEKLY CASH REPORT

	Cash in Hand (as counted) brought forward		6 46
	Gross Weekly Takings (Col 1 + Col 2 + Col 3)		2105 02
Add {	Other Receipts (Col 4)		121 08
	Cash Drawn from Bank		
	Total		2232 56
	Stock Payments (cash)(Col 9)	109 00	
Deduct {	Other Payments (cash)(Col 11)	229 01	
	Amount paid to Bank (Col 8)	1126 60	
	Total		1464 61
	Cash Balance on books		767 95
	Cash in hand (as counted) carr. fwd		767 60
	Difference on books (+ or −)	—	· 35

Fig. 3.2 *Entries recorded on the Simplex Weekly Page*

The word 'Gross' indicates that if the trader is registered for VAT the figures are to include the VAT charged to customers (so that some of the money received must in due course be passed on to the VAT officer).

'Daily Gross Takings' would be the cash flowing in from cash sales, i.e. a turnover flow. 'Other Receipts' would be chiefly debts collected, and occasionally rent paid by a sub-tenant, or tax refunds received.

A most important entry under 'Other Receipts' would be the cash or balance in the bank brought in as capital on the day the business commences. What to do at Dawn on Day 1 is explained fully in Chapter 4. For the moment we are simply looking at the layout of the weekly page.

Another type of entry in this column would be loans received from outside bodies such as banks or finance houses, while a fourth type would be 'fees received' or 'commission received'. All such receipts should be entered at once.

The 'Particulars' column enables a short note to be made of any special items received. This is of great help when details of an item are called for at some future date—if, for example, it is queried by an inspector of taxes. Indeed, a brief note here may be self-explanatory to the inspector.

Part of this 'Receipts' section is a 'Paid to Bank' column in which daily payments into the bank are recorded. Whenever cash is banked it must be recorded in the paying-in book, and the amounts paid in are then entered in the 'Paid to Bank' section, and totalled in the end column (Col. 8).

To summarize the 'Receipts' section, we can record each of the cash in-flows shown in Fig. 2.1 as follows:

Table 3.1 Recording cash inflows

Inflow No.	Type of inflow	Column where recorded
1	Capital contribution	'Other Receipts'
2	Loans from outsiders	'Other Receipts'
3	Cash sales received in cash	'Daily Takings (cash)'
4	Cash sales received by cheque	'Daily Takings (cheques)'
5	Cash sales received as credit card vouchers	'Daily Takings (credit cards)'
6	Debts settled by customers	'Other Receipts'
7	Sundry earnings	'Other Receipts'

(b) The 'Payments for Business Stock' Section

In this section we record any payments made to suppliers for goods which are to be resold, or used in the business if it is a service trade. Many of these payments may be made in cash, or by cheque, direct to the carman at the time of delivery. Others will be made at a later date, depending on the creditworthiness of the businessman and the custom of the trade. Usually the credit period is very short in trades where the goods are perishable; it is often longer for durable goods where the rate of turnover is slower.

Many businesses do not buy and sell goods, but instead offer a service. Thus a builder and decorator is not, like a retailer of electrical goods, buying appliances for resale to customers. Instead he buys bricks, lime, sand, paint, paper and other materials which will be embodied in the work done for his customers. All such purchases of stock 'to render a service' must be recorded as 'Payments for Business Stock' and will eventually appear in the Trading Account as one of the expenses to be charged against profits.

Whenever payments are made to suppliers, the name of the supplier is entered in the 'To Whom Paid' column, and the amount is entered in either the 'By Cash' or 'By Cheque' column, according to the method of payment used.

(c) The 'Payments Other than for Stock' Section

This section is used to record all payments other than 'turnover' payments for stock for resale or stock to render a service. Many of the items, such as rent and rates, are listed individually. There is a gap further down the page which separates items which are losses (i.e. expenses) of the business from items that are not. Capital items, for example, are used permanently in the business and cannot be written off the profits except as depreciation. Drawings are not an expense of the business, nor are payments to the Inland Revenue. A more detailed explanation of these items is given later.

Note that if the business is a partnership there is a line available for up to three partners. A special explanation about partnership affairs is given later (see Sections 22.3-22.5).

To summarize these payments sections, we can record each of the cash outflows shown in Fig. 2.1 as follows:

Table 3.2 Recording cash outflows

Outflow No.	Type of outflow	Section where recorded
1	Purchase of assets	Capital items lines (lower section)
2	Consumable items and other expenses	Top part of 'Other Payments' column
3	Purchase of stock for resale or to render service	'Business Stock' column
4	Drawings	Lower part of 'Other Payments' column
5	Tax payments	Inland Revenue line
6	Private payments of the proprietor(s)	Treat as Drawings

(d) The Weekly Bank Report

The Bank Report opens with a balance brought forward from the previous week. To this is added the total paid into the bank during the week, and then various sums spent are deducted. These will all be cheques drawn, either for cash for office use, payments to suppliers or payments for business expenses. There will also be deductions for any standing orders payable by the bank, and for bank charges. These items are explained more fully in Chapter 8.

(e) **The Weekly Cash Report**

The Cash Report begins with a balance of cash brought forward from the previous week. To this is added the weekly takings, any other cash receipts and the cash drawn from the bank (if any). This is then reduced by the amount of cash paid out for goods supplied and for business expenses, and by the total sums banked for the week. The balance of cash in hand is then checked against the till itself to ensure agreement. If the figure according to the Weekly Cash Report differs from the Cash in Hand (as counted) the difference is recorded as a 'difference on books'. This may be a + or a − difference. The Cash in Hand (as counted) is then carried forward to the Weekly Cash Report of the following week as the Opening Balance. Any difference between the calculated book figure and the actual cash in hand would have to be carefully investigated.

There is an important point about any 'difference on books'. If this item appears regularly the Inland Revenue are likely to take the view that it is 'undeclared drawings'. After all, if cash is missing it is your job to find out why. Are staff stealing the takings? Are they so incompetent that they give wrong change? It is your job to solve these problems. If you do nothing they will conclude you are using the money personally and will add the total missing to your profits and tax it as profit you have taken as drawings, but not declared.

Some examples of the entries necessary to record all these receipts and payments are given in Fig. 3.2 (see page 10).

3.4 Conclusion

Each of the sections listed above is dealt with in detail in a special chapter (Chapters 5 to 8). The main point of the Simplex layout is its simplicity in recording every financial aspect of the business (except the VAT commitments) on a single page each week. Special arrangements for dealing with VAT are discussed in chapter 18.

Before looking at the detailed arrangements for these weekly page records we must learn what to do at Dawn on Day 1 (i.e. the moment that the business starts up, or changes over to the Simplex System).

3.5 Exercises on the Layout of a Simplex Page

1. Write a sentence or two about each of the items listed below saying where you would record it on the Simplex page.
    (a) Cash takings of £495.65 on Wednesday, 3rd July.
    (b) Cash takings of £672.50, takings by cheque of £38.75 and credit card takings of £396.50 on Friday, 5th July.
    (c) Goods delivered from Wholesale Supplies Ltd., for £395.60, which you paid for by giving a cheque to the delivery man on 4th July.
    (d) Payment of a month's rent, by cheque, £420.00 on 3rd July, by post.
    (e) Payment of income tax to the Inland Revenue on July 5th, £1 728.50.

2. Write a sentence or two about each of the items listed below saying where you would record it on the Simplex page, and how much the entry would be.

(a) On Monday, August 4th the till totals £326.50. There was a £20 float in the till at the start of the day. Cash was £185.40, cheques £49.25 and credit card sales £91.85.

(b) A delivery man delivers goods valued at £482. You return him packing cases on which there is a £24.80 refund, and the balance is paid by cheque to the delivery man.

(c) The delivery man, whose lunchtime is due, agrees to help you move some heavy stock. You give him £4 to pay for his lunch.

(d) The V.A.T. Account for the quarter £3 758.60 is paid by cheque to H.M. Customs.

(e) £220 is paid for a new till for the shop by cheque.

3. Explain why the Simplex system makes a special point of not carrying figures for receipts, payments for business stock etc., forward from week to week.

Chapter Four

Opening Your Simplex D
Account Book

4.1 Records start at Dawn on Day 1

One of the worst mistakes made by those who start up in business is to overlook the fact that records start from the very first moment that business begins. It is essential to have your accounting system (and your VAT records if you intend to register for VAT) ready to go from Day 1, for those little pieces of paper that are so vital for proper records begin to arrive immediately.

Every transaction begins with a document of some sort, an invoice or a credit note or a till receipt or some other piece of paper. Unless you have some system to record these pieces of paper immediately (or at least preserve them until the time you have a spare moment to record them) you will be losing vital records. Don't become submerged in production problems, or display problems or marketing problems without first of all having in readiness a system of accounting records and VAT records. Let us consider the practical problems which need solving before Day 1 dawns. Dawn on Day 1 is a crucial moment—we shall see—in the control and management of our affairs. Before you even start, get it fixed into your head that Dawn on Day 1 is a moment to prepare for.

4.2 Preparing for Day 1

We need a proper system of records to be actually in situ when Day 1 begins. The easiest thing of all is to buy a Simplex D Account Book, a Simplex VAT book if we are going to register for VAT and a Simplex Wages Book if we are going to have any employees. If the business we are to run is a public house we could use the Simplex Licensee's Book instead of the Simplex D and the VAT book.

Other essential items are a lever arch file and a concertina file. A lever arch file is the best way to preserve your VAT documents. Since 1985 it is necessary to keep these records for six years, (formerly three years only). If you record each year's records in a Simplex VAT book and have the documents safely filed in a lever arch file—clip the small ones onto sheets of A4 paper with a small stapling machine—you will be able to preserve the records easily, at a total cost of about £8 per year. The concertina file consists of a set of about 30 pockets, all joined together like a concertina. These pockets make it easy to preserve your documents in good order. Have a separate section for each type of document—purchases invoices in one pocket, till receipts in another. Get into the habit of putting each document as it arrives *behind* the others in the file. They will then be in correct date order when you get a spare moment to make your entries.

If you are going to be in retail trade you will need a **till** or tills. This is another item you must have ready for Day 1, so do not delay about obtaining it. If you are not taking over the tills of an existing business see a local office equipment firm and discuss various types of tills with them. Obviously a sophisticated till gives you all sorts of electronic advantages, automatic totalling, analysis of sales activity to show you which lines are selling best, etc., etc. On the other hand they do break down, or are affected by power failures, etc. You want an agreed package of servicing coverage—replacement of faulty tills with a minimum of delay, etc. Take plenty of time weighing up the pros and cons before you place an order and put in writing what you want and the sort of back-up you require. Keep copies of all letters you write as a matter of course.

A **filing cabinet** quickly becomes an essential part of anyone's organisation. You need not only the cabinet itself but a a small supply of files, file guides, etc. Buy one that has a top section which can be locked as a cabinet to keep your account books in, and also has a safety device so that only one drawer can be opened at a time. Filing drawers get very heavy, and if two are pulled out at once they can tip and crush you. Always put the heaviest stuff in the bottom drawer. If you are only using one drawer fill the bottom drawer with house bricks and you will be safer.

VAT is explained fully later in this book (see chapter 18) but you do have to decide before Dawn on Day 1 whether or not you intend to register for VAT. You must register if your takings are likely to be in excess of the compulsory figure set by the Chancellor of the Exchequer on Budget Day. At present this is £25 400 per annum, about £490 a week. If you are unlikely to take that amount of money each week you do not have to register for VAT, but you may still register voluntarily if you wish. If you register you must keep VAT Records (which are easy enough using the Simplex VAT book) but you can reclaim the VAT you pay out on purchases, and capital items. You must collect VAT from your customers and pay it over to H.M. Customs at regular intervals, after deducting the money you are reclaiming.

For VAT records we must know what system we are using. We shall almost certainly use the Normal Method for our input records, because our suppliers will give us an invoice every time they make a supply. The Normal Method, remember, is based on the recording of invoices and credit notes (if any). If we ourselves always issue an invoice with every supply we make, our Output records too will be invoiced based—and will therefore use the Normal Method. If we are not issuing invoices then we have to use one of the twelve special schemes. Read Chapter 18 of this book and decide which scheme to use. Send to the VATman for the scheme leaflets, and other background booklets and fill up the VAT Registration Form, VAT 1. You will then be sent a VAT Registration Number, and the computer will start to see you are supplied with VAT Returns every month, or quarter, as the case may be.

For the Inland Revenue it can be helpful to notify the local tax office of your intention to set up in business and a preliminary interview may be arranged—though at times of heavy activity they may simply be content with opening a file on you and working you into the system. Their leaflet *Starting in*

Business is helpful. Mention whether you are likely to employ anyone and they will send you the necessary information about an employer's liability to deduct tax etc., from wages paid, under the PAYE system.

These are the chief things you must do to be ready for Dawn on Day 1. We must now find out why Dawn on Day 1 is a crucial moment in the life of any business.

4.3 Dawn on Day 1—the Opening Balance Sheet

Any system of book-keeping leads eventually to the Final Accounts of a business, a Trading Account, Profit and Loss Account and a Balance Sheet. The Trading Account and the Profit & Loss Account are the accounts where we work out the profit made (or the loss suffered) in any financial year. A Balance Sheet is a statement of the affairs of a business, and it shows what the state of affairs is on the last day of the old year, and what is being handed-on to the first day of the new year. In order to work out the Balance Sheet on the last day of any financial year we need to know how we started at the beginning of the year. It follows that when we start up a new business we must start by drawing up a Balance Sheet as at 'Dawn on Day 1'. This is also true of anyone who is already in business but has decided to turn over to a different system of accounting. You must start your new system with an opening Balance Sheet position. So if you have just decided to start using the Simplex System, or if you are starting a brand new business, you must begin by drawing up an 'Opening Balance Sheet' position.

To draw up an Opening Balance Sheet the procedure is as shown below. Before drawing up your own list to start your own books consider the following points:

(a) Premises. If you are setting up your business in your own home do not count the premises as a business asset; they are a domestic asset. You may, if you like, claim some of your household expenses as business expenses but there are disadvantages. These are explained later. If you do have business premises separate from your domestic premises, and if you own them, count them as an asset of the business at the cost price, or current valuation if you have had them for some time. If you rent the premises they are not your property and are not one of your business assets. If you have paid for a lease the lease is an asset. Put it on your list of assets contributed.

(b) Shared items; part business; part domestic. Some assets such as cars are often shared between the business and domestic use. It is usual to regard the full value of the asset as a business asset, especially in the first year, and to keep a record of the use made for each purpose (for example the business mileage and the domestic mileage). The Inland Revenue will use these records to decide how much of the asset is a business asset, and will allow that part of the expenses to be deductable as a business expense. Some simple fraction, $\frac{1}{2}$ and $\frac{1}{2}$, $\frac{2}{3}$ and $\frac{1}{3}$, $\frac{3}{4}$ and $\frac{1}{4}$ is usually chosen. In the meantime put the full value on the books.

(c) *Enterprise Allowances.* Many unemployed people starting up in business ask for an **Enterprise Allowance** for the first year. In order to qualify they must have at least £1 000 in capital and they often borrow this from a bank. What happens is that the bank puts £1 000 in their Current Account (an asset Cash at Bank = £1 000) but opens up an equal and opposite Loan Account of £1 000—a liability of £1 000. If you have done this to get started the asset Cash at Bank will appear on your list of assets contributed, but the Loan Account will come on your list of liabilities.

Some people who borrow £1 000 in this way don't really need it (a window cleaner does not need £1 000 to buy a bucket and a few cloths). It is easy enough to repay it once the Enterprise Allowance has been agreed. This is explained later (see page 230).

To draw up a Balance Sheet at the start of the business we proceed as shown below.

(a) Prepare a list on a piece of paper of everything you are bringing into the business: cash, money at the bank and other assets of various sorts. A typical list might be as follows:

Assets Contributed

	£
Cash in hand	125
Cash at bank	1 625
Motorcar	5 400
Shop fittings	2 455
Stock	8 230
Total assets	£17 835

Thinking about these assets a little more carefully we note that some of them, the shop fittings and the motor car are long-lasting durable assets which may serve the business for many years. We call these **'Fixed assets'**, they stay in the business a long time. The others, cash in hand, cash at bank and stock are called 'current assets'. The word 'current' comes from French word for running (courrant). They are assets which are always on the move. We sell our stock and it turns into cash. We sell our stock and take a cheque or a credit card voucher and it turns into 'cash at bank'. We buy more stock, etc., etc. Current assets do not stay in the business a long time. The dividing line between current assets and fixed assets is one year. If an asset stays in the business longer than one year it is a fixed asset.

(b) Against this list of 'Assets Contributed' we must have an equal and opposite 'List of Liabilities'. A Balance Sheet is a statement of the affairs of a business, showing the assets owned and the liabilities owed. They are always equal, and this is what gives us the name 'Balance Sheet'; the two sides always balance.

Suppose, we have borrowed £1 000 from the bank for 'enterprise allowance' purposes and £4 000 from a Finance Co to buy the car. Our list of liabilities is as follows:

List of External Liabilities

	£
Loan (Helpful Bank PLC)	1 000
Loan (Helpful Finance Co Ltd)	4 000
	£5 000

We have said that the assets and liabilities always balance, but it is clear that £5 000 does not balance £17 835. The difference is £12 835. This is the capital of the proprietor; you. The capital of a business is a liability of the business; it is what the business owes to the proprietor. True it is a debt that will not be paid until the proprietor ceases to trade, and either retires from business altogether or sells the business and moves on to some other enterprise activity. By that time, too, the original investment may have grown as profits were ploughed back into the business year after year. Capital may be called an 'internal' liability. It is owed to someone inside the business; the proprietor.

4.4 Entering the Balance Sheet at the start of the business/year

At the front of the Simplex D Account Book you will find a Balance Sheet for you to complete to start your books off for the year. Using the figures provided in Section 4.3 above our opening Balance Sheet is as shown in Fig. 4.1.

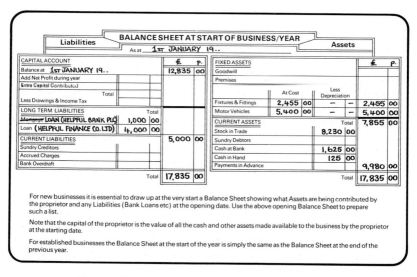

For new businesses it is essential to draw up at the very start a Balance Sheet showing what Assets are being contributed by the proprietor and any Liabilities (Bank Loans etc) at the opening date. Use the above opening Balance Sheet to prepare such a list.

Note that the capital of the proprietor is the value of all the cash and other assets made available to the business by the proprietor at the starting date.

For established businesses the Balance Sheet at the start of the year is simply the same as the Balance Sheet at the end of the previous year.

Fig. 4.1 *The Opening Balance Sheet of a new business*

4.5 Opening the books at the start of the business/year

Although the Balance Sheet shown in Fig. 4.1 records the opening position of the business it does not actually open the books of the business because the book-keeping only starts on the first weekly page, when we make the first set of entries for receipts and payments. The opening situation has to be recorded on this first weekly page and the figures have to be carried to the summaries at the back of the book at the end of the first week.

The details of these entries are as follows:

(a) We pretend that everything to do with the opening of the business is done at the first moment of 'Dawn on Day 1'. At this moment the business received three lots of money, the 'Loan from Helpful Bank PLC', the 'Loan from Helpful Finance Ltd' and the capital subscribed by the proprietor. These are all entered as 'Other Receipts', and the details are written in the 'Particulars' column. You will see this done on a weekly page in Fig. 4.2.

(b) At the first moment of 'Dawn on Day 1' we also pretend that the business obtains all the assets. This means that we need to make the following entries:

  (i) Enter the £2 455.00 for fixtures and fittings on the first 'capital items' line in Payments other than for Stock. Treat all these payments as cash payments.

  (ii) Enter the £5 400 for the motor vehicle on the second 'capital items' line in Payments other than for Stock.

  (iii) Enter the £8 230.00 stock on the first line of 'Payments for Business Stock'.

  (iv) Enter the £1 625.00 which is in the bank in the Paid to Bank Section, pretending it is all 'Cash'.

There is no need to enter the £125.00 cash because it has already been entered. If you can't see why the explanation is as follows:

  (i) We have entered a total of £17 835 as Other Receipts.

  (ii) We have spent £8 230 on stock, £7 855 on capital items and we have banked £1 625. This makes a total of £17 710 spent. The balance of £125 is the cash we have left after all these expenditures. There is no need to enter it anywhere—it is already in the till.

These various entries can all be seen in Fig. 4.2.

4.6 Carrying these entries to the summaries

In the Simplex System at the end of every week we carry the various figures on the weekly page to the various summaries at the back of the book. These opening entries will of course get muddled in with the normal week's entries of Week 1; for example if we buy more goods for resale and enter them in the 'Payments for Business Stock' section the £8 230 of stock recorded on 1

RECEIPTS	Week No. 1.		Commencing: 1ST JANUARY 19..		

RECEIPTS

Day/Date	Daily Gross Takings			Other Receipts Col 4	Particulars
	Cash Col 1	Cheques Col 2	Credit Cards Col 3		
Sun : 1.1		'		1,000 00	LOAN - HELPFUL BANK
Mon : 2.1				4,000 00	LOAN - HELPFUL FINANCE
Tues : 3.1				12,835 00	CAPITAL FROM PROPRIETOR.
Wed : 4.1					
Thur : 5.1					
Fri : 6.1					
Sat : 7.1					
Totals					

PAID TO BANK

Cash Col 5	Cheques Col 6	Credit Cards Col 7	TOTAL Col 8
1,625 00			1,625 00
Totals			

PAYMENTS FOR BUSINESS STOCK

Date or Chq. No.	To Whom Paid	Amount Paid	
		By Cash Col 9	By Cheque Col 10
1ST JAN	SUNDRY SUPPLIERS	8,230 00	
Totals			

PAYMENTS OTHER THAN FOR STOCK

Nature of Payment	Amount Paid	
	By Cash Col 11	By Cheque Col 12
Rent		
Rates		
Light and Heat		
Carriage		
Postages		
Paper		
Motor Expenses		
—do—		
Travelling		
Cleaning		
Printing & Stationery		
Repairs & Renewals		
Insurance (Business)		
Advertising		
Telephone		
Sundries		
Wages (Employees)		
Inland Revenue (PAYE + NI)		
Drawings of the Proprietor (see Note 4)		
Drawings – Partner 1		
Drawings – Partner 2		
Drawings – Partner 3		
Capital Items (see Note 3(1)) FIXTURES ETC.	2,455 00	
—do— MOTOR VEHICLE	5,400 00	
Totals		

WEEKLY CASH REPORT

	Cash in Hand (as counted) brought forward		
Add	Gross Weekly Takings (Col 1 + Col 2 + Col 3)		
	Other Receipts (Col 4)		
	Cash Drawn from Bank		
	Total		
Deduct	Stock Payments (cash) (Col 9)		
	Other Payments (cash) (Col 11)		
	Amount paid to Bank (Col 8)		
	Total		

© GEORGE VYNER LTD

COPYRIGHT RESERVED REPRODUCTION OF THIS BOOK IN WHOLE OR IN PART STRICTLY FORBIDDEN

Cash Balance on books	
Cash in hand (as counted) carr. fwd	
Difference on books (+ or −)	

WEEKLY BANK REPORT

	Opening Balance brought forward		
Add	Total Paid to Bank during week (Col 8)		
	Total		
Deduct	Cash drawn from bank		
	Stock Payments (Col 10)		
	Other Payments (Col 12)		
	Standing Orders/Direct Debits		
	Bank and Interest Charges		
	Total		
	Closing Balance carried forward		

Fig. 4.2 *Entries to get the books open*

January will get muddled in with these extra purchases and the total will be carried to the summary of Payments for Business Stock. The capital items will be carried to the summary 'Capital Expenses incurred during the Year' (see Chapter 7, page 54) and the Other Receipts will be carried to the Summary of Other Receipts, or the Loan Summary (see Chapter 5, page 36). The £1 625 paid to the bank will be muddled in with any further sums paid to bank in the week and will be carried to the Weekly Bank Report and Weekly Cash Report at the foot of the Weekly Page.

You have thus recorded your Opening Balance Sheet position and are ready to start your business. Whatever happens in your business now, you are ready for it. If invoices arrive put them in your concertina file and in the next quiet moment record them in the VAT book if you are VAT registered and your Simplex D Account Book on the weekly page for your financial records. If you make out an invoice and send the top copy to a customer put the second copy in your concertina file, and in due course enter it. If you buy anything, demand a till receipt and put it in your concertina file, before entering it in the VAT records, etc.

4.7 Starting with Simplex from some other accounting system

Many people who set up in business do not start with the Simplex System and only find out later that this simple system is available. They may for example have been advised by an accountant to buy some other system that uses analysis books of one sort or another. The trouble is with such 'plain' books—in other words there are only ruled lines and no indications of where, or how, to record receipts and payments of different sorts—unless you know double-entry book-keeping you don't know where to put anything. We are constantly meeting people who look at the Simplex page and see all those lines labelled with rent, rates, light, etc, and say "It looks very complicated". We have to explain that having a place for everything, and everything in its place, isn't complicated, it's easy. The complicated book is the one with a lot of lines and no indication of what to put where.

If you are converting to Simplex from some other system it is quite easy really. You simply draw up a list of all the assets and liabilities exactly as already described and enter them at the 'Dawn on Day 1' position. Only now it isn't Day 1 of your new business, it is Day 1 of your Simplex system.

To give an example, take the position of Jim Hargreaves who is only in business in a small way as a road haulage operator and wishes to change to a system so that he can keep his own books to a considerable extent. The existing system must show somewhere the values placed upon the various assets and he must know who owes him money, (his debtors) and whom he owes money to (his creditors—both short and long-term). He draws up his list of assets and liabilities as follows:

Assets		Liabilities	
	£		£
Premises	42 000	Mortgage	29 500
Vehicles	19 250	Motor Finance Ltd	9 650
Office Equipment	1 500	Barclaycard	1 375
Tools etc	3 850	Trade creditors	
Debtors		Rex Garages	152
M Higgs	250	Spares Ltd	84
P Dark	380		
Cash at Bank	4 925		£40 761
Cash in hand	184		
	£72 339		

The assets and liabilities must of course balance, and the missing item is the capital, owed by the business back to J. Hargreaves. This works out at £31 578.

	£
Total assets	72 339
Total external liabilities	40 761
Capital owed to proprietor	£31 578

Jim is now in a position to draw up his Opening Balance Sheet as in Fig. 4.1. Remember though that he has to carry all the items into the books to start the Weekly Pages going. What we pretend is that the whole thing starts at Dawn on Day 1, and at that moment all the funds are supplied by the mortgage people, the finance company and the proprietor, etc and used to buy all the assets. The following entries would be made on Page 1 of Jim's new Simplex D book.

(a) Enter in 'Other Receipts' and the 'Particulars' column

29 500	Mortgage
9 650	Motor Finance
1 375	Barclaycard
152	Rex Garages
84	Spares Ltd
31 578	Capital contributed

Having entered these in the Other Receipts section they have to be carried to the summaries, as follows:

(i) Carry the mortgage and the motor finance figures to the Loans Summary at the back of the book.

(ii) The Barclaycard and the items for Rex Garages and Spares Ltd do not need to be carried to any summary, because you haven't actually paid these bills yet, but there should be some paper evidence to show you owe the money. Your Barclaycard statement will be the evidence for this liability, and there will be an invoice or a statement from the other two creditors. Wherever you have these, perhaps in a 'payments pending' file or even in a Creditors Ledger somewhere those records constitute a summary of payments due.

(iii) The capital contributed doesn't go to any summary—it becomes the Capital at start for the Balance Sheet at the end of the Book for the Final Accounts at the end of the year. If you like you can actually carry it now to your final Balance Sheet (but it will just stay there until the last day of the year).

Now we must spend all this money (in our imagination) buying all the assets at Dawn on Day 1.

(b) Now spend the money on buying all the assets by entering as follows:

(i) Premises £42 000 on the 'Capital Items' line in 'Payments other than for Stock' (and carry this to the Summary of Capital Expenses).

(ii) Vehicles £19 250 on the other 'Capital Items' line and carry it to the Summary of Capital Expenses.

(iii) Do the same with Office Equipment and Tools etc. Use one of the spare lines for each of them on the 'Payments other than for Stock' section and carry them to the Summary of Capital Expenses.

(vi) The two debtors don't need to be entered anywhere (until the debtors actually pay) but there must be some documentary evidence of these debts, probably in a file (accounts uncollected) or perhaps in a Debtors Ledger.

(v) Put £4 925 in the Paid to Bank Section.

(vi) You don't actually need to put the £184 cash in hand anywhere, it is actually there already. We have contributed £72 339 to Other Receipts and have only 'spent' £72 155—what is left is £184 cash in hand.

There is one small point to make about VAT registered businesses. If you are VAT registered and use the Simplex VAT book the debtors will be recorded in your VAT book and the output tax will be calculated there; while the creditors will be recorded in the 'Input Account' section and the input tax will be calculated there. You might have a balance due to the VAT officer as a result. A full consideration of VAT is given later (see Chapter 18).

4.8 Buying a business—Goodwill

If you are buying a business you may be asked to pay a sum for the 'Goodwill', and even if you are not asked to pay anything for goodwill you may finish up with goodwill on your books as an asset, for the reason explained below. It is therefore necessary to understand goodwill.

What is goodwill? Goodwill may be defined as a payment to the vendor of an existing business over and above the actual net value of the assets, to compensate the vendor for hard work done in the past to establish the business. One judge said 'Goodwill is a payment to recognise the fact that the old customer will return to the old place for further supplies when the purchaser of a business has done nothing to deserve this custom'. In other words some of the profits you make in the first few years of your new business will be the result of the vendor's hard work building up the business and you should pay him/her for this advantage.

How much should be paid for Goodwill is always a matter for negotiation; the seller will naturally claim as large a sum as possible and the buyer will try to pay as little as he/she can. Goodwill is often called an intangible asset, one that you cannot touch. Whether Mrs. Smith, Jones and Robinson do bear a trader goodwill is almost impossible to prove. If the business records are available for the last—say—five years, and show a growing turnover and rising profitability then Goodwill probably does exist. Of course inflation must be taken into account, a rising turnover may only reflect higher general prices and in real terms the business might actually be declining. If the previous owner cannot produce convincing figures it is advisable to pay only a nominal sum for goodwill, and a local valuer who knows the trends of business in the area should be consulted if the sum asked seems excessive.

As far as book-keeping is concerned Goodwill is a strange asset. Suppose we pay £2 000 for Goodwill. It is a fixed asset (really an intangible asset), but in fact of course no-one does bear *us* any goodwill. The £2 000 has been paid for the Goodwill local people feel to the *previous* owner. For this reason is it usual to write off Goodwill out of the Profits (as a type of Drawings; not on the Profit and Loss Account). Usually we reduce it by about one quarter each year for the first four years. By the time Goodwill is reduced to nothing on the Balance Sheet people have grown to know and trust us, and do bear us some Goodwill. So accountants talk about the paradox of Goodwill. When it is worth most on the Balance Sheet it is really worth nothing, and when it is valued at nothing on the Balance Sheet it is quite valuable.

Leaving aside the question about depreciating goodwill (it is dealt with in Chapter 21) there are one or two things we need to know about it as far as the opening day of our business is concerned.

Suppose we are asked to pay £2 000 for goodwill, this will of course be an asset of the business (an intangible asset because we have nothing really to touch or use, just an impression in the minds of customers). However, the correct figure for goodwill may not be £2 000 and even if we did not pay anything for goodwill in the purchase of the business it may still appear on our books. The explanation is most easily followed if we take an example:

On January 19 M. Laidlaw purchased for £98 000 the business of R. Buchanan, a manufacturer. At that date the assets and liabilities appearing in the books of Buchanan were:

	£
Buildings	36 560
Plant	34 800
Motor Vans	2 650
Stock-in-Trade	14 800
Debtors	950
Creditors	1 615
Loan from bank	2 000

The agreement about the sale was that all the assets would be taken over by Laidlaw, but the creditors and the bank loan would not be transferred, but would be paid up privately by R. Buchanan.

Now although these were the agreed terms, there is nothing to stop the new owner of the business taking on the assets at what he/she considers to be a fairer valuation, because the book values on the old business may be quite unlike the true value. Suppose Laidlaw decides that the real values are as follows:

	£
Buildings	50 000
Plant	25 000
Motor Vans	2 500
Stock	12 500
Debtors	475
	£90 475

What this means is that the premises on the books of the old business were undervalued, and were still at the price they cost the vendor some years ago. Laidlaw has no doubt been told by a valuer that they are in fact worth £50 000 today. However, the plant, the motor vans and the stock were all overvalued on the books of the vendor, while Laidlaw reckons half the so-called debtors are probably bad debts and will never be collected. When he revalues these assets the total is £90 475, for which Laidlaw paid £98 000. What did he get for the extra £7 525? It can only be the intangible asset 'Goodwill'. So Goodwill is valued at £7 525.

Supposing that Laidlaw contributed £50 000 capital, and borrowed £30 000 as a mortgage on the premises and £20 000 as a loan from the bank. His Balance Sheet (supposing all the capital except £100 cash in hand was banked, and the vendor was paid in full) would be as follows:

Liabilities	BALANCE SHEET AT START OF BUSINESS/YEAR As at __1st JANUARY 19..__			Assets				
		£	P.				£	P.
CAPITAL ACCOUNT				FIXED ASSETS				
Balance at 1st JANUARY		50,000	00	Goodwill			7,525	00
Add Net Profit during year				Premises			50,000	00
Extra Capital Contributed					At Cost	Less Depreciation		
Total								
Less Drawings & Income Tax				Fixtures & Fittings PLANT	25,000 00	— —	25,000	00
LONG TERM LIABILITIES	Total	50,000	00	Motor Vehicles	2,500 00	— —	2,500	00
Mortgage	30,000 00			CURRENT ASSETS		Total	85,025	00
Loan	20,000 00			Stock in Trade		12,500 00		
CURRENT LIABILITIES		50,000	00	Sundry Debtors		475 00		
Sundry Creditors				Cash at Bank		1,900 00		
Accrued Charges				Cash in Hand		100 00		
Bank Overdraft				Payments in Advance		— —	14,975	00
	Total	100,000	00			Total	100,000	00

Fig. 4.3 *The Opening Balance Sheet when an existing business is purchased by a new owner*

4.9 A word about 'Capital'

Before we leave the opening situation at Dawn on Day 1 and go on to see how the everyday receipts and payments are entered in the books of the business we must just re-emphasise what capital is. Capital is not money. Capital is the total value of the assets put into a business by the proprietor, whatever form they were in. It is a liability of the business to the owner of the business. This idea is worth stating, for it reminds us that the business is regarded in accountancy as something separate from the owner of the business, even though the owner works in the business and is legally liable for all its affairs. The true relationship between the proprietor and the business is one of debtor and creditor. The business owes the proprietor back all the money invested in it, and the return of all other assets contributed. Since, with a prosperous business the proprietor earns good profits and draws out only enough to live on, we say that some of the profits are 'ploughed back' into the business. This means that the value of the business to the proprietor rises year by year. This increase in the capital repayable is called the increase in 'Net Worth'. If profits are ploughed back Net Worth rises. On the other hand, a trader who draws out more in drawings than is being earned in profits is said to be 'living on his/her capital'. The 'Net Worth' of the business to the owner of the business declines, and if this goes on for several years the business will go bankrupt.

4.10 Exercises on 'Opening Balance Sheets'

1. R. Faulkner sets up his business with the following assets, on 1 April, 19.. He has Premises £35 000; Fixtures and Fittings £3 820; Motor Vehicles £1 950; Stock of goods for re-sale £4 775; Cash at bank £1 216 and cash in hand £130.

He owes A. Supplier £282.50. Other liabilities owing are a loan from Helpful Bank PLC of £2 000 and a mortgage on premises of £25 000. Draw up the Opening Balance Sheet of the business.

2. Gillian Jossaume sets up in business with the following assets, on 1 May, 19.. She has Computers £1 600; Fixtures and Fittings £2 475.50; Motor Vehicles £725.60; Stock of goods for re-sale £11 846.55; Cash at bank £387.50 and cash in hand £19.65.

She owes A. Supplier £137.50. Other liabilities owing are a loan from Helpful Bank PLC of £1 400 and another from Hairdressing Finance Ltd of £2 500. Draw up the Opening Balance Sheet of the business.

3. Lightfoot (Cambridge) Ltd set up in business with the following assets, on 1 July, 19.. They have Premises £65 000; Fixtures and Fittings £4 500; Motor Vehicles £2 850; Stock of goods for re-sale £3 750.50; Cash at bank £4 929.75 and cash in hand £116.95. They owe A. Supplier £426.50. Other liabilities owing are a loan from Helpful Bank PLC of £3 000 and a mortgage on premises of £40 000. Draw up the Opening Balance Sheet of the business.

4. George Shah buys the business of Abdul Akram for £94 750 on 1 January 19.. The assets on the books of the vendor were:

	£
Premises	45 000
Fixtures and Fittings	3 250
Motor Vehicles	4 840
Stock for re-sale	13 250
Debtors	660
Cash at Bank	5 994
Cash in Hand	425

Shah will not take over one of the vehicles valued at £1 800 and will value the stock at only £10 000. He will not take over the debtors, or the Cash at Bank or Cash in Hand. He decides to value the Premises at £78 000, and Fixtures and Fittings at £2 500.

He brings in capital of £100 000, putting £99 750 in his Bank Account, and the balance in the cash box. The vendor is paid by cheque the same day. Draw up the opening Balance Sheet of George Shah's new business.

5. Garry Peters buys the business of Susan Metcalfe for £90 000 on 1 July 19.. The assets on the books of the vendor were:

	£
Premises	40 000
Fixtures and Fittings	3 000
Motor Vehicles	8 000
Stock for re-sale	12 250
Debtors	120
Cash in Bank	15 590
Cash in Hand	140

Peters will not take over one of the vehicles valued at £4 500 and the debtors are to be collected privately by Susan Metcalfe. She will also keep all the cash. Peters decides to value the Premises at £68 000 and the Fixtures at £2 000.

He brings in capital of £100 in cash and £69 900 in his Bank Account. He borrows £30 000 by a mortgage on the property. The vendor is paid by cheque that day. Draw up the opening Balance Sheet of Garry Peters' new business.

Chapter Five
Recording Receipts

5.1 The Receipts Section of the Weekly Page

The section of the weekly page which is used for recording receipts is shown in Fig. 5.1. It has four columns which are directly concerned with receipts: three are headed 'Daily Gross Takings' in cash, in cheques and by credit cards. The fourth column is headed 'Other Receipts'. There is also a space for 'Particulars'. A separate sub-divided column headed 'Paid to Bank' is provided for the proprietor to record any sums paid into the bank account during the week.

Types of Receipt

The chief purpose of book-keeping records is to determine whether the business is profitable or not. In attempting to discover this, we must know about and follow certain guide-lines used since time immemorial to determine profit. These traditional criteria have been reaffirmed in recent years by decisions of the courts in inland-revenue cases. For better or worse, the profits of every business are a matter of keen interest to the Chancellor of the Exchequer and his representative—the local tax inspector. It follows that accounts prepared along unusual lines at the whim of the individual businessman can lead to disputes with the Inland Revenue authorities over the tax payable.

The basic formula in the calculation of profit is:

$$\text{RECEIPTS } less \text{ EXPENSES} = \text{PROFIT}$$

However, the words 'receipts' and 'expenses' are too wide, and must be narrowed by a careful definition. For example, there are *capital receipts* which the business receives from the proprietor at the start of the enterprise, and there are *revenue receipts* which flow into the business as trading activities proceed and services are rendered to clients. Similarly, we can distinguish *capital expenditure* (such as the purchase of business assets) from *revenue expenditure* (such as the purchase of consumable items necessary to the conduct of the firm, payment of wages, telephone and motor-vehicle expenses). This distinction is important because *capital* receipts and *capital* expenditure are *not* taken into account in a proper calculation of profit. Profit is in fact determined by the formula:

$$\text{REVENUE RECEIPTS } less \text{ REVENUE EXPENDITURE} = \text{PROFIT}$$

The separate identification of capital items and revenue items is a fundamental principle of accounting, and is essential to the keeping of correct records.

RECEIPTS	Week No. 1		Commencing: 1st JANUARY 19..			PAID TO BANK			
	Daily Gross Takings			Other Receipts Col 4	Particulars	Cash Col 5	Cheques Col 6	Credit Cards Col 7	TOTAL Col 8
Day/Date	Cash Col 1	Cheques Col 2	Credit Cards Col 3						
Sun : 1-1	—	—	—	1,000 00	LOAN - HELPFUL BANK	1,625 00			1,625 00
Mon : 2-1	238 60	17 25	21 19	4,000 00	LOAN - HELPFUL FIN.				
Tues : 3-1	452 17	129 60	38 76	12,835 00	CAPITAL FROM PROP.	600 00	146 85	59 95	806 80
Wed : 4-1	318 54	54 72	45 50						
Thur : 5-1	586 70	136 60	124 62						
Fri : 6-1	989 42	184 20	365 80			1,500 00	310 32	493 62	2,303 94
Sat : 7-1	763 60	38 50	285 60						
Totals	3,349 03	560 87	881 47	17,835 00		3,725 00	457 17	553 57	4,735 74

Fig. 5.1 *The 'Receipts' record on the weekly page*

(a) **Revenue receipts** consist of all those receipts which result from the normal activities of the business. They may be

  (i) daily takings resulting from the sale of goods,

  (ii) daily takings resulting from the provision of services, or

  (iii) miscellaneous receipts.

Miscellaneous receipts are those which arise from some incidental activity other than the main business activity, and which ought properly to be regarded as income of the proprietor. For example, if a businessman sub-lets part of his premises, the rent he received represents an income to him which should be included in the profits of the business.

A rather special case of a revenue receipt is the *'Enterprise Allowance'* paid to new businesses whose proprietors have been unemployed before setting-up in business, and trying self-employment, not unemployment. Such people find it impossible to move off the unemployment register without a bit of help, because businesses cannot usually be immediately profitable. The Enterprise Allowance of £40 per week (£80 for a partnership business where both husband and wife were unemployed) is definitely regarded by the Government as a contribution to the revenue income of the firm, not a capital receipt, and is taxable. However, to prevent it distorting the takings of a business and giving a false impression, it is taxed under a separate heading, and is therefore shown separately from takings. If you will look at your Simplex D Account book at the back you will find a Summary of Other Receipts where there is a special column for Enterprise Allowances. The money is actually paid by 'Bank Giro' credit transfer directly into the business bank account, and is brought into the books each month as a bank statement arrives. This is explained later (See Chapter 16). The item 'Enterprise Allowance' is also included in the Profit and Loss A/c at the back of the book, and the total figure of the Summary column is carried there at the end of the year. The Enterprise Allowance is only paid for one year from the commencement of the business, and can therefore only affect the profits in the first accounting period, or perhaps the first two accounting periods. The publishers of this book do sell a book called 'Self-employment *not* Unemployment' by the present author. It costs £3.95 and may be ordered from George Vyner (Distributors) Ltd., Freepost, Holmfirth, Huddersfield HD1 2RB, cash with order, please.

(b) **Revenue expenditure** includes all those expenses *incurred directly in the earning of the revenue receipts listed above,* provided that the benefits received from the expenditure do not last longer than one year. Thus the purchase of goods for resale is a revenue expense, but the purchase of furniture or motor vehicles is not, since these items are expected to last for longer than one year.

A full discussion of the calculation of profits will be easier to understand after we have considered receipts and expenditure, and is therefore left until Chapter 21 Let us now return to examining the 'Receipts' section of the weekly page. As we do so, bear in mind that we must distinguish between those receipts of a 'revenue' nature, which will need to be used in calculating the profits, and those which can be properly disregarded when profits are worked out at the end of the financial year.

5.2 The 'Daily Gross Takings' Columns

The daily takings of the business are the total amount of cash that has flowed into the tills during the day, less any float which may have been put there at the start of the day. Whether this money arrives as actual cash, or in the form of cheques or credit card vouchers it is counted as cash for the purpose of deciding what is the 'daily gross takings'. The word 'gross' is important here. It means 'inclusive of VAT'. Under the Simplex System VAT is treated rather differently from other systems. This is explained separately in 5.3 below. Ignore this for the moment. We do our entries for daily takings at the end of the day, but there is one important point. If we go to the bank during the day we might decide to bank the cheques and credit card vouchers that have already been taken up to the time of banking, and possibly some of the money as well. If we do this we must put a slip of paper in the till saying how much of each type of cash has been banked. For example:

Banked at 1.30 Friday 5 June

Cash	180.00
Cheques	82.50
Credit card vouchers	163.65
	£426.15

As these sums have not yet been recorded as 'Daily Takings' it would mean they might be overlooked unless we leave this note in the till.

Instead of waiting until the actual moment of closing the premises to discover the daily-takings figure, it is often more convenient to cash up a little before closing time and extract from the tills all that has been taken so far that day. Any further takings that day will be treated as takings of the following day, and will be placed in the till with the float the following morning. The daily takings are recorded in the appropriate columns of the Simplex page as shown in Fig. 5.1.

Some readers may be thinking that as they do not run a shop, or keep a till, all this explanation is not really applicable to them. This is not so. Every business receives money or cheques from time to time and these are simply entered as they arrive, and the cheques are taken to the bank for collection. For example the author of this book only gets paid about ten times a year, when publishers pay royalties for the previous year's sales. There are many weeks when there are no 'Receipts' at all, and a few weeks when a reasonably big cheque arrives. Such a 'Daily Gross Takings' section is shown in Fig. 5.2.

Safety Measures with Daily Takings

Business premises are a common target for thieves, and every precaution should be taken to ensure that if burglaries are unavoidable they are at any rate

RECEIPTS		Week No. **15**		Commencing: **APRIL 15**		
Day/Date	Daily Gross Takings				Other Receipts Col 4	Particulars
	Cash Col 1	Cheques Col 2		Credit Cards Col 3		
Sun : 15						
Mon : 16		4,295	60			HEINEMAN (INCL. VAT)
Tues : 17						
Wed : 18						
Thur : 19		1,875	56			VYNERS (INCL VAT)
Fri : 20						
Sat : 21						
Totals		6,171	16			

Fig. 5.2 *Takings for a firm that does not use a till*

unfruitful. Both the daily takings and the cash floats should be removed from the tills after business hours—and the tills should be left open. (A till that is left open is less liable to be broken or even removed bodily by the thief; the loss of a till can be both expensive and inconvenient).

The daily takings may be deposited in the night-safe of a local bank. A charge is made for this service, but it might well prove to be the most satisfactory method of safeguarding cash overnight. Takings may instead be taken home, at some risk to the proprietor, who should certainly install a good safe if this is his/her regular practice. The cash floats for the tills next day should also be taken home, preferably in separate bags indicating to which till they belong. Obvious safeguards, such as taking different routes to the bank each night, should never be neglected.

The Problem of Debtors

If a customer is given time to pay we say they are given credit. They become a debtor on our books, and immediately present two problems, a credit control problem and a book-keeping problem. This is a book-keeping book, and it is the book-keeping problem which is of most concern to us, but first a general word about credit control.

Credit control. In strict law we do not have to give anyone credit, and many traders display notices saying 'Please do not ask for credit as a refusal may offend'. A trader is entitled to exercise **a lien** on goods on which the charges have not been paid. A lien (the word rhymes with the boy's name Ian) is a passive right to retain goods until the charges on them have been paid. Thus dry cleaners and shoe repairers may retain these goods until the customer offers payment in full, and innkeepers may retain luggage until charges for accommodation have been paid. If we do give people time to pay we must exercise credit control in two ways:

(a) Set a limit beyond which they cannot have further supplies until previous supplies are paid for. It is not uncommon for a customer to place one or two small orders and pay promptly and then place a very large order for which there is no intention to pay.

(b) Keep adequate records of the transaction so that

    (i) the customer is a debtor on the books;

    (ii) the customer knows what the settlement terms are and has been informed in writing)—for instance pay within 30 days of invoice—and

    (iii) we pursue the debtor in a known way. For example some traders have a simple policy. Payment of an overdue debt is requested once by letter. If this produces no results a solicitor is told to pursue the debt. Most solicitors have a computerised system which puts the collection procedure in hand automatically in a sequence which increases the pressure on the debtor. Debtors pay the person who presses them, and do not pay the other creditors who are more lenient. Using a solicitor does not cost the earth, and the cost is a business expense which is tax deductible—which reduces the effective cost to a profitable business.

The accounting problem. The nature of the accounting problem is whether the goods should be regarded as *(a)* sold (in which case the amount of this 'credit sale' must be included in the daily takings), or *(b)* not sold until they are actually paid for (in which case the goods must be imagined as still being in stock, even though in reality the debtor has them and may be using them).

The second method is the simpler, since the goods are not yielding any profit until they are actually paid for. On the whole, however, the first method is preferable, since in law the goods become the property of the buyer at the moment that the parties intend the property to pass; it makes no difference if the payment is postponed by giving the buyer credit.

In a business which keeps a full double-entry system the goods would be regarded as sold and the debtor would have an account opened in his/her name in the Debtor's ledger. In the Simplex System there are no ledger accounts, and debtors do present a problem. There are several simple ways to overcome the problem. Let us consider each in turn.

(a) **VAT registered traders who issue invoices for goods supplied or jobs done.** If you are registered for VAT, and either issue invoices for all goods supplied or jobs done, or issue invoices to those customers who are given time to pay—i.e. your debtors, the VAT records can be your debtors' record. Since under VAT law you must keep 'output-tax' records of every invoice issued the record you make of out-going invoices is a complete record of supplies. You will probably be using a Simplex VAT book, and there are spare columns not in use in that book—for example the Positive Rate B column. If you head up that column 'Date paid' you can use it to record the date when the customer pays. By looking at the VAT Book you can see at a glance which debts are outstanding and you can see the date the invoice was issued. If the customer has fallen behind with the payment you start the credit control procedure to collect the overdue account.

Besides this indication you can use the second copy of your invoice as a control. In the normal way this must be filed in a lever arch file as documentary evidence for the VAT inspector, properly numbered in sequence. If you file the unpaid invoices in a 'customers' invoices 'pending' file and only transfer them to the VAT file when the invoice is actually paid your file of unpaid invoices clearly signals which debtors have not yet paid.

(b) **The 'butcher's book' method.** In the days before supermarket trading the local butcher was often a source of credit and supplied meat to customers for payment at the end of the week, the debts being recorded on a simple cash book with a single cash column on the right hand side. The butcher could use either of the methods mentioned above. These were:

(1) **Regarding goods as not sold until paid for, but as 'Stock out to Customers'.** In this method credit sales are entered in a debtors' record book as described above, but are disregarded for 'takings' purposes.

When a debtor pays a debt the following action should be taken:

   (i) Cross out the debt in the debtors' book by scoring it through.

  (ii) Record the cash in the 'Daily Takings' column in the normal way.

(2) **Regarding goods sold on credit as sold.** When goods (or services) are supplied the debt is recorded in the book in the normal way. At the end of every week we draw a clear line across the debtors' book, add up the week's debts and add the total to the week's takings in the summary of Daily Gross Takings at the back of the book. This is explained more fully below.

When a debtor pays a debt the following action should be taken:

   (i) Cross out the debt in the debtors' book by scoring it through.

  (ii) Record the cash paid, not as 'Daily Takings' but as 'Other Receipts'. This ensures that the cash will not be counted twice, since we have already included the sale of the goods in the weekly takings during the week they were sold. Now that the goods are actually being paid for, the cash is entered as an 'Other Receipt'. This is explained more fully below.

The 'butcher's book' method is illustrated in Fig. 5.3.

19..		Paid on	£	
Nov	1	~~Mrs. Smith, 2, River Road~~	5 Nov	5	48
	1	Mrs. P. Jones , 3, Hill Road		3	25
	3	R. Tyler (Mr.), 4, Combe Close		7	28
	4	L. Brown (Miss), 27, High St.		1	52
	4	R. Johnson (Mrs), 48 Parker Place	p	0	48
	5	Total for week	£	18	01

Include this total in the week's takings by entering any debts very small in the total column (see Fig 5.4)

Fig. 5.3 *A simple debtor's record book*

5.3 Transferring 'Daily Takings' to the 'Weekly Summary of Takings'

At the end of each week the total figure of the 'Daily Takings' columns (cash, cheques and credit card vouchers added together) must be transferred to the 'Weekly Summary of Daily Gross Takings' page, near the end of the Simplex book. This is shown in Fig. 5.4.

If you allow credit to some customers, and regard the goods as sold at once (method (2) above), the total debts accepted in the week—found by adding up the Debtors' Record Book—should be added to the total of the 'Daily Takings' columns to give the correct total sales for the week. The summary shown in Fig. 5.4 is shortly to be modified to give an extra column where any total of debtors for the week can be inserted, but if you are using one of the older Simplex D Account books the debtors should be entered in the total column, rather small, with a letter D (for debtors) alongside.

The layout of this summary page (Fig. 5.4 overleaf) in the Simplex book permits the trader to draw up quarterly and annual figures, from which he/she may prepare the Trading Account (see Section 21.2). Note that if you use method (1) for debtors, the outstanding debtors at the end of the year must be added to the total sales for the year in the box provided. This is because they have not been included as Sales in the Daily Takings section.

What to do with Cheques and Credit Cards received in the Daily Takings

Cheques and credit cards received as part of the daily takings are entered in the 'Gross Daily Takings (cheques and credit cards)' columns and are then carried to the back of the book and recorded in the summary. They will of course be paid into the bank, and consequently will appear in the 'Paid to Bank' column, along with the cash paid in at regular intervals. Proprietors whose takings are considerable should bank daily, using the night-safe service if necessary.

5.4 Other Receipts

Four main types of receipt come under the heading 'Other Receipts'. These are listed below:

Type of Receipt	*Explanation*
(a) Payments by debtors	The goods being paid for may have been regarded as 'sold' when they were supplied to the debtor. If so, no action is necessary now to include the receipt in daily takings, for it will already have been included in 'takings' at an earlier date. The money received must be included in the Weekly Cash Report.
	If goods sold to debtors were not treated as 'sold' until paid for, the receipt must now be treated as cash takings and should therefore be included in the 'weekly takings' figure. The cash or cheques received must also be carried to the Cash Summary. This is explained in Chapter 8.

WEEKLY SUMMARY OF DAILY GROSS TAKINGS

WEEK No.	CASH		CHEQUES		CREDIT CARDS		TOTAL		WEEK No.	CASH		CHEQUES		CREDIT CARDS		TOTAL	
1	1,326	42	425	60	156	84	1,908	86	14	1,971	07	459	72	516	77	2,947	56
2	1,372	56	388	45	197	24	1,958	25	15	1,485	90	621	36	429	74	2,537	00
3	1,428	60	396	26	238	60	2,063	46	16	1,276	13	385	42	326	37	1,987	92
4	1,418	55	725	80	198	54	2,342	89	17	1,732	50	427	61	429	26	2,589	37
5	1,422	30	496	85	672	42	2,591	57	18	1,426	50	516	74	714	49	2,657	73
6	1,384	60	721	63	589	64	2,695	87	19	1,388	60	713	81	386	54	2,488	95
7	1,732	60	845	26	721	64	3,299	50	20	1,785	60	294	73	342	76	2,423	09
8	1,426	50	196	74	138	86	1,762	10	21	1,685	60	426	62	516	35	2,628	57
9	1,372	80	298	74	198	60	1,870	14	22	1,526	60	531	54	483	45	2,541	59
10	1,688	80	569	60	228	75	2,487	15	23	1,430	40	618	71	392	53	2,441	64
11	1,725	60	421	36	731	25	2,878	21	24	1,480	40	724	86	167	27	2,372	53
12	1,642	40	438	60	493	65	2,574	65	25	1,492	60	429	75	273	19	2,195	54
13	1,486	30	518	20	726	45	2,730	95	26	1,721	60	615	94	426	21	2,763	75
Total 1st Qtr.	19,428	03	6,443	09	5,292	48	31,163	60	Total 2nd Qtr.	20,403	50	6,766	81	5,404	93	32,575	24

WEEK No.	CASH		CHEQUES		CREDIT CARDS		TOTAL		WEEK No.	CASH		CHEQUES		CREDIT CARDS		TOTAL	
27	1,784	60	426	74	381	27	2,592	61	40	1,721	30	431	27	275	55	2,428	12
28	1,886	20	383	68	422	36	2,692	24	41	1,562	55	526	33	326	65	2,415	53
29	1,634	40	716	72	274	42	2,625	54	42	1,472	80	387	48	419	38	2,279	66
30	1,420	50	549	36	126	54	2,096	40	43	1,459	60	429	52	528	41	2,417	53
31	1,428	50	126	49	318	71	1,873	70	44	1,473	28	516	61	614	21	2,604	10
32	1,556	60	724	51	479	86	2,760	97	45	1,426	40	714	64	736	37	2,877	41
33	1,495	90	338	42	526	92	2,361	24	46	1,389	85	628	75	521	43	2,540	03
34	1,480	01	174	44	428	74	2,083	19	47	1,427	30	495	38	164	95	2,087	63
35	1,630	27	295	38	114	81	2,040	46	48	1,625	46	384	42	729	65	2,739	53
36	1,680	48	462	97	197	56	2,341	01	49	1,752	80	721	36	518	13	2,992	29
37	1,690	25	381	79	681	74	2,753	78	50	2,120	50	169	94	724	27	3,014	71
38	1,685	72	421	38	384	82	2,491	92	51	2,750	25	425	71	326	95	3,502	91
39	1,738	60	526	66	642	28	2,907	54	52 53	1,408	39	176	89	419	15	2,004	43
Total 3rd Qtr.	21,112	03	5,528	54	4,980	03	31,620	60	Total 4th Qtr.	21,590	48	6,008	30	6,305	10	33,903	88

SUMMARY	CASH		CHEQUES		CREDIT CARDS		TOTAL	
1st Qtr	19,428	03	6,443	09	5,292	48	31,163	60
2nd Qtr	20,403	50	6,766	81	5,404	93	32,575	24
3rd Qtr	21,112	03	5,528	54	4,980	03	31,620	60
4th Qtr	21,590	48	6,008	30	6,305	10	33,903	88
TOTAL	82,534	04	24,746	74	21,982	54	129,263	32

TOTAL SUMMARY FOR YEAR		
Gross Takings for Year	129,263	32
Plus Debtors at end of Year	121	60
Sub-total	129,384	92
Less Debtors at start of Year	166	30
Gross Takings for Year	129,218	62

Fig. 5.4 *The Simplex 'Weekly Summary of Daily Gross Takings'*

(b) Capital receipts   The capital provided by the proprietor when a business is launched is obviously a capital receipt. However, many small businesses are kept going in the first few months by the proprietor paying out of his/her private funds for goods and services, and it is important to realize that these payments are in fact capital contributions which should be recorded as 'Other Receipts'. We may also have capital receipts from the sale of surplus assets or worn-out assets. These receipts must be collected together in one place for inclusion in the capital of the business.

A special 'Summary of Other Receipts' in the back of the Simplex D Book can be used to record these capital receipts. The column is headed 'Extra capital introduced'.

One special point about capital contributions. We are often asked at the Simplex Advice Bureau why a receipt like the Enterprise Allowance eventually appears on the Profit and Loss Account, but capital contributions do not. It is very important to get clear in your mind the difference between the two words 'capital' and 'revenue'. A revenue item, whether it is a revenue receipt or a revenue expense is an item that affects this year's current activities. Thus a revenue receipt is a profit of the business and must appear in either the Trading Account or the Profit and Loss Account, and a revenue expense is a loss of the business and must similarly appear on the Final Accounts and be used in the profit calculations. Capital receipts are not receipts that affect the profits of any one year—the money goes into the business to help the long-term activity over many years, and similarly capital expenditure (the purchase of assets of the business) is beneficial in the long term. These capital movements do not come into the profit calculations—but they do appear on the Balance Sheet, either as assets or liabilities (we owe the capital back to the proprietor when he/she ceases to trade).

(c) Revenue receipts   These are similar to daily takings, but are not the usual type of items included under that heading. Common examples are rent and commission received. Another example is the 'Enterprise Allowance'. As this is paid by Bank Giro transfer it is explained in Chapter 8. Revenue receipts must be included when calculating the profits at the end of the year.

On rare occasions we receive money which is

accountable for tax purposes, because it has avoided tax beforehand. The most likely example is a 'bad debt recovered'. (Where a debt has been previously written off as bad, it has been deducted as a loss in the accounts.) If such a debtor pays up, the sum received is treated as a revenue receipt, since it is taxable.

A special summary column for these miscellaneous receipts will be found in the 'Summary of Other Receipts' at the back of the Simplex book. They will then be brought into the Profit and Loss Account at the end of the year.

Finally, most traders do have at least one Deposit Account at a bank, which will earn interest. One use of such Deposit Accounts is to hold business funds. It is vital to keep such funds available—even on a turnover of only £1 500 per week VAT is nearly £200, which amounts to £2 600 in a quarter. Finding £2 600 which has been muddled in and used for ordinary business funds can be a problem. Even current accounts at banks earn interest these days and this interest must not only be added to the account concerned but recorded as a 'Miscellaneous Receipt' in the 'Summary of Other Receipts'.

(d) Occasional non-revenue receipts

On rare occasions we receive money which is not accountable for tax purposes, since it has been used to calculate tax already. Examples are income-tax refunds. These occasional non-revenue receipts are best recorded in the same place as 'capital receipts' (see above), since they are like profits of former years ploughed back into the business. Similarly 'Loans' arranged are not taxable, and should be taken to the special summary at the back of the Simplex book.

5.5 Summary: What to do to record Receipts

The actions to be taken by the user of a 'Simplex' system to record various types of receipts are summarized diagrammatically in Fig. 5.5 overleaf.

5.6 Keeping Separate Bank Accounts for Personal and Business Items

A great many people get into difficulties with bank accounts because they muddle up personal and business items. It is highly desirable to run separate bank accounts—preferably with different banks if you live in an area which is well served for banking purposes. Since most of us start up with a bank's help and bankers do not like to lose customers there can be an initial difficulty in

RECEIPTS							Week No. **5**		Commencing: **29ᵀᴴ JANUARY 19..**

Day/Date	Daily Gross Takings						Other Receipts Col 4		Particulars
	Cash Col 1		Cheques Col 2		Credit Cards Col 3				
Sun : 29·1	275	27	98	24	94	54	160	00	ENTERPRISE ALLOW.
Mon : 30·1	381	34	36	78	63	70	35	60	TAX REFUND
Tues : 31·1	224	42	128	60	107	24	19	65	DEBTOR P. FOX
Wed : 1·2	379	51	129	70	196	36			
Thur : 2·2	426	90	136	50	175	24			
Fri : 3·2	735	75	274	20	199	50			
Sat : 4·2	516	36	326	30	238	60			
Totals	2,939	55	1,130	32	1,075	18	215	25	

Cash up the till each evening, including cheques and credit card vouchers; deduct any float and record the daily takings here.

Carry the total of these figures to the Cash Summary since the cheques and vouchers are treated as cash and are paid into the bank with the cash takings.

Carry the total of these figures to the weekly summary of daily gross takings at the end of the book If you treat credit sales as 'goods sold', you should include the weekly total of your Debtors' Record Book e.g.

	£
Cash takings	2,939.55
Cheque takings	1,130.32
Credit vouchers	1,075.18
Debtors' total	97.14
	£5,242.19

The enterprise allowance is paid direct to the Bank Account and picked up on the Bank Statement. Enter it on the Sunday line and it will also be entered in the Paid to Bank section. Carry the entry to the summary of other receipts. The Tax Refund is a cheque. Since this is the property of the proprietor it is carried to the summary of other receipts as 'Extra Capital contributed'. The sum from the debtor has to be crossed off in the Debtors Book. It does not need to be carried to a summary if you are treating credit sales as goods sold. If you are treating credit sales as stock out with debtors you must add the amount collected to your gross daily takings figure now you have received the money.

Fig. 5.5 Recording receipts under the Simplex system

changing to another bank. To avoid this at least get clearly separate accounts for business and personal use with your present banker and avoid using the wrong cheque book. It is also very helpful to have a separate deposit account for VAT and Inland Revenue money. Put your tax away in the deposit account every week or month, and you will always have it available on the due date. When it is time to pay you simply transfer enough out of the Deposit Account and into the Current Account and pay it by cheque at once. The Deposit Account earns interest, which is of course a little profit for the business.

Some management books and some accountants will tell you that the availability of VAT money and tax money eases the 'cash flow' of small businesses. This is of course true if you can budget your affairs in such a way as to know with absolute certainty that the funds will be available when needed. It is reckless and unwise to use such short term moneys to buy fixed assets such as machinery or vehicles if it leaves you unable to pay VAT and Taxes as they fall due. Remember in particular that VAT money is not your money—you have only collected it for H.M. Customs and they require it to be paid on the due date.

5.7 Payments to the Bank

Most retailers bank daily, large firms bank two or three times a day. Care should be taken when banking takings, and times and routes to the bank should be varied. The cash to be banked, and any cheques received, are listed in the paying-in book, and credit card vouchers are paid in as you were shown when you became a credit card trader. The amounts paid in are then entered in the 'Paid to Bank' section of the Simplex book (see Fig. 5.6). The weekly total of takings banked is then transferred to both the Weekly Bank Report and the Weekly Cash Report. It represents an increase in the 'Bank' balance and a decrease in the 'Cash' balance in hand.

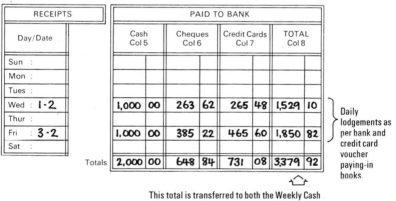

Fig. 5.6 *The Simplex 'Paid to Bank' section*

5.8 Earnings paid net of tax

Some traders who are self-employed only receive payments net-of-tax, at the basic rate, because Inland Revenue rules require the person for whom they are doing sub-contracting work to deduct basic rate tax before payment. Any over-payment or under-payment is sorted out later at the end of the financial year. Recording such receipts is a little tricky, because the income earned is really the gross figure but the amount received is only the net figure. The best way to resolve the problem is as follows:

(a) Enter the gross income (including tax) in the Daily Takings column and carry it to the Summary of Takings at the back of the book (which will therefore show the full earnings).

(b) Enter the tax as a Payment other than for stock, on one of the spare lines as Tax deducted at source. Carry this to the Summary of Expenses at the back of the book, using one of the spare columns headed 'Tax deducted at Source'. This is not a normal business expense, and will not appear on the Profit and Loss Account at the end of the year, but if you tell the tax office about it when you send in your accounts they will give you credit for it, and arrange a refund if you have in fact had too much deducted.

5.9 Exercises on the recording of 'Receipts'

Traders who wish to practice their use of a Simplex D book may feel it is worthwhile using a spare copy of the D book to practice the exercises in this book. There are some at the end of each chapter. If you consider this wasteful it is permitted to photocopy pages for educational or training purposes— anything further is a breach of our copyright. Teachers and lecturers should read the special Foreword in the front of this book.

1. Tom Brown uses the Simplex D Account Book. It is week No. 27 and the week commences on Sunday 1st October. Sales in cash each day are as follows: Monday £117.20; Tuesday £185.50; Wednesday £48.90; Thursday £386.50; Friday £477.25 and Saturday £562.00. On Monday he also sold goods for a cheque £73.65. This is paid in by cheque. On Wednesday he is notified that he has won £728.50 on the Football Pools and decides to put £500 in as extra capital. Credit card sales were Monday £48.60; Tuesday £139.25; Wednesday £97.75; Thursday £126.50; Friday £246.24 and Saturday £380.65. He banks on Tuesday £200 cash, the cheque for £73.65 and credit card vouchers worth £148.60. On Friday he banked cash £750, the football pools £500 by cheque and credit card vouchers worth £350.62. Make all these entries and total the various columns.

2. M. Lipton uses the Simplex D Account Book. It is Week No. 15 and the week commences on July 9th. Sales in cash each day are as follows: Monday, £148.65; Tuesday £272.65; Wednesday £184.50; Thursday £229.75; Friday £347.50; Saturday £492.85. Credit card sales were as follows: £98 on Monday; £137.56 on Tuesday; £213.60 on Wednesday; £84.56 on Thursday; £395.60 on Friday and £338.25 on Saturday.

He also takes a cheque on Tuesday for £100.00. On Friday he recieved a sum of money by cheque from a tenant for rent £52.00. He pays £701.16 into the bank on Wednesday, consisting of cash £250.00, cheques £100 and credit card vouchers £351.16. On Friday he banks £650 cash and credit card vouchers worth £678.16. Make all these entries and total the various columns.

3. R. T. Crafty uses the Simplex D Account Book. Her week No. is 52 and the week commences on 26th March. Sales in cash each day are as follows:

Monday £137.50; Tuesday £246.20; Wednesday £384.50; Thursday £374.00; Friday £386.50; Saturday £596.55. She also takes a cheque for £198.64 on Tuesday, and another on Thursday for £118.45. On Friday she receives a sum of money in cash from A. Debtor £18.25. Credit card sales were as follows: Monday £92.64; Tuesday £106.70; Wednesday £496.32; Thursday £521.16; Friday £424.75; Saturday £198.26. She pays into the bank on Wednesday cash £450.00, cheque £198.64 and credit card vouchers worth £495.66. On Friday she banks £750 in cash, a cheque for £118.45 and credit card vouchers worth £945.91. Make all these entries and total the various columns.

4. Anne Accountant uses the Simplex D Account Book. It is Week No. 17 and the week commences on 23rd July. Fees received are mostly paid by cheque and each day are as follows: Monday £25.00; Tuesday £482.50; Wednesday £36.50; Thursday nil; Friday £28.50. Only Friday's payment was in cash.

She also receives a cheque on Wednesday for £42.50 from a debt collection agency. On Friday she received a sum of money in cash £14.50 for the use of a machine loaned to a fellow accountant. She pays £586.50 into the bank on Thursday, all in cheques. Make all these entries and total the various columns.

Chapter Six

Recording Purchases of Stock for Resale or to Render a Service

6.1 Purchases

The word 'purchases' has a special meaning in book-keeping. In everyday language anything that is bought is a 'purchase', but in business use the word is understood to mean 'a purchase of goods for resale or to render a service'. Depending on the type of business, it is the opposite of the word 'sales' or the opposite of the phrase 'fees for services rendered'. 'Purchases' come into the business, and require to be paid for by the proprietor; 'sales' go out of the business, and are paid for by the customer. The difference between the two gives the profit of the enterprise, and is found by the formula.

$$\text{SALES} - \text{PURCHASES} = \text{PROFIT}$$

However, the costs of its 'purchases' is far from being the only expense that a business incurs: there are of course running costs and overheads to be considered. Similarly, sales are not the only receipts. Accountants talk therefore about 'gross profit' and 'net profit'. Gross profit means 'fat' profit, or total profit. Net profit means 'clean' profit, or clear profit.

$$\text{GROSS PROFIT} = \text{SALES} - \text{PURCHASES}$$
$$\text{NET PROFIT} = \text{GROSS PROFIT} + \text{MISC. RECEIPTS} - \text{EXPENSES}$$

In Chapter 5 we saw that the daily takings, or 'sales', are recorded in the 'Receipts' section of the Simplex page. The 'purchases' are recorded in the 'Payments for Business Stock' section of the Simplex page, as shown in Fig. 6.1.

6.2 Recording Purchases

When goods are purchased they may be paid for in cash or by cheque. Payment may be made to the driver who delivers the goods, or by post. There will usually be some document available to inform the businessman of the value of the consignment, and on which a receipt can be obtained. Cheques are, in themselves, receipts once they have been stamped 'paid' by the banker, but the trader is still entitled under the Cheques Act, 1957, to ask for a receipt for the sum paid. The types of document used in the transaction are described in detail below. Here we are solely concerned with the record made of payments for purchases.

As shown in Fig. 6.1 the amounts paid are recorded by writing down the name of the payee, and the amount. If the payment was a cash payment it is recorded in the 'By Cash' column. If the payment was by cheque it is recorded in the 'By Cheque' column. At the end of the week the two columns are

| Date or Chq. No. | To Whom Paid | Amount Paid | | | |
		By Cash Col 9		By Cheque Col 10	
	PAYMENTS FOR BUSINESS STOCK				
3/4	J. CONLAN & SONS.	48	50		
3/4	J. BREWER & CO. LTD.			36	50
4/4	A.J. GOOD LTD.			136	85
5/4	J. BROWN & CO. LTD.	33	80		
7/4	F. LIVESEY & CO.	26	70		
7/4	A. NEWCOMBE			86	25
	Totals	109	00	259	60

Fig. 6.1 *The recording of 'purchases' in the Simplex system*

totalled. The two amounts, 'total cash paid' and 'total cheques paid', are added together and entered in the 'Weekly Summary of Payments for Goods Purchased' (see Fig. 6.2) as the total purchases for the week. Once again the system permits quarterly totals and an annual total to be prepared. This annual total is transferred to the Trading Account, where it is used to find the Gross Profit of the business.

6.3 Documents for Goods Purchased

(a) **Invoices.** An invoice is defined as 'a document which is made out by the seller when he/she sells goods to a customer'. Most suppliers use a multi-copy system of invoices similar to the batch shown in Fig. 6.3. Such a multi-copy system enables the supplier to start in motion the various activities that are required to deal with the fulfilment of an order. The distribution of invoices from the popular five-copy system is as follows:

(i) The *top copy* is sent by post to the customer to notify him/her that the order is in hand and should be delivered shortly.

WEEKLY SUMMARY OF PAYMENTS FOR BUSINESS STOCK

WEEK No.	AMOUNT	WEEK No.	AMOUNT	WEEK No.	AMOUNT	WEEK No.	AMOUNT	Summary and Reconciliation for Year	
1	285 50	14	368 60	27	880 60	40	860 25		
2	292 70	15	572 32	28	884 40	41	526 30		
3	324 26	16	426 24	29	552 60	42	539 45		
4	315 30	17	380 50	30	380 42	43	542 60		
5	444 25	18	515 30	31	520 32	44	532 75		
6	385 00	19	472 40	32	640 62	45	674 50	Summary and Reconciliation for Year	
7	362 60	20	658 20	33	806 82	46	779 25	1st Qtr.	6,655 06
8	358 60	21	800 50	34	1,240 20	47	638 40	2nd Qtr.	8,764 60
9	327 20	22	572 40	35	820 15	48	1,268 27	3rd Qtr.	8,877 67
10	1,236 40	23	786 30	36	430 24	49	1,272 30	4th Qtr.	12,057 02
11	295 55	24	980 42	37	840 25	50	1,428 50	Purchases Creditors at end of Year	142 50
12	1,226 30	25	825 30	38	400 60	51	1,784 25	SUB-TOTAL	36,496 85
13	801 40	26	1,406 12	39	480 45	52	1,210 20	Less Purchases Creditors at start of Year	342 60
						53		TOTAL	36,154 25
Total 1st Qtr.	6,655 06	Total 2nd Qtr.	8,764 60	Total 3rd Qtr.	8,877 67	Total 4th Qtr.	12,057 02		

Fig. 6.2 *The Simplex 'Weekly Summary of Payments for Business Stock'*

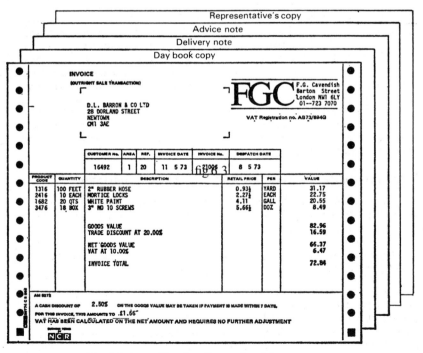

Fig. 6.3 *A set of invoices for goods sold to a customer*

(ii) The second copy or *day-book copy* is sent to the supplier's accounts department. Here it is used to debit the customer's account now that he/she has become a debtor.

(iii) and (iv) The third copy or *delivery note* is sent with the fourth copy or *advice note* to the stock department. Here they are used to authorize the removal of the goods from stock, and to send them with the documents to the dispatch department. The advice note is packed with the goods, to inform the buyer of the contents of the parcel or consignment. The delivery note is given to the driver, who gets a signature for the goods on delivery.

This acknowledgement of safe delivery is returned to the stock department or dispatch department.

(v) The fifth copy or *representative's copy* is sent to the commercial traveller who took the order to inform him/her that it has been fulfilled.

Invoices should always be preserved, either in an indexed lever-arch file or in a 'concertina' file. Since the trader usually receives two copies—the top copy and the advice note—they should be clipped together when both are available.

(b) **Credit Notes.** A credit note is a document made out whenever one person returns goods to another. The credit note is always made out by the seller, who is now receiving back the goods which are unsatisfactory for some reason. It leads to a reduction in the debt of the customer or, if payment was made in cash to a reduction in the amount payable on the next occasion that the customer places an order. Credit notes should be filed in the same way as invoices in a lever-arch file or a concertina file.

Note re VAT and Documents. Invoices and credit notes become very important to VAT registered traders because they are tax documents on which VAT is charged. VAT is explained later in this book (see Chapter 18).

(c) **Statements.** A trader who is given credit is expected to pay, not on delivery, but when a *Statement of Account* is rendered—usually at the end of the month. These days statments are often prepared by a computer at the same time that the customer's account is up-dated.

A trader who receives this type of statement can use it to check his/her own records of the goods invoiced in the trading period covered by the statement. Returns credited should also be shown as a reduction in the amount owed. A typical statement of account is shown in Fig. 6.4.

6.4 Purchases taken from Stock for Use by the Proprietor

An item which indirectly affects the 'Payments for Business Stock' is the taking home of goods for use by the proprietor. The method of dealing with this item is given later (see Section 21.2).

6.5 Transferring 'Payments for Business Stock' to the 'Weekly Summary of Payments for Goods Purchased'

As with the Weekly Summary of Takings, the Weekly Summary of Payments for Business Stock (Fig. 6.2 p46) enables the trader to collect together the total quarterly and yearly figures for purchases. The 'purchases' for the year will then be used to work out the profits of the business in the Trading Account. Note that if there are any trade creditors, whose bills have not yet been paid, they must be included in the final figures by recording the total trade creditors

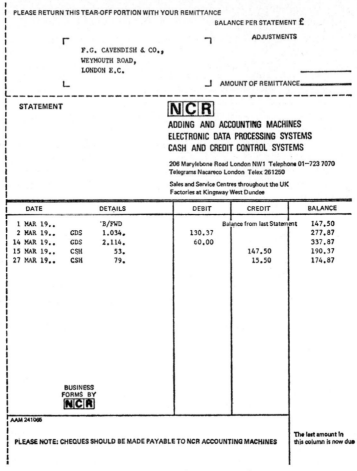

PLEASE RETURN THIS TEAR-OFF PORTION WITH YOUR REMITTANCE

BALANCE PER STATEMENT £

ADJUSTMENTS

F.G. CAVENDISH & CO.,
WEYMOUTH ROAD,
LONDON E.C.

AMOUNT OF REMITTANCE

STATEMENT

NCR

ADDING AND ACCOUNTING MACHINES
ELECTRONIC DATA PROCESSING SYSTEMS
CASH AND CREDIT CONTROL SYSTEMS

206 Marylebone Road London NW1 Telephone 01–723 7070
Telegrams Nacareco London Telex 261250

Sales and Service Centres throughout the UK
Factories at Kingsway West Dundee

DATE		DETAILS	DEBIT	CREDIT	BALANCE
1 MAR 19..		·B/FWD		Balance from last Statement	147.50
2 MAR 19..	GDS	1.034.	130.37		277.87
14 MAR 19..	GDS	2.114.	60.00		337.87
15 MAR 19..	CSH	53.		147.50	190.37
27 MAR 19..	CSH	79.		15.50	174.87

BUSINESS
FORMS BY
NCR

AAM 241065

PLEASE NOTE: CHEQUES SHOULD BE MADE PAYABLE TO NCR ACCOUNTING MACHINES

The last amount in
this column is now due

Fig. 6.4 *A computerized statement of account*

in the box provided before adding up the total for the year. Trade creditors at the start of the year will be deducted because, although paid in the present year, they are really payments for the previous year's purchases.

6.6 What to do with a credit note for goods returned

When a credit note is received for goods returned it is in effect a reduction in the charge previously made. It depends what this charge was for, as to the remedial action that should be taken. If it was a charge for business stock, the credit note may be deducted from the cost of the next supply made, and this will mean that the total charge made for 'Payments for Business Stock' will be reduced to the correct figure. If the credit note is not for stock, but is for a 'Payment other than for Stock' it will be dealt with in the 'Payments other than for Stock' section. This is explained in Chapter 7.

The actual entries for a credit note for stock returned by you to a supplier depend upon whether you regularly deal with the supplier concerned. If you do, wait until the next invoice (or statement) due for payment arrives. If it is an invoice deduct the value of the credit note from it and enter the invoice at the reduced figure, so that the total carried to the summary is reduced by the amount of the credit note. If the accounting document is a monthly statement, check that the credit note is deducted from it. If it isn't, deduct it from the statement and only pay the net amount.

If you do not intend to deal with the supplier again the supplier must repay you the amount due. Phone or write for a cheque in settlement. In the meantime enter the credit note in red ink and carry it to the summary at the back of the book, and deduct it from the quarterly total when you add up the quarterly figure.

6.7 Exercises in Recording Payments for Business Stock

1. M. Phillips records in his Simplex page under the heading 'Payments for Business Stock' the following items during the week.

July   7. Paid to R. Corbett by cheque £25.74 and to S. Tims in cash £5.40.
July   8. Paid to McKrill Biscuit Co., by cheque £85.50 and to Prepared Foods Ltd., £46.50 by cheque.
July   9. Paid to R. Masterson by cheque £27.25 and to The Mineral Water Co. Ltd., in cash £25.85.
July 13. Paid to M. Laws by cheque £17.25.

Enter these items and total the 'cash' and 'cheque' columns.

2. R. Walford records on his Simplex page under the heading 'Payments for Business Stock' the following items during the week.

Aug. 14. Paid to M. Rogerson by cheque £27.55 and to B. Laker by cheque £13.50.
Aug. 16. Paid to A. Waterson in cash the sum of £25.80 for materials supplied.
Aug. 18. A delivery from R. Cook & Co., is valued at £48.50 but returns amounting to £7.25 are given by Walford to the van driver. The net amount is paid in cash.

Enter these items and total the 'cash' and 'cheque' columns.

3. Mary Toft records on her Simplex pages under the heading 'Payments for Business Stock' the following items during the week.

Oct.   7. Paid to T. Ludd by cheque £28.74 and to S. Thames in cash £5.46.
Oct.   8. Paid to Water Biscuit Co. Ltd., by cheque £88.50 and to Novel Foods Ltd., £48.50 by cheque.
Oct.   9   Paid to R. Smiley by cheque £112.00 and to Fresh Vegetables Ltd. in cash £7.35.
Oct. 13. Paid to M. Lawson by cheque £14.25.

Enter these items and total the 'cash' and 'cheques' columns.

4. R. Bliss records on his Simplex page under the heading 'Payments for Business Stock' the following items during the week.

May 24. Paid to M. Lawrence by cheque £24.25 and to K. Mayman by cheque £27.20.

May 26. Paid to R. Brett in cash the sum of £13.25.

May 28. A delivery from Utopia Ltd., is valued at £42.80 but returns amounting to £5.00 are given by Bliss to the van driver. The net amount is paid in cash.

Enter these items and total the 'cash' and 'cheques' columns.

Chapter Seven

Recording Payments Other than for Stock

7.1 Payments Other than for Stock

We have already seen in Chapter 6 that stock for resale and stock to render service is purchased throughout the year and is recorded in the 'Payments for Business Stock' section of the weekly page. In addition, many items which are not for resale, but are for use in the business, are purchased when required. These may be either *consumable items* (such as petrol and oil, office stationery and postage stamps) or *capital items* (such as machinery, typewriters, furniture and fittings). A third kind of payment is that made for *services rendered* to the business (such as wages, rent and insurance). All these payments, which may be called *working expenses*, must be recorded on the weekly page, in the section shown in Fig. 7.1.

Finally there are some rather specialized items, such as payment of income tax to the Inland Revenue, or Value Added Tax to the Customs & Excise, and drawings by the proprietor. These are not 'working' expenses, but are recorded on the weekly page in the same way.

PAYMENTS OTHER THAN FOR STOCK				
Nature of Payment	By Cash Col 11		By Cheque Col 12	
Rent	35	00		
Rates				
Light and Heat			63	50
Carriage	9	45		
Postages £1·70, 24p· £2·38	4	32		
Paper				
Motor Expenses PETROL	16	12		
—do— REPAIRS			54	50
Travelling	7	32		
Cleaning	5	00		
Printing & Stationery			23	20
Repairs & Renewals			15	78
Insurance (Business)				
Advertising				
Telephone				
Sundries	1	05		
Wages (Employees)	65	75		
H.M. CUSTOMS & EXCISE (VAT)			1,436	20
Inland Revenue (PAYE + NI)			27	96
Drawings of the Proprietor (see Note 4)	85	00		
Drawings – Partner 1				
Drawings – Partner 2				
Drawings – Partner 3				
Capital Items (see Note 3(1)) SHELF UNIT			32	00
—do—				
Totals	229	01	1,680	60

Fig. 7.1
Recording payments other than for stock

SUMMARY OF PAYMENTS

Week No.	Rent and Rates	Light and Heat	Carriage and Postages	Paper	Motor Expenses	Motor Expenses	Travelling	Cleaning	Printing and Stationery	Repairs and Renewals
1	520 00		12 36					32 00		
2			4 56		16 95			32 00		
3	236 50		7 32		9 12			32 00		
4			6 15		13 15			39 50		
5		86 26	5 29		16 12			32 00		36 25
6		42 60	2 34	27 63			13 24	32 00		
7			13 75		14 10			32 00		
8			12 94		15 12			32 00		
9			4 25		11 27			42 50		
10			6 25		36 19			32 00	36 38	
11			7 13		14 12			32 00		
12			8 01		15 06			32 00		
13			9 94		13 72			35 00		
1st Qtr.	756 50	128 85	100 29	27 63	174 92	– –	13 24	437 00	36 38	36 25
14			11 36		17 46			32 00		
15	520 00		5 17		12 37			32 00		
16			8 64				23 68	32 00		
17			6 25		8 54	168 54		34 50		
18		62 30	17 83	27 63	18 49			32 00		127 32
19		35 14	1 75		13 28			32 00		
20			24 40				16 28	32 00		
21			13 25		11 63			32 00		
22			16 01		9 17			39 50		
23			19 14	14 92	19 51			32 00		
24			14 60		14 42			32 00		
25			1 75		11 72			42 50		
26			7 99		16 58			32 00		
2nd Qtr.	520 00	97 44	148 14	42 55	153 17	168 54	39 96	436 50	– –	127 32
27	520 00		14 27		15 24			35 00		
28			3 18				14 92	41 25		
29			2 46		18 57			35 00		
30			15 25		27 32			35 00		
31	236 50	44 60	6 13	28 14	12 54			35 00	47 22	
32		25 50	5 73		14 46			46 25		
33			28 82				16 25	35 00		
34			7 87		16 68			35 00		
35			19 54		23 17			40 30		
36			6 75		45 76			35 00		
37			11 46	28 32	39 24			35 00		
38			4 21		15 76			35 00		
39			12 54	15 04	21 83			35 00		
3rd Qtr.	756 50	70 10	138 21	71 50	250 57		31 17	477 80	47 22	– –
40			4 42		23 74			35 00		
41	520 00		14 86		12 49			35 00		
42			7 71		14 62			35 00		
43			19 39	28 32	25 57			35 00	18 15	
44			7 19				86 71	48 50		
45			13 58		26 38			35 00		
46		79 85	12 88		10 26	131 26		35 00		28 94
47		62 80	2 29		12 43			39 50		
48			3 84		27 51			35 00		
49			8 14		15 17			35 00		
50			4 12	15 14	19 36			43 25		
51			14 61		18 20			35 00		
52			17 16		11 44			35 00		
53										
4th Qtr.	520 00	142 65	130 19	43 46	217 17	131 26	86 71	481 25	18 15	28 94
Annual Total	2553 00	439 04	516 83	185 14	795 83	299 80	171 08	1832 55	101 75	192 51

Fig 7.2 *A typical summary*

FOR EXPENSES

Week No.	Insurance (Business)	Advertising	Telephone	Sundries & Bank Charges	Wages	Inland Revenue	Total
1					68 00		632 36
2					68 00		121 51
3					68 00		352 94
4					69 00	148 50	275 30
5	50 00				78 00		303 91
6			324 00		78 00		519 81
7					85 00		144 85
8		272 50			85 00	156 20	573 76
9				24 30	165 00		247 32
10					165 00		275 82
11					165 00		218 25
12					165 00	176 30	396 37
13					165 00		223 66
1st Qtr	50 00	272 50	324 00	24 30	1423 00	481 00	4285 86
14					165 00		225 82
15					165 00		734 54
16					165 00	176 30	405 62
17				1 52	165 00		384 35
18			423 00		124 50		833 07
19				3 56	124 50		210 23
20					124 50	138 20	335 38
21		86 40			124 50		267 78
22				29 62	124 50		218 80
23					168 00		253 57
24					168 00	143 40	372 42
25					168 00		223 97
26					168 00		224 57
2nd Qtr	— —	86 40	423 00	34 70	1954 50	457 90	4690 12
27					168 00		752 51
28					168 00	159 90	387 25
29					168 00		224 03
30					168 00		245 57
31			375 00		168 00		953 13
32	95 20				168 00	86 54	441 68
33					85 55		165 62
34				29 85	85 55		174 95
35					85 55		168 56
36					85 55	112 25	285 31
37					85 55		199 57
38					85 55		140 52
39					85 55		169 96
3rd Qtr	95 20	— —	375 00	29 85	1606 85	358 69	4308 66
40					173 40	147 27	383 83
41					173 40		755 75
42				12 17	173 40		242 90
43			416 00		173 40		715 83
44					173 40	169 50	485 30
45		163 60			173 40		411 96
46					173 40		471 59
47				14 97	173 40		305 39
48					173 40	108 24	347 99
49					173 40		231 71
50					168 00		249 87
51					168 00		235 81
52					168 00	106 72	338 32
53							
4th Qtr	— —	163 60	416 00	27 14	2238 00	531 73	5176 25
Annual Total	145 20	522 50	1538 00	115 99	7222 35	1829 32	18460 89

of payments for expenses

7.2 Recording Working Expenses

Working expenses, i.e. payments for consumables and services received, may be paid in cash or by cheque. It will often be the case that only one entry per week appears under each heading. For example, rent is unlikely to be paid twice in one week; possibly it will only be paid once a quarter or once a month. But some items (such as postage) are paid more frequently than once per week. In this case it is usual to jot down at some convenient spot on the page such items as they occur. The total can then be entered in the cash or cheque column on the last day of the week. This method may be seen on the 'postages' line in Fig. 7.1.

Summarizing the Expenses of the Business

The Simplex weekly page is designed to record each week's receipts and payments on a single sheet of paper. To calculate the profits of the business we must collect together all these items into an annual figure. We have already seen how the daily takings are summarized (see Section 5.3 and Fig. 5.4) and how purchases of business stock are summarized (see Section 6.2 and Fig. 6.2).

Fig. 7.2 shows the 'Summary of Payments for Expenses' page which appears near the end of the Simplex book. The weekly figures are transferred from the 'Payments Other than for Stock' columns (Fig. 7.1) to this summary, where they are added together to give quarterly totals. The quarterly totals are eventually added to give annual totals, which can then be transferred to the Profit and Loss Account to determine the profits for the year.

7.3 Recording Capital Items

The 'Payment Other than for Stock' section is divided by the printer into two

	CAPITAL EXPENSES INCURRED DURING THE YEAR						
DATE	NATURE AND FULL DETAILS OF EXPENSE	INVOICE VALUE		NET VALUE OF ASSET		VAT	
19.. JAN 31	WEIGHING MACHINE (REF 2/5/17405)	234	75	204	14	30	61
JUNE 7	ELECTRONIC TILL (MICROLEADER 4/732/5A)	438	20	381	04	57	16
NOV 7	SHELF UNITS (6 × 6ᶠᵀ× 6 SHELVES)	136	00	118	26	17	74
NOV 14	SHELF UNIT (1 × 4ᶠᵀ× 4 SHELVES)	32	00	27	83	4	17
	TOTALS						

Fig. 7.3 *Recording additions to assets during the year*

parts, the top part being used to record payments for working expenses, and the lower part for other payments. Capital items, which are unlikely to occur very frequently once the business is actually under way, are recorded at the bottom of the page. Some indication of the item purchased should be written in the space next to the words 'Capital Items'. Thus (taking an example from Fig. 7.1) a typical entry might be: 'Shelf unit ... £32. It does not matter whether the item is new or second-hand: provided that it is one of permanent use to the trader in the conduct of his/her affairs, and likely to last more than one year, it is treated as a capital asset.

Capital expenses are not losses of the business, and are not therefore summarized in the same way as expenses. There will not be many of them, and those there are will merely add to the value of the assets of the business. They are recorded near the back of the Simplex book in a table headed 'Capital Expenses Incurred During The Year'. This is shown in Fig. 7.3.

7.4 Recording Drawings for Self

The proprietor of a business draws sums of money in expectation of profit, for the support of himself and his family. These payments by the business to the proprietor are therefore quite different from any other type of payment. A full explanation of these drawings is given later; at the moment it is only necessary to note that they are recorded in the lower part of the 'Payments Other than for

SUMMARY OF DRAWINGS FOR SELF

Week No	Partner 1	Partner 2	Partner 3	Week No	Partner 1	Partner 2	Partner 3	Yearly Summary
1	150.00			27	150.00			**Partner 1**
2	150.00			28	150.00	750.00		1st Qtr 1950.00
3	150.00			29	150.00			2nd Qtr 4124.00
4	150.00	750.00		30	150.00			3rd Qtr 1950.00
5	150.00			31	150.00			4th Qtr 1950.00
6	150.00			32	150.00	750.00		Total 9974.00
7	150.00			33	150.00			
8	150.00	750.00		34	150.00			
9	150.00			35	150.00			
10	150.00			36	150.00	750.00		
11	150.00			37	150.00			
12	150.00	750.00		38	150.00			
13	150.00			39	150.00			**Partner 2**
1st Qtr	1950.00	2250.00		3rd Qtr	1950.00	2250.00		1st Qtr 2250.00
14	150.00			40	150.00	750.00		2nd Qtr 5106.00
15	150.00			41	150.00			3rd Qtr 2250.00
16	150.00	750.00		42	150.00			4th Qtr 3000.00
17	150.00			43	150.00			Total 12606.00
18	150.00			44	150.00	750.00		
19	150.00			45	150.00			
20	150.00	750.00		46	150.00			
21	150.00			47	150.00			
22	150.00			48	150.00	750.00		**Partner 3**
23	150.00			49	150.00			1st Qtr
24	150.00	750.00		50	150.00			2nd Qtr
25	150.00			51	150.00			3rd Qtr
26	150.00			52	150.00	750.00		4th Qtr
TAX	2174.00	2856.00		53				Total
2nd Qtr	4124.00	5106.00		4th Qtr	1950.00	3000.00		

Fig 7.4 *Summary of drawings for self—two partners shown*

Stock' columns, just above capital items. The drawings are then carried to a Summary of Drawings for Self, as shown in Fig. 7.4 opposite. Space is available for up to three partners.

7.5 Recording Tax Payments

Every trader or business pays a variety of taxes indicated as follows. In the Simplex System they are all recorded in the 'Payments Other than for Stock' section as shown in Fig. 7.1.

(a) Self Employed Trader. A proprietor is liable to pay tax on his/her profits. The amount due is paid in two equal half yearly instalments on January 1st and July 1st. If the tax due is paid out of business funds the half yearly payments should be treated as extra 'Drawings' since the proprietor is using some of the business's funds to pay his/her tax.

(b) PAYE (Pay as you earn). A proprietor who is also an employer must deduct tax from employees' wages and remit it to the Inland Revenue, along with National Insurance Contributions, monthly (or quarterly if the sums involved are small). The total sums for Income Tax and NICs are collected together for convenience in the 'Summary of Payments for Expenses' sheet as shown in Fig. 7.2. They are different from other tax payments as they are really part of the employees' wages and as such are a deductible expense of the business. They can be deducted from the profit at the end of the year in the Profit and Loss Account and are shown 'grossed up' ....i.e. added on to the Wages (see the Profit and Loss Account on Page 156).

(c) Limited Company. Companies are liable to pay Corporation Tax as explained on page 83..

(d) VAT (Value Added Tax). All businesses whose turnover exceeds £25 400 per annum must register with H.M. Customs & Excise. They must then charge their customers with VAT and account for it to H.M. Customs & Excise at the end of each quarterly period. VAT payments are carried to the Summary of VAT Quarterly Payments at the back of the book as shown in Fig. 7.5. A full description of VAT and the way in which it is dealt with in the Simplex System is given in Chapter 18.

Note: Zero rated traders do not pay VAT quarterly. Instead they get a monthly refund from H.M. Customs & Excise (because they do not collect any output tax from their customers but are allowed to reclaim input tax paid on their inputs). These repayments appear in the Summary of Other Receipts.

7.6 Recording Payments of Wages

For our present purpose it is necessary only to notice that wages, and the National Insurance contributions which an employer must pay, are recorded in the 'Payments Other than for Stock' columns as shown in Fig. 7.1. They represent an expense of the business which may be deducted when calculating the profits for the year. If the number of staff exceeds two, their wages should also be entered in a separate Wages Book (see Chapter 17).

SUMMARY OF VAT QUARTERLY PAYMENTS		
Note: VAT refunds for Zero Rated traders are dealt with in the Summary of Other Receipts.		
Week No.	Quarter Ending	Amount
4		1436 20
17		1,527 60
30		1,175 80
43		1,926 30
	Total for Year	6,065 90

Fig. 7.5 *The VAT Summary at the back of the Simplex D book*

Where a wife (or a husband) is employed in a family business, the payments made to her/him are treated like ordinary wages of other employees; they are deductible from the profits of the business. However, this wage paid to the spouse has to be included in her/his earnings as part of her/his income for tax purposes. Since wives and husbands now have separate assessments for tax purposes the spouse who has been employed in the other's business must be given the usual P60 (end of year statement of income received, etc) so that she/he can complete the tax return in a proper manner.

Where the spouse is a partner in the business, the sums paid are not wages but 'drawings'. They are recorded just like the drawings of any other proprietor as outlined in Section 7.4.

7.7 Self Employed Stamps

If business funds are used to buy self-employed stamps their value must be treated as 'drawings' since these are a use of the business's profits to meet the personal expenses of the proprietor, and are not the same as the employer's National Insurance contributions for employees.

7.8 Credit notes for expenses

If you receive a credit note for an expense item, for example for an overcharge from a garage or something like that, it presents a little problem. The expense has already gone through your books and been carried to the Summary of Expenses at the back of the book. If you deal regularly with the person concerned you can wait until the next time you get a bill from them, and then deduct the credit note from it (the new expense therefore going to the Summary of Expenses at the reduced figure).

If you do not deal regularly with the firm, and they actually refund the amount due, enter it in the Other Receipts column, but do not carry it to the Summary of Other Receipts. Instead use a red ball point pen to enter a red ink item on the Summary of Expenses in the column concerned; for example (− £7·92 refund). This will be deducted when you add up the quarterly total for the expense concerned.

7.9 Credit notes for capital items

Where a credit note is received for an allowance on a capital item or for the return of a capital item it depends once again whether the supplier concerned is likely to supply further goods in the near future. If so the value of the credit note could be deducted from the value of the next invoice, the new item going through to the Summary of Capital Expenses at the reduced rate. However this is really rather unsatisfactory, and the better method is to make a red ink entry in the Summary of Capital Expenses to bring the existing capital item down to the correct value (or remove it altogether if it was returned). We then have to remember that we have a supplier who is really a debtor (he/she owes us for the returned item). This could be cleared up:

(a) When we receive a further invoice, the credit note not being deducted from the actual payment although the new capital item would be entered in the Summary of Capital Expenses at the full price or

(b) If we are not likely to order more goods from the supplier in the near future we can ask for a refund of the money owed—which will come in as an 'Other Receipt'.

7.10 Refunds to customers

Sometimes we make a refund to a customer when it is not possible to do it from the money in a till. For example an ordinary trader who uses a till would solve the problem of a dissatisfied customer by taking the goods back into stock and refunding money from the till (thus reducing the daily takings to give a correct figure in the Summary of Gross Daily Takings. Where we cannot do this, and have to make a refund in cash or by cheque without taking the money from today's takings, it is important to remember the two things that are happening:

(a) Stock is going back on the shelves, and consequently total takings for the year must be reduced by the amount of the refund.

(b) Cash (or a cheque) is going out as we return it to the customer.

The entries therefore are as follows:

(i) Enter the refund as a 'Payment Other Than For Stock' using one of the spare lines provided and labelling it. 'Refund of Cash (or Cheque) to a Customer'.

(ii) Instead of carrying this to the Summary of Expenses carry it to the Summary of Gross Daily Takings as a red ink entry which will be deducted from the takings as we add up the quarterly total.

7.11 Cheques returned by a supplier who is for some reason unable to supply

Sometimes we order something and enclose a cheque, but the supplier is unable to supply for some reason and the cheque is returned. This leaves a bit of a problem because we have deducted the cheque some time ago but the money has never gone out of our Bank Account because the Supplier did not present it for payment but simply returned it. Suppose the cheque was for £50 and it was for Stationery.

(a) We make a red ink entry in the 'Stationery' line 'cheque returned £50'. This will be deducted from the other cheques paid this week and will bring our weekly Bank Report correct, because it will compensate for the £50 deducted a few weeks earlier.

(b) We go to the Summary of Expenses at the back of the book and put a red ink entry (−£50) in the stationery column to reduce the amount spent on stationery in the quarter. When we add up the quarterly total we deduct £50.

It may also be necessary to go to our cheque book (where the counterfoils will have been deducted from the running balance) and add back £50 to get the cheque book balance correct—since the £50 has never really been deducted from our Bank Account.

7.12 Pension and Life Assurance Payments

If pensions and life assurance payments for the benefit of the proprietor or his/her dependants are paid out of the business bank account they must be treated as extra drawings since they are not a business expense.

7.13 Conclusion

We have now seen how to record on the Simplex page the following matters:
- *(a)* The daily takings ('sales') and other receipts.
- *(b)* The purchases of goods for resale or to render service ('business stock').
- *(c)* The payments for consumable items and for services rendered to the business.
- *(d)* The purchases of capital assets.
- *(e)* The payment of tax, and VAT.
- *(f)* The drawing of cash by the proprietor.

It only remains to calculate the cash balance and the bank balance, by recording our receipts and payments in the 'Weekly Cash Report' and 'Weekly Bank Report'.

7.14 Exercises in Recording Payments Other than for Stock

Using paper ruled as in Fig. 7.1, or a spare Simplex D Account Book make the following entries in the 'Payments Other than for Stock' section.

1. Martin Brown is in business as a greengrocer. In Week 42 he pays the following items in cash: rent £45; postages 27p, 32p, 46p and £1·40; petrol

£8·75 and insurance £15·20. He also pays wages £87·50 in cash. He pays by cheque for a weighing machine £69·75 and for sundries £8·50. He also draws for his own use the sum of £60·00 by cheque. Enter the above items and total the two columns to find the total 'Cash' and 'Cheque' payments.

2. Ella Goodtaste is in business as a fashion designer. In Week 37 she pays the following items in cash: postages £2·47 and £1·32; art materials £4·65 and travelling £12·50. She also pays wages £82·50 in cash. She pays by cheque for stationery £7·42 and a telephone bill for £281·74. She also draws for herself the sum of £100 in cash. Enter the above items and total the two columns to find the total 'Cash' and 'Cheque' payments.

3. Michael Beltaine is in business as a chiropodist. In Week 37 he pays the following items in cash: postages 27p, 32p, 66p and £1·46; advertising £32·50 and sundries 25p. He also pays travelling expenses £13·28 in cash. He pays by cheque for rates £248·50, VAT to Customs and Excise £765·60, and also draws for his own use the sum of £85·00 by cheque. Enter the above items and total the two columns to find the total 'Cash' and 'Cheque' payments.

Chapter Eight
The Weekly Cash and Bank Reports

8.1 Introduction

At the end of each week's work it is advisable to check on the cash and bank positions. For this reason the Simplex system incorporates a 'Weekly Bank Report' and a 'Weekly Cash Report'. These two sections of the weekly page enable you to check the accuracy of your cash record, your record of cheques drawn and your daily entries in the 'Paid to Bank' column. Assuming that they have been kept in the manner shown below, the weekly reports can be compared with the actual cash in the till and with the statement as rendered by the bank. Any discrepancy should of course be investigated.

8.2 The Weekly Bank Report

A typical 'Weekly Bank Report' is shown in Fig. 8.1. It starts with the opening balance brought forward from the previous week. This is then increased by the total amount paid in during the week, which is found from the 'Paid to Bank' column (see Section 5.7). These two figures are then added, and their sum gives the total amount in the bank account.

From the total in the bank account we must now deduct the total of cheques drawn. This is made up of the cheques drawn for 'Payments for Business Stock', plus the cheques drawn for 'Payments Other than for Stock', plus the total (if any) of cash drawn from the bank. Of course a firm which was taking considerable sums in cash from customers, as in the example shown in Fig. 8.1 would not have much need to go to the bank to draw out cash.

It may also be necessary to deduct any standing orders or direct debits that have been paid by the bank, and also any bank charges and interest charges. These items are explained below. They cannot be dealt with every week; only in the week when we receive a bank statement. Deducting the total paid out from the bank from the total in the account gives the 'Closing Balance carried forward'. This is taken over to the next page, ready to start the new week. Study Fig. 8.1 now.

Although the result of these calculations gives us the balance to carry forward, there are still two points to be borne in mind: one concerns 'bank reconciliation statements', the other concerns overdrafts.

(a) Bank Reconciliation Statements

In fact, although we have found the balance on the bank account according to our records, the bank may not agree with us for a number of reasons. First, the bank deducts 'charges' for keeping our account. Secondly, it automatically makes payments by 'standing orders' or 'direct debits' which we have

WEEKLY BANK REPORT				
	Opening Balance brought forward		1,343	56
Add	Total Paid to Bank during week (Col 8)		4,126	60
	Total		5,470	16
	Cash drawn from bank	—	—	
	Stock Payments (Col 10)	1,259	60	
Deduct	Other Payments (Col 12)	1,244	40	
	Standing Orders/Direct Debits	—	—	
	Bank and Interest Charges	—	—	
	Total		2,504	00
	Closing Balance carried forward		2,966	16

Fig. 8.1 *The Weekly Bank Report*

authorised. Recurrent charges such as rates, mortgage repayments and annual subscriptions are often dealt with in one of these two ways. All such deductions will be made on our account without the bank informing us. Similarly, the bank may receive money into our account from customers who pay hire-purchase instalments or trade debts to us by 'credit transfer'. The result is that we may either have more money or less money in the bank than we think. The actual position will be known when we inspect our bank statement, which we usually receive monthly.

The process of reconciling the 'Weekly Bank Report' with the bank statement is explained in Section 16.4. It requires us to draw up a 'bank reconciliation statement' after checking the various differences between the two sets of records. A Bank Reconciliation Statement is usually worked out once a month when the Bank Statement arrives.

(b) Overdrafts

It is important to note that if you are trading on overdraft, the balance brought forward will be an 'overdraft balance', i.e. one that you *owe* to the bank. Therefore sums paid in will reduce the overdraft balance (instead of increasing a credit balance), and sums paid out must be added to the overdraft balance (instead of being deducted from a credit balance). Consequently you must reverse the words 'Add' and 'Deduct', as shown in Fig. 8.2. In this example the sums paid into the bank during the week reduce the overdraft, but it is raised again by the further payments made for Stock and Other Payments.

8.3 The Weekly Cash Report

The 'Weekly Cash Report' shown in Fig. 8.3 is very similar to the 'Weekly Bank Report'. It starts with the opening balance (cash in hand—as counted) brought forward from the previous week. To this cash in hand we add the combined total of the 'Daily Takings' columns (1, 2 and 3). We also add the 'Other Receipts' and any cash that has been drawn from the bank for office use.

WEEKLY BANK REPORT					
	Opening Balance brought forward			1568	47
~~Add~~ DEDUCT	Total Paid to Bank during week (Col 8)			1126	60
			Total	441	87
	Cash drawn from bank	—	—		
	Stock Payments (Col 10)	259	60		
~~Deduct~~ ADD	Other Payments (Col 12)	244	40		
	Standing Orders/Direct Debits	—	—		
	Bank and Interest Charges	—	—		
			Total	504	00
	Closing Balance carried forward			945	87

Fig. 8.2 *The 'Weekly Bank Report' when trading on overdraft*

Now we must deduct, first, the 'Payment for Business Stock' which were made in cash, secondly, the 'Payments other than for Stock' which were made in cash, and finally the total 'Paid to Bank'. What remains after these deductions is the *cash balance according to our books.*

This cash balance is now checked by counting the cash balance actually in the tills. In doing so any cheques and credit card vouchers not yet paid in must be treated as part of the cash in hand. Any difference on the books should be investigated to discover the error, or the cause of the cash loss from the till. If blame cannot be assigned to anyone, and the missing amount recovered, it is recorded as a 'difference on books'. In Fig. 8.3 the difference is 35 pence.

WEEKLY CASH REPORT					
	Cash in Hand (as counted) brought forward			6	46
Add	Gross Weekly Takings (Col 1 + Col 2 + Col 3)			2105	02
	Other Receipts (Col 4)			121	08
	Cash Drawn from Bank			—	—
			Total	2232	56
Deduct	Stock Payments (cash)(Col 9)	109	00		
	Other Payments (cash)(Col 11)	229	01		
	Amount paid to Bank (Col 8)	1126	60		
			Total	1464	61
©GEORGE VYNER LTD	Cash Balance on books			767	95
COPYRIGHT RESERVED REPRODUCTION OF THIS BOOK IN WHOLE OR IN PART STRICTLY FORBIDDEN	Cash in hand (as counted) carr. fwd			767	60
	Difference on books (+ or −)			— •	35

Fig. 8.3 *The Weekly Cash Report*

Note: Readers are asked to note that the illustrations used in this book are not supposed to be from the same business or relate to one another. Because it is necessary to illustrate all the different situations that might arise figures have been chosen from any number of different businesses. Please do not try to relate one illustration to another.

8.4 Differences on books

It is useful at this point to say a word or two about differences on books. The tills can be wrong in either direction, a shortage or a surplus. A shortage may mean the following things:

(a) Theft from the tills by outsiders

(b) Theft from the tills by staff

(c) Careless giving of change—a customer has been given too much change

(d) Errors in the book-keeping. Money paid out has not been recorded.

A surplus may mean that a customer has been given too little change. Clearly a shortage is a 'loss' to the business and a surplus is 'a profit'. However the Inland Revenue refuses to admit that this type of loss is really a legitimate expense of the business. It argues (a) that the most likely thing is that any serious loss is undeclared drawings by the proprietor. (b) that incorrect change giving and poor book-keeping are really the responsibility of the proprietor. So is theft from the tills, since supervision must be lax. For these reasons it is usual to treat 'differences on books' as undeclared drawings, and they are added at the end of the year to the proprietor's drawings figure. Only in the case of burglaries and other crimes reported to the police would these losses be considered as business expenses, and even then it would be usual to recover them from insurance in many cases. There is a special summary at the back of the book for differences on books. This is illustrated in Fig. 8.4.

WEEKLY SUMMARY OF DIFFERENCES ON BOOKS															
Week No.	+ or −	Balance		Week No.	+ or −	Balance		Week No.	+ or −	Balance		Week No.	+ or −	Balance	
1	+	5	00	14		0	00	27	−	1	56	40	−	4	26
2	−	2	72	15		0	00	28	+	3	00	41	+	5	00
3	−	3	50	16	−	1	50	29		0	00	42	−	4	33
4		0	00	17	+	5	00	30		0	00	43		0	00
5		0	00	18	+	0	23	31	−	5	50	44		0	00
6	−	10	00	19		0	00	32		0	00	45		0	00
7	−	0	50	20	−	1	50	33		0	00	46	−	20	00
8		0	00	21	−	10	50	34	−	5	62	47	−	5	60
9	+	0	50	22		0	00	35	−	1	00	48	−	4	25
10		0	00	23	−	2	50	36	−	0	50	49		0	00
11		0	00	24	−	1	32	37	+	5	00	50		0	00
12		0	00	25		0	00	38	−	1	61	51	+	1	50
13	−	1	52	26	−	20	00	39		0	00	52		0	00
												53			
1st Qtr	−	12	74	2nd Qtr	−	32	09	3rd Qtr	−	7	79	4th Qtr	−	31	94

Yearly Summary

1st Qtr	−	12	74
2nd Qtr	−	32	09
3rd Qtr	−	7	79
4th Qtr	−	31	94
Final Balance	−	84	56

Fig. 8.4 *The Summary of Differences on Books*

8.5 Withdrawing cash from the Bank

At times a business runs short of cash, or draws cash from its current account at the Bank to meet a particular requirement such as paying wages, or going to a sale of bankrupt's assets etc. In these circumstances the trader merely draws a cheque to 'cash', and the only entries required are those in the 'Weekly Bank Report' (cash drawn from Bank) which deducts the money from the Bank Account and the entry in the Weekly Cash Report (cash drawn from Bank) which adds the money drawn to the 'Cash in hand'.

The cash drawn does not go in the receipts section, because of course we received it long ago and put it in the bank. We are simply transferring it from the bank account to the cash box, till, etc. If drawing cash from the bank for office use is a fairly rare event (as it would be for example in a retail shop where takings are largely in cash and consequently we are rarely short of cash) we can enter the figure on the day we draw the money in the 'Cash Drawn from Bank' section on both the Weekly Cash Report and the Weekly Bank Report. If we are likely to draw cash more than once a week it is best to enter it on the lines concerned, but not in the end column. By the end of the week the lines might read, £50, £30, £170 and we could total these up to £250 in the end column.

8.6 The use of a Deposit Account

Many proprietors find it is advantageous to place sums on Deposit Account at the Bank. In this way the money earns a reasonable rate of interest, yet is available at seven days notice when required. In fact the bank will usually make it available at once, but charge seven days interest on it if notice is not given. Certain sums of money which are only paid intermittently, such as Income Tax (payable twice yearly), Value Added Tax (payable quarterly), Corporation Tax (payable annually) etc., are best accumulated in this way so that they are not confused with Current Account moneys. Some advisers and some text-books will tell you that such funds are of use to the business because they represent extra working capital for use in the business. This is all very well but in our experience it is unwise to leave such sums in the ordinary Current Account, even if it is an interest bearing Current Account. The favourable balance gives an impression of riches which is not in fact the case. The money is committed to pay VAT, income tax etc and is not really available to finance the purchase of extra assets or stock. If put into a Deposit Account it is clearly not available for Current Account use, and it earns a better rate of interest.

The amount to be put into the Deposit Account should be entered on one of the spare lines in the 'Payments Other than for Stock' section, as follows:

Transferred to Deposit Account £725.00. The entry could be in the 'cash' or the 'by cheque' column.

At the back of the Simplex D Account Book there is a section headed 'Movements in and out of Deposit Account'. It is in the style shown in Fig. 8.5. The balance on the account is worked out after every entry. Banks now add interest every three months to this type of account, and when notified by a Bank Statement that interest has been added this should be entered on the Simplex record as a movement into Deposit Account, to bring the balance on our books into line with the balance as shown on the Bank Statement. Note that this interest is a profit of the business which must be accounted for at the end of the financial year, but it will have had tax deducted from it at the standard rate. It should be shown as a Miscellaneous Receipt in the Summary of Other Receipts.

Where money previously deposited is required back in the Current Account to pay VAT or tax we simply transfer it from the Deposit Account back into the Current Account. The entry is made as an 'Other Receipt', writing 'Transfer from Deposit Account' in the Particulars Column. It is entered in the Paid to Bank section and carried to the Summary of Movements in and out of Deposit Account (where of course it reduces the balance available).

Movements in and out of Deposit Account								
Date		Details	Withdrawals (debits)		Deposits (credits)		Balance in hand	
JAN	1	Balance at Start					3284	00
JAN	31	VAT OUTPUT TAX			3214	70	6498	70
	31	TAX			460	00	6958	70
FEB	28	VAT OUTPUT TAX			2736	40	9695	10
	28	TAX			420	00	10,115	10
MAR	25	TO PAY VAT (QTR ENDING 28 FEB)	6140	00			3,975	10
		ETC, ETC.						

Fig. 8.5 *Deposit Account*

Where a Deposit Account *is not part of the business accounts,* but is the personal account of the proprietor, any sum of money taken from the Deposit Account and put into the business is like extra capital contributed. It should therefore be entered in the 'Other Receipts' section and carried to the 'Extra Capital Contributed' summary at the end of the book.

In any case, the sum transferred from Deposit Account will come into the Weekly Bank Report as an extra sum of money in the Current Account. It should be added into the 'Paid to Bank' section so that it becomes part of the 'Total Paid to Bank during Week'.

8.7 Problems with Cheque Payments

Many customers today pay by cheque, and since the development of the credit card system there is no real reason for a trader to refuse payment of small sums by cheque if the customer has a credit card from his/her bank. The banks will always honour a cheque up to the limit stated on the credit card, which at the time of writing is usually £50. The acceptance of cheques in payment of sums greater than the limit on the card is unwise, unless the goods are being withheld until the cheque has been cleared.

Despite this guarantee of eventual payment cheques can still be inconvenient if they are not properly made out, and staff should be trained in the checking of cheques. Sometimes the proprietor or a floor manager insists on personally confirming that a cheque is correctly made out before goods are wrapped. The chief difficulties are:

- *(a)* Incorrect date or no date at all.
- *(b)* Incorrect name on the line which begins 'Pay...........' The name should be the correct business name, either of the company, or the partnership or the sole trader. If the business trades under a name which is not the same as the name of the trader(s) the correct name is the name displayed at the business premises, under the new rules laid down in the Business Names Act, 1985. A leaflet about this is available from Companies House, 55 City Rd., London EC1Y 1BB.
- *(c)* The wording and the figures of the amount should be the same.
- *(d)* It is frequently the case that the word 'pounds' is left out; the drawer of the cheque writing 'Thirty seven 21' instead of 'Thirty seven pounds 21'.
- *(e)* The cheque may not be signed. Even if it is signed the signature should be compared with the signature on the credit card and any doubts raised with the drawer. He may be asked to sign it a second time.
- *(f)* It is best to cross the cheque if it is not crossed, or ask the drawer to do so.
- *(g)* Any alterations should be initialled, or a full signature is even better.

Dishonoured Cheques

Dishonoured cheques are a problem both from the book-keeping point of view and the pursuit of the debtor. From the viewpoint of keeping the books correct the difficulty is that the cheque has been included in the Daily Takings and carried to the Weekly Summary of Takings. This will mean that the total takings for the year is eventually too high. The best thing to do is to enter the cheque in red on the day it is received in the Other Receipts Particulars Column, explaining that it has been dishonoured. Then carry this red ink entry to the Weekly Summary of Takings and deduct it from the quarterly total. It is also necessary to get your Bank Report right because this money has never reached your Bank Account. In this week's Bank Report on the line reading 'Cash drawn from bank' write in red ball point (Dishonoured cheque) and insert the amount. This will bring your Closing Balance into agreement with the Bank's statement, and the dishonoured cheque will cross-check with the debit to your account made by the bank.

Dishonoured cheques are a great nuisance but the problems they cause will be much reduced if cheques are only accepted from customers who have a banker's credit card. Where a cheque is dishonoured it should be entered in the Debtors' Record Book, to record the debt, and suitable action taken to 'refer the cheque to the drawer'. This means approach him and ask him what he means by it. In most cases he will be suitably apologetic, phone his bank and make arrangements for the cheque to be honoured. It is then re-presented as part of the 'Daily Takings' of the day it is paid in for the second time. If no satisfaction can be obtained it is of course an offence to write cheques knowing that they will not be honoured and the police may be informed. If the sum is trivial and the proprietor wishes to avoid publicity he/she may prefer not to pursue the matter, and the debt will then become a bad debt, which may be written off the profits at the end of the year. (see page 165).

8.8 Bank Reconciliation Statements

There are many things that happen when we use the full services offered by a bank, which do not come to our attention until we receive a bank statement. This should be supplied at regular intervals, usually on a 'cyclical billing' basis. This means that customers are sent a bank statement on the same day each month (but not necessarily on the convenient 'last day' of the month). The items that may not come to our attention until that moment are:

(a) The bank may pay 'standing orders' for us.

(b) The bank may pay 'direct debits' authorised by us.

(c) The bank may collect bank giro credits for us from customers or dividend warrants, gilt-edged securities' interest, etc.

(d) The bank may pay us interest on current or deposit accounts.

(e) The bank may charge us bank charges, or interest on loans, etc.

All these situations are explained in Chapter 16, and we need not deal with them for the moment.

8.9 Exercises in Preparing Weekly Bank Reports and Weekly Cash Reports

1. Tom Smith is in business as a builder. At the end of Week 15 his bank transactions have been as follows: Opening Balance £1 727·46; total paid to bank during week £498·50; Stock payments £84·95 and payments other than for stock £176·50. He also knows that his Bank deducts a mortgage payment of £84·50 during this week, as a standing order. Work out the Weekly Bank Report on special paper ruled as in Fig. 8.1 and thus discover the 'Closing Balance' to be carried forward to week 16.

2. Mary Baker owns a restaurant. At the end of week 23 her bank transactions have been as follows: Opening Balance £2 725·62; total paid to bank during week £895·50; Stock payment £326·56 and Payments other than for stock £48·50. She also knows that bank charges of £38·50 were charged on certain investment dealings during the week. Work out the Weekly Bank

Report on the special paper, and thus discover the 'Closing Balance' to be carried forward to week 24.

3. Ivor Waywivem is in business as a garage owner. At end of week 45 his bank transactions have been as follows: Opening Balance £3 728·52; total paid to bank during week £985·70; Stock payments £525,60 and payments other than for Stock £824.65. He also knows that he withdrew cash from the bank £150 during the week. Work out the Weekly Bank Report on the special paper, and thus discover the 'Closing Balance' to be carried forward to week 46.

4. Martin Reed is in a business as a thatcher. At the end of week 36 his cash transactions have been as follows: Cash in hand (brought forward from previous week) £7·52; total weekly takings £465·50; Other Receipts £15·00. Payments for stock were £38·25 and other payments in cash came to £44·50. He had paid £375·00 into the bank. Using special paper ruled as for Fig. 8.3 work out the Weekly Cash Report and hence discover the Cash Balance. How would you check that this balance was correct?

5. Alison Knitwell is in business as a draper. At the end of Week 4 her cash transactions have been as follows: Cash in hand (brought forward from previous week) £15·56; total weekly takings £678·75; other receipts £8·40. Payments for stock were £232·50 and other payments in cash came to £84·35. She had paid £332·00 into the bank. Using the special paper work out the Weekly Cash Report and hence discover the Cash Balance. Cash in hand as counted came to £58·86. What was the difference on books?

6. Alan Groves is in business as a funeral director. At the end of week 37 his cash transactions have been as follows: Cash in hand (brought forward from previous week) £45·00; total weekly takings £2 762·00; Other receipts £34·00. Payments for stock were £198·00 and other payments in cash came to £836·00. He had paid £1 800·00 into the bank. Using the special paper work out the weekly Cash Report and hence discover the Cash Balance. The cash in hand (as counted) came to £6·50. What was the difference on books?

Chapter Nine

The Simplex System and Various Types of Business

9.1 Introduction—Which Type of Business is Yours?

Into which of the following categories does your business fall?

(a) **A farm, livestock** or **market-garden** business, which has for its main aim the raising of produce for sale to the general public.

(b) A **manufacturing** business, which has for its main activity the conversion of purchased raw materials into a finished product which is then sold at a profit.

(c) A **trading** business, which derives its main profit from the buying and selling of goods.

(d) A **service** business which requires purchase of materials *as well as* the use of skills. A typical example is the builder and decorator who must purchase materials and work them into the customer's property or assets to produce a visible final effect.

(e) A **pure service** business, where your expertise or skill in making arrangements is the vital part of the business, and little or no material is required to provide the service.

The Simplex system is suitable for each of these types of business. The following list is designed to help you decide which type of business yours is. There are bound to be some businesses which overlap and could come under two or more different headings. If this is so in your case, it is advisable to read as many of Chapters 10-15 as are appropriate. You will need to read every chapter if your business is concerned with all five kinds of activity.

9.2 Farms, Livestock and other Primary Production

Read Chapters 10 and 15 if your type of business is like any of those named below:

beekeeper	farriers
bird breeders and dealers	fish farms
bloodstock agencies	fisherman
budgerigar breeder	forage merchants
bulb grower	fruit grower
chicken raiser	grain merchants
dairy farmer	granite merchants
dog breeder	gravel pits
egg and poultry packers	hatchery
farmer	hay and straw merchants

insemination services
livestock breeder
market gardener
mushroom grower
nature conservance
nurseryman
pick-your-own market gardeners
pig breeder/dealer
potato grower
poultry farmer
quarries
rabbit breeders
sand and aggregates
seedsman
smallholder

sheep breeders
shellfish suppliers
slate quarries
stables
straw suppliers
soft-fruit grower
stud farm
tomato growers
trout farms
turf supplier
turkey farmer
vegetable growers
vineyards
yeast suppliers

9.3 Manufacturing Business

Read Chapters 11 and 15 if your type of business is like any of those named below:

aquarium manufacturer
armature winders
artificial flowers
automatic control engineers
bacon curer
battery manufacturers
balustrades and hand rails
barbecues
bearings
brake linings
building systems
button manufacturer
cabinet maker
capstan lathe operators
car spares
carbon products
catering equipment
compact discs
component manufacturers
computers
contact lenses
crane manufacturers
detergents
distillers
doors

electric motors
electroplaters
embossers
embroidery
engines
engineers' tools
etchers
exhaust systems
explosives
fabrics
fans and blowers
fibreboards
film processors
filters
fire alarms
fireproof materials
fireworks
fish curers
flavourings
flocks and fillings
forgings
footwear
foam products
foundries
garden craftsman

gas bottles
garment manufacturer
gearboxes
glazes
gloves
glues
gown maker
grinders
hairpieces
hand driers
handbags
handcarts
handling equipment
ice-cream manufacturer
instruments
jewellery
jigs and tools
kitchen equipment
knitting machines
labelling machines
ladies wear
lighting goods
locks
loose-cover maker
machinery
magnets
matches
materials handling equipment
mattress makers
meat products
medical equipment
metal trades
meters
millinery
mortar manufacturers
mouldings
musical instruments
nailmakers
netmakers
novelties
number plates
nylon
office equipment
optical goods
packing cases
packing materials

paints and varnishes
pallet manufacturer
paper-bag maker
paper sacks
paving stones
pet foods
pipes and tubes
plastics manufacturer
precision engineers
polythene
pottery
poultry houses
power tools
press tools
razor blades
records and cassettes
rubber-stamp maker
rustic woodworker
saddler and harness maker
safety equipment
sail maker
sanitary appliances
sausages
scaffolding
sea-moss dyers and processors
seating manufacturers
shock absorbers
shop fittings
shutter manufacturers
skirts
slipper makers
soap manufacturers
stationery manufacturers
steel makers
storage equipment
structural engineers
surgical goods
tag labels
telecommunication equipment
testing apparatus
textiles
ties and scarves
toolmakers
towelling
trailers
transformers

travel goods
tubes
turbochargers
tyres
ultrasonic devices
underwear

vacuum cleaners
wigmakers
window frames
windscreens
wires and cables
wrought ironwork

9.4 Trading Businesses

Read Chapters 12 and 15 if your type of business is like any of those named below:

antique dealer
aquarium supplier
artist's sundries
audio dealers
automobile trader
babyware shop
bait and tackle shop
baker
boats and small-craft dealer
bookseller
boutique
building centres
builders' merchants
butcher
camping-equipment shop
cane merchants
car-accessory dealer
car breaker
car salesman
card shops
carpets and rugs
'cash and carry'
CB radio
cellular radio
chemist
china and glassware shop
Chinese restaurant
church furnishings
coffee machine suppliers
compact discs
computer shops
computer spares
confectioner
cycle shops

dairy
decorator's merchant
delicatessens
do-it-yourself shop
draper
dress shop
electrical supplies
engineers' merchants
fancy goods
fashions shop
filling station
fish and chip shop
fish merchant
fishmongers
fishing-tackle shop
florist
freezer centres
fruiterer
furniture retailer
furriers
garage
garden centre
general dealer
general merchant
general store
gift shop
gown shop
greengrocer
greetings-card shop
grocer
haberdashery
hardcore merchants
hardware shop
hatter

health-food shop
hi-fi dealers
hobby shop
home-improvement centre
horticultural sundriesman
ice-cream parlour
infants' wear
ironmonger
jeweller
joke shops
knitwear shops
ladies' wear
launderettes
leather-goods shop
lighting goods shops
lightning conductors
lingerie shop
maternity wear
men's wear
milk bar
milliner
model shops
motor traders
music shops
newsagent
night club
novelties and carnival goods
off licence
office-equipment retailers
optical goods
outfitter
paint and wallpaper shop
pet shop
petrol station
pharmacies
philatelic dealer
picture framers
pizza parlours
photographic goods
plumbers' merchants

public house
radio and electrical-goods shop
rag merchant
rain wear
record shop
regalia
restaurant
salvage dealer
scrap merchant
seed merchant
sheet metal merchants
shoe shops
snack bar
sports shop
stamp dealer
stationer
supermarket
surgical goods
sweet shops
surplus store
tableware
take-away restaurants
tea room
telephone shops
television supply and servicing
tailors
teenwear shops
timber supplier
tobacconist
trophy shops
tropical-fish shop
typewriter supplies
video shops
wallpaper merchants
wine and spirit merchant
wine bars
wool shops
wrought-ironwork trader
yacht chandlers

9.5 Service Businesses which require Materials

Read Chapters 13 and 15 if your type of business is like any of these named below:

acoustic engineers   aerial (TV) installer

agricultural contractor
air conditioning
alarm systems
amusement machinery
animal boarding
anodisers
antique restorer
architectural-model maker
anti-corrosion treatments
artexing
asbestos removal
assembler and fabricator
automobile service
banqueting services
barber
battery servicing
beauty salon
blacksmith
boarding-house
boat builder
boiler cleaning
bookbinder
bricklayer
builder and decorator
cable television
calibration services
café
car breakdown
car engine tuning
car hire
car leasing
car park
car spraying
car valeting
caravan park
caterer
cavity wall insulation
ceilings (suspended)
cleaner
closed circuit TV
cold storage
contract furnishers
contract packers
contractor plant hire
cobbler
copying service

crop-spraying contractor
cycle shops
damp proofing
decorator
dental repairs
dentist
descaling services
direct mail
divers
door entry systems
doctor
double-glazing firm
drainage consultants
draught exclusion
drilling contractors
dry cleaning
dry lining
dyeline printing
duplication and office services
electrical contractor
electroplater
energy conservation
engineer
effluent treatment
estate developers
exhaust replacement service
export packers
fencing contractor
ferries
floor-laying service
forestry maintenance
freight forwarders
french polishers
fumigation services
galvanisers
garden contractor
gilding
glass silvering
glazier
gown hire
grainers
graphic designers
grit blasters
hairdresser
health farm
heating contractor

hi-fi sales and service
home improver
hotel
insulation contractor
insurance agent
insurance broker
intercom systems
kitchen consultants
joiners
kennels
keycutting
label printer
laboratory
landscaping
lift engineers
lighting hire
locksmith
loft insulation
machinery installers
marblers
milliner
motor-vehicle service/repairs
music systems
office-cleaning contractor
paging systems
paint sprayer
painter and decorator
pawnbroker
photocopying service
photographer
pile driving
photo agencies
pipework contractors
plasterer
plumber
poster site maintenance
pregnancy-testing service
printer
public address systems
public analysts
rat-catcher

ready mixed concrete
refrigeration engineer
road contractors
roofing contractors
rot proofing
rough casting
school (private)
secretarial services
shop repairer
shopfitter
sign maker
sign writer
silver plater
slater
sound equipment installers
steam cleaning
swap agents
swimming-pool supplier
tailor
tar paving contractor
taxidermists
television repairs/service
thatcher
tiler
tiling contractor
timber preservation
turf contractor
tyre service
upholsterer
vacuum-cleaner repairs
van hire
vending machines
ventilation services
video makers
waste merchants
welder
well-borers
window consultants
window dressers
windscreen replacement
woodworm control

9.6 Pure Service Businesses

Read Chapters 14 and 15 if your type of business is like any of those named below:

abattoir

acapuncture practitioners

accommodation address agencies
accommodation agency
accountant
actuaries
advertising agency
adoption agencies
air-charter service
aerial surveys
aerobics
ambulance services
archaeologists
architect
artist
astrologers
auctioneer
audio-visual services
average adjusters
baby-sitter
bacteriologists
bailiffs
band
boat hire
bookmaker
bureaux de change
business consultancy
business entertainment
business-transfer agent
camping hire
chauffeurs
chimney sweep
chiropodist
chiropractor
circular and sample distributors
claims assessors
clairvoyants
cleaning contractor
clinics
coach service
commodity brokers
company registration agents
composer
computer bureaux
computer consultants
computer training
conference facilities
confirming houses

courier services
credit trader
credit investigation
customs clearers
dance band
dancing teacher
data banks
data processors
dating agencies
day nursery
debt collector
delivery services
dental surgeon
dental technician
design consultants
detective agency
direct mail
disco services
dog handler
domestic agency
drain clearer
driving school
dry cleaner
dyslexia centres
economic forecaster
editorial services
educational consultancy
electrician
electronic information
elocution
embalmer
employment agency
entertainer
entertainment agency
escort agency
estate agent
estate management
export agents
export finance
express deliveries
factoring
fax bureaux
film producers
finance brokers
finance houses
flying school

football pool promoters
forecasting services
fund raising
funeral director
furniture remover
geologists
golf professional
golf school
graphologists
'group' (musical)
gutter cleaner
hair consultants
haulage contractor
heating consultant
holiday accommodation
homeopaths
horse trainer
industrial (HASAWA) consultants
inquiry agent
journalist
just-in-time services
kennels
kissograms
ladder hire
land clearer
landscape gardener
lawyers
launderette
legal services
leisure centres
library
life assurance consultants
literary agent
lithographic platemaker
loss adjusters
magician
mail-order firm
management consultancy
manufacturer's agent
marine consultants
market research
marketing consultants
marriage bureau
marriage guidance
martial arts
mercantile-protection agency

messenger services
minibus hire
model agency
modelling schools
money-lender
mortgage brokers
motel
musical arranger
music teacher
musician
naturopaths
noise and vibration consultants
notaries
nursery school
nursing home
oculist
optician
osteopath
parcel delivery
patent agency
pension consultants
pet services
physiotherapists
piano tuner
plant hirer
plastic consultants
private detective
property valuation
property management
public-address equipment hire
public-relations consultancy
publishing
quantity surveyor
radio therapists
recording services
recovery services
relocation agents
remote control consultants
removals
researchers
riding school
road haulage
scaffolding
school (private)
security firm
self-drive cars

singing teacher
site clearing
snooker centres
solicitor
software houses
staff bureau
statistical services
steeplejack
stock-taking service
storage services
systems analysts
tarpaulin hire
tatooists
tax consultants
taxis
teachers
telecommunications consultants
tent hire
therapists
ticket agencies
tour operators

towing service
town planning
trade mark agents
training services
travel agent
tree feller
trichologist
tutors
typesetters
typing bureau
undertaker
valuer
van hire
veterinary service
vocalist
waste clearance
watch repairer
window cleaner
woodworkers
word processing
yacht hire

Chapter Ten

The Weekly Page for Farms, Livestock and Market-garden Businesses

10.1 Receipts

(a) Gross Daily Takings

Whenever you receive money (either cash, cheques or credit card vouchers) for goods or stock which you have sold, put it in the till. At the end of each day cash up the till, deduct any float you may have used to start the till off, and enter the 'Daily Takings' in the appropriate column (cash, cheques or credit card vouchers) of the 'Receipts' section of the weekly page.

(b) Debtors

Where goods are being supplied on credit there are, as we have seen in Section 5.2, two ways of looking at the problem. If you adopt the recommended method, which is to record the credit sale in a Debtors' Record Book and regard the goods as sold, you must remember to add the weekly total of 'debtors supplied during the week' to the week's takings when you transfer the latter to the 'Weekly Summary of Takings'.

(c) Other Receipts

(i) *Capital contributions.* Any extra money you put into the business, such as payments out of your private funds to keep the business going in its early days, represents an additional contribution of capital and should therefore be recorded in the 'Other Receipts' column. If, as is often the case, you make this contribution to pay a specific bill or purchase a specific item, you must record it as an 'Other Receipt' as well as making the relevant entry in the 'Payments for Business Stock' or 'Payments Other than for Stock' columns. Carry the figure to the Summary of Other Receipts at the back of the book.

(ii) *Loans from outsiders.* Since loans become liabilities of the business, they have to be recorded as 'Other Receipts', and are then carried to the Loan Summary at the back of the book. If the loan is put into your bank account put it in the 'Paid to Bank' section as well as in 'Other Receipts' and the Loan Summary.

(iii) *Debts settled.* If you have adopted the method referred to above for dealing with debtors, the cash you receive when the debt is settled should be entered as an 'Other Receipt'. It must not be included in 'Daily

Takings' as this would result in the sale being counted twice in the takings. Mark up the debt as 'paid' in the Debtors Record Book.

(iv) *Sundry earnings*. Examples of sundry earnings include rent received from a sub-tenant, commission received, dividends on investments held and repayments of VAT from HM Customs & Excise. All of these should be entered as 'Other Receipts'. They will be carried to the Summary of Other Receipts.

(d) Particulars Column

You may find it useful to record the names of debtors who paid, the source of 'other receipts' such as VAT refunds, extra capital contributed, and similar details for future reference.

10.2 Paid to Bank

These columns, where you record day by day all sums paid into your bank account, enable you to prepare your Weekly Bank Report at the end of the week. They also help you very much with your bank reconciliation statement (see Section 16.4).

10.3 Payments for Business Stock

Farmers, livestock dealers, market gardeners and those in similar kinds of business need to consider the 'Payments for Stock' columns in some detail.

(a) You may 'buy in' certain lines expressly to sell again. Thus a chicken hatchery might at times buy in day-old ducklings in season for customers who require them, and a nurseryman will often buy in trees and plants for resale. Such purchases are just like stock bought for resale by a trading enterprise, and are dealt with in Chapter 12.

(b) Many other items will be purchased and worked into the stock finally sold. A nurseryman may buy timber to 'knock up' into seed boxes, or a beekeeper may buy sugar to feed his bees through the winter months. These items come under the heading of 'stock to render a service to the business'. As they are an expense of the business, they must of course be recorded at their full cost price.

Both types of item should be recorded as they occur, in date order, using the cash or cheque column according to which method of payment was used. If you receive goods and do not pay for them at once, because for example you pay on monthly credit terms, put the unpaid invoice or delivery note in your filing system until the 'statement' arrives from your supplier. Record the payment in your Simplex book only when you actually pay it. Always check the statement against the invoices (and credit notes, if any) in your file.

10.4 Payments Other than for Stock

Payments made by a business 'other than for stock' comprise the running expenses, capital items and special items. Most of the entries made under this heading are perfectly straightforward, but some are listed below as worthy of special mention.

(a) **Rent.** If your place of business is separate from your own home, then all the rent, lighting and heating costs, etc., incurred at this place of business are expenses of the business and may be deducted from the profits at the end of the year. Just record them in the 'By Cash' or 'By Cheque' column, whichever is appropriate.

Special rules apply if you operate from your own home. You may claim only a proportion of the rent, cost of heating, etc. (The actual portion may be calculated on floor area). Often about one-fifth or one-sixth of such expenses are chargeable against profits. It is obviously a benefit to claim allowances in this way, but note that, if you ever sell your house, you may be liable to pay capital gains tax on one-fifth or one-sixth of any profits you make on the sale of the property. Normally an owner-occupier house is not liable to capital gains tax, which is a distinct advantage. At present capital gains tax stands at the marginal rate of tax of the person paying it, so that a person paying basic rate tax would pay the basic rate on one-fifth or one-sixth of the gain on the property.

(b) **Motor Expenses.** If a vehicle is used exclusively for business purposes, the whole of the running costs are an expense of the business. This includes fuel, servicing, repairs, road tax and insurance. An allowance for depreciation may be given as well; your inspector of taxes will advise on how much.

If a vehicle is used for both private and business purposes, the expenses will have to be apportioned between the two in some agreed ratio, perhaps two-thirds to one-third or half and half. Your inspector of taxes will advise you on this point when he goes through the accounts at the end of the first year. In the meantime enter the full expenses in the Weekly Page.

(c) **Telephone.** If you work from your own home, an appropriate portion of the telephone bill may be charged as a business expense. Once again this must be by arrangement with the tax inspector, and is usually decided at the end of the first year.

(d) **Value Added Tax.** All businesses whose turnover exceeds £25 400 per annum are obliged to register for VAT, and become agents for the Government in the collection of VAT. Full details of this procedure are given in Chapter 18. Because the tax collected has to be paid quarterly to the Customs & Excise authorities, there will be a 'Customs & Excise (VAT)' entry once every three months in the 'Payments Other than for Stock' section. (For traders dealing largely in zero-rated goods there may be a monthly refund from the VATman instead, in 'Other Receipts').

(e) **Wages of Employees.** Wages of employees, national insurance deductions (including the employer's part) and any Trade Union subscriptions or charitable contributions that are deducted from wages and sent off to such organisations are counted as wages. If you have employees (even if it is only

one or two) you would be well-advised to keep a Simplex Wages Book for them. This is explained later in Chapter 17. If you do this you only need to enter the gross wages figure from that book in your Weekly Page on the 'Wages' line. If you do not use a Wages Book it is better to enter the net wages on the wages line, the tax and National Insurance on the line provided and any payments to charities, etc on one of the spare lines. However, these various payments must be added together and carried to the wages column of the Summary of Other Expenses as the 'grossed up' wages for the week (or month) as the case may be.

(f) **Spouse's Wages.** Where a husband employs a wife or a wife employs a husband the spouse is treated just like any other worker and their wages will be included on the wages line as explained above. They must be given the same tax records as other workers and at the end of the year will need to include these earnings as 'Income from employment' on their tax return forms.

(Note: If the business is being operated as a partnership the spouse is not an employee, but a partner, and will not be paid wages—any money paid out to the spouse is then 'drawings' and will be recorded on one of the 'Drawings' lines).

(g) **National Insurance.** The NIC payments of employees are like extra wages payable, and are chargeable against the profits at the end of the year. Your own national insurance contribution is not. It is regarded as further drawings, and should be included in the 'Drawings' and carried to the 'Summary of Drawings' at the back of the book.

(h) **Inland Revenue.** Payments to the Inland Revenue usually come under one of three headings:

(i) *Your own tax payments.* These are due in two parts: on January 1st and July 1st each year. We regard income tax payments made by the proprietor as extra 'Drawings'. He/she has drawn these amounts to satisfy the tax requirement, and paid them out of business funds. They are entered on the 'Drawings' line and carried to the 'Summary of Drawings'.

(ii) *PAYE payments.* These are the tax deductions made from the pay packets of employees. Since they are a part of the wages you pay to employees, they should be included in the wages figure, as explained in *(e)* above.

(iii) *Corporation Tax.* Your business will only be liable to pay Corporation Tax if it is trading as a limited company. The tax is payable in two ways; (a) as **advance corporation tax** which is the tax deducted from dividends distributed to shareholders (payable within 14 days of the end of the quarter when the dividend is paid, currently at 25/75 of the dividend) and (b) as **mainstream corporation tax,** payable 9 months after the end of the financial year. The rate of tax is 25% for small companies (those earning profits of less than £150 000 per year) and 35% for other companies. To prevent hardship to companies in the band of profits immediately above this cut off figure, a special marginal relief is given on profits from £150 000 to £750 000. This has the effect of gradually raising the tax from 25% to 35%. If you pay Corporation Tax the amount should be entered in the 'Payments Other than for Stock' section of your Simplex Book.

(i) **Drawings.** When the proprietor draws from the business sums of money for living expenses, some people say he/she is drawing out his/her capital. This is not strictly true; what is being drawn is the profit the proprietor hopes the business is making. Since profits are not finally calculated until the end of the year, we do not know for certain that we have made any profits. We therefore say that drawings are 'in expectation of profits made'.

Since partners need to keep their drawings separate, three 'Drawings for Self' lines are provided in the Simplex Book. Note that if your spouse is a true partner in the firm you must regard his/her remuneration as drawings and not as wages.

One further point is this. You can draw 'Drawings' in two different ways. (a) You can take the money you require from the till, or cash box, if you have enough funds available to do so. The entry will then be in Col. 11 (the cash column) and will be carried from there to the Summary of Drawings. (b) If you do not have enough funds for this in the cash box or till you will need to draw the money from the bank. Whether you write a cheque and cash it over the bank counter or use a bank card to obtain the money from a cash dispenser, enter the amount drawn in the By Cheque column (Col. 12 on Fig. 7.1. page 51). Such a withdrawal does not need to appear on the lines 'Cash Drawn from Bank' in the Weekly Cash Report and Weekly Bank Report, since this only refers to cash drawn for office use (not for drawings).

If you pay personal tax, or national insurance contributions, these are of course not a business expense. If paid from business funds they must be recorded as drawings, and carried to the Summary of Drawings at the back of the book. The cheques made out would go in Col. 12.

(j) **Capital Items.** Every purchase of a capital asset, whether new or secondhand, must be entered on the 'Capital Items' line. The details of each purchase should also be recorded in the 'Capital Expenses Incurred During The Year' page near the back of the Simplex Book. It is wise to include serial numbers of all machines, office equipment, etc., since these may be required for police purposes in the event of burglaries.

(k) **Other Items.** Spare lines are provided in the 'Payments Other than for Stock' columns so that you can record any expenses which are additional to those listed. An example is 'commission paid' on odd occasions to someone who has rendered a service. Many such extraordinary expenses may occur which are legitimate charges against the profits of the business.

10.5 The Weekly Cash Report

Some businessmen do not understand why a 'Weekly Cash Report' is necessary. They assume that by simply counting the cash in the till they know how much cash they have got, and that is all they need to know. Of course this is not good enough. Errors on the till can occur by cashiers who give the wrong change, either deliberately or because they are incompetent when handling money. Theft from tills is one of the commonest petty crimes, and millions of pounds a year are stolen in this way.

It is also very easy to overlook an entry. If you pay out and do not record it, or receive money and do not put it into your receipts section, then clearly your cash balance will not be right at the end of the week.

Details of how to keep the Weekly Cash Report are given in Section 8.3, and you should refer to this section as you make your entries. Any difference between the expected cash balance and the actual till balance as counted should be investigated. If it cannot be put right (for example by making the necessary entry for a payment that has been overlooked) the difference must be entered as a 'difference on books' and carried to the 'differences on books' summary.

10.6 The Weekly Bank Report

Instructions for completing the Weekly Bank Report are given in Section 8.2. Remember that, while theft from your bank account is less likely than theft from your till, you should never leave cheque-books or bank credit cards lying about where members of staff or the public might be able to steal them. In one recent trial it was revealed that a burglar who found both a cheque book and an 'Access' card on the mat in a house he was burgling purchased goods worth over £4 000 in a few weeks. Although the bank concerned accepted full responsibility, it shows how important it is not to leave such items around.

Remember too, that you cannot check your bank account as easily as your till. You should therefore know how to draw up a 'bank reconciliation statement' (see Section 16.4).

10.7 What to do at the End of the Week

Various book-keeping activities have to be carried out at the end of each week's trading—although some can be postponed if necessary. Since these activities are the same for all types of business, they are discussed collectively in Chapter 15.

10.8 Exercises on Keeping the Weekly Page

1. R. Johnson is a market gardener and keeps his Simplex D Account Book to record all the details of his day-to-day transactions. Enter the following items for Week 4 April 30th-May 6th 19...

   (a) *Cash Receipts.* Monday: Cash £249·50; cheques £21·30; Tuesday: Cash £199·65; cheques £48·25; credit card vouchers £86·50; Wednesday: Cash £254·20; Thursday: Cash £389·70; cheques £42·61; credit card vouchers £154·80; Friday: Cash £195·65; cheques £246·20; credit card vouchers £175·85; Saturday: Cash £236·48; cheques £497·60; credit card vouchers £295·45.

   (b) *Paid to Bank.* Wednesday: Cash £380·60; cheques £69·55; credit card vouchers £86·50; Friday: Cash £600·00; cheques £142·61; credit card vouchers £204·80.

(c) *Payments for Business Stock*. May 3rd T. Nelson & Co. Ltd. Cheque £146·50; May 5th R. Bloom £230·25 cheque.

(d) Other Payments Postages 27p, 35p, £1·35; Motor Expenses (cheque) £34·86; Wages £142·50 cash.

(e) *Weekly Cash Report* began with Balance of £5. *Weekly Bank Report* began with balance £2 975.97.

Total the items at the end of the week and do the Cash and Bank Reports. The cash in hand (as counted) came to £1 470·21.

2. Mary Shaw keeps poultry and uses her Simplex D Account Book to record all her day-to-day transactions. Enter the following items in her weekly page, which is Week 38, December 16-22 19...

(a) *Receipts* Monday 17th: Cash £284·50; cheques £35·00; credit card vouchers £86·50; Tuesday: Cash £333·50; cheques £105·50; credit card vouchers £198·20; Wednesday: Cash £246·20; cheques £148·50; credit card vouchers £137·25; Thursday: Cash £495·60; cheques £48·24; Friday: Cash £326·30; cheques £89·65; credit card vouchers £295·60; Saturday: Cash £526·30; cheques £172·60; credit card vouchers £848·21. Other Receipts: Dividend cheque from Growfast PLC £192·80.

(b) *Paid to Bank* Tuesday: £350·00 in cash; £35·00 cheque and £186·50 in credit card vouchers; Friday: Cash £1 000; cheques £302·24; credit card vouchers £286·05.

(c) *Payments for Business Stock* Monday Corn & Maize Co Ltd. £23·40 cash; Thursday A. Naylor and Co. Ltd. £185·55 by cheque.

(d) *Other Payments* Postages 78p, 24p, 85p; Timber poultry house purchased (capital item) £140·00 cheque. Drawings in Cash £60·00.

(e) *Weekly Cash Report* began with a balance of £132·50. *Weekly Bank Report* began with a balance of £3 484·29.

Total the times at the end of the week, and do the Cash and Bank Reports. The cash in hand (as counted) came to £2 437·89.

Chapter Eleven

The Weekly Page for Manufacturing Businesses

11.1 Receipts

The rules for making entries in the 'Receipts' column are exactly the same for a manufacturing business as for any other kind of business. The relevant information will be found in Section 10.1.

11.2 Paid to Bank

Record in these columns any amounts paid to bank, on the day you pay them in. You will find the 'Paid to Bank' columns of great help when you come to prepare a bank reconciliation statement (see Section 16.4). They also enable you to prepare your Weekly Bank Report at the end of the week.

11.3 Payments for Business Stock

Manufacturing businesses do not often purchase stock for resale, since the vast majority of their purchases are raw materials and components which are embodied in the product during manufacture. Therefore the usual items to be entered in this section will be raw materials and components to render services in manufacture. When you do 'buy in' finished goods from suppliers (for example, because your own production capacity cannot meet a sudden demand) you should still record such purchases as 'stock for resale'.

Record all purchases of stock, whether to render a service or for resale, in date order as they occur. Use the 'cash' or 'cheque' column according to which method of payment is used. If you receive goods on credit, as when you are trading with your suppliers on monthly terms, do not make any entry in the Simplex book at this stage. File the invoice or advice note and, when the 'statement' arrives from your supplier, use it to check that the statement is correct. The money paid for the month's supplies should be recorded in your Simplex weekly page at the time you actually pay the statement.

11.4 Payments Other than for Stock

The method of recording 'Payments Other than for Stock' is exactly the same for all types of business. A detailed account of the entries under this heading is given in Section 10.4.

11.5 The Weekly Cash Report

The reason why a 'Weekly Cash Report' is necessary is explained in Section 10.5.

In Section 8.3 you will find a detailed description of how to prepare the Weekly Cash Report, and you should refer to it as you make your entries. Any difference between the expected cash balance and the actual till balance as counted should be investigated. If the problem cannot be resolved (for example by remembering a payment that has not been recorded) the difference must be shown as a 'difference on books'.

11.6 The Weekly Bank Report

The Weekly Bank Report should be completed in accordance with the instructions given in Section 8.2. Remember that cheque-books and bank credit cards are a temptation to thieves: the danger of leaving them lying around is stressed in Section 10.6.

Finally, you should refer also to Section 16.4 so that you will know how to draw up a bank reconciliation statement.

11.7 What to do at the End of the Week

Various book-keeping activities have to be carried out at the end of each week's trading—although some can be postponed if necessary. Since these activities are the same for all types of business, they are discussed collectively in Chapter 15.

11.8 Exercises on Keeping the Weekly Page

1. R. Coppersmith is a manufacturer and keeps his Simplex D Account book to record all the details of his day-to-day transactions. Enter the following items for week 5, May 7th–13th.

(a) *Receipts* All by cheque: Monday £449·50; Tuesday £472·60; Wednesday £486·50; Thursday £1 438·20; Friday £2 356·70. Other Receipts Wednesday Rent from sub-tenant £445·00 by cheque.

(b) *Paid to Bank* Wednesday Cheques £1 408·60; Friday Cheques £4 239·90.

(c) *Payments for Business Stock* May 8th Metal Supplies Ltd. Cheque £266·50; May 10th Components Ltd. £585·25.

(d) *Other Payments* Postages 85p, 85p, £1·35; Motor Expenses (cheque) £148·86; Wages £442·50 cash; Drawings £100 in cash.

(e) *Weekly Cash Report* began with balance of £45. Cash drawn from bank on Friday £600·00. *Weekly Bank Report* began with balance £2 989·98.

Total the items at the end of the week and do the Cash and Bank Reports. The cash in hand (as counted) came to £94·05.

2. Ann Overton is a fashion designer with a small factory. She keeps her Simplex D Account Book to record all her day-by-day transactions. Enter the following items in her weekly page, which is Week 37, December 9-15th.

(a) *Receipts* Monday 10th, cash £215·29; Tuesday cash £326·30, cheque

£3 054·70; Wednesday cash £115, cheques £284·50, credit card vouchers £96·50; Thursday cash £714·80, cheque £142·50, credit card vouchers £275·60; Friday cash £484·50; Saturday cash £332·50. Other receipts— Thursday Tax refund £39.74 by cheque.

(b) *Paid to Bank* Friday cash £1 500, cheques £3 521·44, credit card vouchers £372·10.

(c) *Payments for Business Stock* Monday Newstyles & Co. Ltd. £826·50 by cheque; Thursday Colourful Accessories £214·25 by cheque.

(d) *Other Payments* Postages 85 pence; Sundry Expenses £2·75 cash; Wages £284·20 cash; Drawings £200 by cheque.

(e) *Weekly Cash Report* began with a balance of £36.50. *Weekly Bank Report* began with a balance of £1 472·75. Cash in hand (as counted) came to £437·09.

Total the items at the end of the week and do the Cash and Bank Reports.

Chapter Twelve

The Weekly Page for Trading Businesses

12.1 Receipts

The rules for making entries in the 'Receipts' column are exactly the same for a trading business as for any other kind of business. The relevant information will be found in Section 10.1.

12.2 Paid to Bank

These columns, where you record day by day all sums paid into your bank account, enable you to prepare your Weekly Bank Report at the end of the week. They also help you very much with your bank reconciliation statement (see Section 16.4).

12.3 Payments for Business Stock

Trading businesses make their profits by purchasing goods *for resale*. The vast majority of the items purchased are simply passed on to the consumer after the traditional retailer's function of breaking bulk has been performed. Just occasionally a retailer may purchase items which are worked up into some new form before being passed on to the customer. Chemists, for example, buy oil to make up into lotions and ointments; cafés buy bread which they resell in the form of sandwiches. Such purchases of raw materials may be described as purchases *to render service*.

Both these types of stock purchases are entered in the 'Payments for Business Stock' columns, in date order as they are paid for. Record the amount paid in either the 'By cash' column or 'By Cheque' column, whichever is appropriate. If you receive goods and do not pay for them at once (perhaps because you deal on monthly credit terms with your supplier), you should file the invoice or advice note until you are rendered a statement by the supplier. Then enter the total payment for the month on the Simplex weekly page.

12.4 Payments Other than for Stock

The 'Payments Other than for Stock' section is exactly the same for the trading business as for all other firms. A full description of the entries to be made under this heading is given in Section 10.4.

12.5 The Weekly Cash Report

The reason why a 'Weekly Cash Report' is desirable is explained in Section

10.5. A detailed description of how to prepare the report will be found in Section 8.3, and you should refer to this section as you make your entries. Any differences between the expected cash balance and the actual till balance as counted should be investigated. If the problem cannot be resolved (for example by remembering a payment that has not been recorded) the difference must be shown as a 'difference on books'.

12.6 The Weekly Bank Report

The Weekly Bank Report should be completed in accordance with the instructions given in Section 8.2. Remember that while it is not likely that theft can occur from your bank account, you should never leave cheque-books or credit cards lying about. The importance of such safeguards is stressed in Section 10.6. Finally, you should refer also to Section 16.4 so that you will know how to draw up a bank reconciliation statement.

12.7 What to do at the End of the Week

Various book-keeping activities have to be carried out at the end of each week's trading—although some can be postponed if necessary. Since these activities are the same for all types of business, they are discussed collectively in Chapter 15.

12.8 Exercises on Keeping the Weekly Page

1. A. Upson keeps a corner shop in Newtown. He keeps his Simplex D Account book to record all the details of his day-to-day transactions. Enter the following items for Week 6 May 14th–20th.

   (a) *Daily Receipts* Monday: cash £349·55; cheques £42·65; credit card vouchers £126·54; Tuesday: cash £472·80; cheques £36·54; Wednesday: cash £158·60; cheques £49·55; Thursday: cash £738·20; cheques £94·60; credit card vouchers £194·62; Friday: cash £656·70; cheques £121·55; Saturday: cash £725·60; cheques £145·90; credit card vouchers £235·50; *Other Receipts* Wednesday Rent from sub-tenant £25·00 in cash.

   (b) *Paid to Bank* Wednesday: cash £900; cheques £179·19; credit card vouchers £328·54; Friday: cash £1 100; cheques £245·70; credit card vouchers £194·62.

   (c) *Payments for Business Stock* May 16th T. Knowles & Co. Ltd. cheque £496·50; May 18th T. Luke £330·25 cheque.

   (d) *Other Payments* Postages 37p, 85p, £4·35; Motor Expenses (cheque) £48·86; Wages £262·50 cash. The Bank deduct £14·50 for charges on investment work on Upson's behalf.

   (e) *Weekly Cash Report* began with Balance of £556. *Weekly Bank Report* began with balance £3 816·42. cash in hand as counted totalled £1 508·28.

   Total the items at the end of the week and do the Cash and Bank Reports.

2. M. Grainger is a newsagent and keeps her Simplex D Account Book to record all her day-by-day transactions. Enter the following items in her weekly page, which is Week 40, December 30th–Jan. 5th 19...

(a) *Receipts* Monday 31st: cash £242·65; Tuesday: cash £238·25; cheque £45·00; Wednesday: cash £147·62; Thursday: cash £283·66; cheque £35·00; Friday: cash £393·75; Saturday: cash £427·28. Other receipts—commission for sale of motor vehicle £45·00 cheque—Wednesday.

(b) *Paid to Bank* Friday: cash £1 400; cheques £125·00.

(c) *Payments for Business Stock* Monday Wholesalers Co. Ltd. £495·00 by cheque Thursday Weekly Press Ltd., £225·50 cheque.

(d) *Other Payments* Postages 85p; Wages to delivery boys and girls £36·50 in cash; Rates £248·95 by cheque.

(e) *Weekly Cash Report* began with a balance of £286·59. *Weekly Bank Report* began with a balance of £2 478·36.

Total the items at the end of the week and do the Cash and Bank Reports. The balance of cash in hand (as counted) was £587·45.

Chapter Thirteen

The Weekly Page for Service Businesses Which Require Materials

13.1 Receipts

(a) Gross Daily Takings

The takings of this type of business consist of fees received for services rendered; usually they will be received at the end of the job, when the work has been completed to the customer's satisfaction. Enter all such items in the 'Gross Daily Takings' 'cash' 'cheques' or 'credit card vouchers' column. If several such items are received in a single day, a till will be necessary; the *total* takings should then be entered as one figure in each column at the end of the day.

(b) Debtors

Any customer who is given goods or (in your case) services on credit will become a debtor of your business. There are two ways of dealing with this problem (see Section 5.2). If you adopt the preferred method, which is to record the debt in a separate debtors' record book, remember to include the weekly total of 'debtors supplied during the week' in your total takings figure when you transfer it to the Weekly Summary of Takings.

(c) Other Receipts

  (i) *Capital contributions.* Any extra money you put into the business, such as payments out of your private funds to keep the business going in its early days, represents an additional contribution of capital and should therefore be recorded in the 'Other Receipts' column.
  (ii) *Loans from outsiders.* Loans must be recorded as 'Other Receipts'. They become liabilities of the business.
  (iii) *Debts settled.* If you have adopted the method referred to above for dealing with debtors, the cash you receive when the debt is settled should be treated as an 'Other Receipt'. It must not be included in the daily takings, otherwise it will be counted twice.
  (iv) *Sundry earnings.* Any earnings which are not the result of normal 'services rendered' should be entered as 'Other Receipts'. Examples include rent received from a sub-tenant, tax refunds, and dividends on investments held by the business.

(d) Particulars Column

You may find it useful to record the names of debtors who paid, the source of 'Other Receipts', and similar details for future reference.

13.2 Paid to Bank

These columns, where you record day by day all sums paid into your bank account, enable you to prepare your Weekly Bank Report at the end of the week. They also help you very much with your bank reconciliation statement (see Section 16.4).

13.3 Payments for Business Stock

Businesses which offer a service where materials are necessary to provide the finished effect required by the customer, may be said to purchase those materials 'to render a service'. Decorators, for example, buy paint and wallpaper for use in the premises of their customers; garages buy oil and brake-fluid to service cars. All such items are *stocks purchased to render a service*. At the same time, you may occasionally buy things to sell at a profit to your customer; these are *stocks purchased for resale*. Both these types of stock should be entered in date order in the 'Payments for Business Stock' section of the weekly page, using the 'By Cash' or 'By Cheque' column as appropriate. If you do not in fact pay immediately for these goods, perhaps because you deal with your supplier on a monthly credit basis, do not make any entry until the statement is received from your supplier. Simply file any invoices or credit notes which you receive. On the date when you actually settle the account, at the end of the month, enter the amount in your 'Payments for Business Stock' column.

13.4 Payments Other than for Stock

The method of recording 'Payments Other than for Stock' is exactly the same for the service business as for all other businesses. A detailed account of the entries to be made under this heading is given in Section 10.4.

13.5 The Weekly Cash Report

The advantages of having a Weekly Cash Report are explained in Section 10.5. A detailed description of how to prepare the report will be found in Section 8.3, and you should refer to this section as you make your entries. Any difference between the expected cash balance and the actual till balance as counted should be investigated. If the problem cannot be resolved (for example by recalling a payment made which has not been entered) the difference must be shown as a 'difference on books'.

13.6 The Weekly Bank Report

The Weekly Bank Report should be completed in accordance with the instructions given in Section 8.2.

While it is unlikely that thefts will occur from your bank account, you should appreciate the risk of leaving cheque-books and credit cards lying about (see Section 10.6).

Finally, you should know how to draw up a bank reconciliation statement. Details are given in Section 16.4, and any reader who is not familiar with banking practice should study the whole of Chapter 16.

13.7 What to do at the End of the Week

Various book-keeping activities have to be carried out at the end of each week's trading—although some can be postponed if necessary. Since these activities are the same for all types of business, they are discussed collectively in Chapter 15.

13.8 Exercises in Keeping the Weekly Page

1. M. Lucas is a builder. He uses his Simplex D Account book to record full details of his day-by-day transactions. Enter the following items on the weekly page, for Week 15, 12th July 19.., 18th July 19... At the end of the week total the various sections and complete the Cash and Bank Reports.

Receipts Wednesday Cash £45·50; Thursday cheque £285·65; Friday cheque £342·65; Saturday Cash £50, credit card voucher £230·35.

Other Receipts Extra capital contributed by Lucas £500 cheque, Wednesday.

Paid to Bank Friday £1 128·30, all cheques.

Payments for Business Stock 14th July Cement Co. Ltd. £108·50 cheque; 16th July United Timber Ltd. £87·55 cheque; General Electric Stores Cash £8·42; McKay's Hardware £83·50, cheque.

Other Payments Wages cheque £184 Drawings cheque £160 VAT payment by cheque £136·52 Motor Expenses Cash £18·54 Sundries £23·62 cash.

Weekly Cash Report Began with a balance of £42·50. Cash drawn from Bank £200. The cash in hand (as counted) comes to £507·77.

Weekly Bank Report Began with an overdraft of £230·50.

2. R. Tobermory is a decorator. He uses his Simplex D Account book to record full details of his day-by-day transactions. Enter the following items on the weekly page, for Week 18, 2nd August–8th August, 19... At the end of the week total the various sections and do the Weekly Cash and Bank Reports.

Receipts Wednesday Cash £116·50; Thursday cheque £185·85; Friday cheque £142·65; Saturday Cash £150.

Other Receipts Extra capital contributed by Tobermory £1 000 cheque on Wednesday. This was a legacy from his aunt.

Paid to Bank Friday £1 328·50 cheques.

Payments for Business Stock Decorators' Suppliers Ltd., were paid £84·60 by cheque on Thursday; Wallpapers Ltd. were paid £76·50 in cash on Saturday.

Other Payments Motor vehicle expenses, cheque £85·65; Lucas bought a ladder (capital item) £67·84 by cheque; Wages £172·50 cash.

Weekly Cash Report Began with a balance of £5·00. Cash drawn from Bank £100·00. Cash in hand (as counted) total £121·00.

Weekly Bank Report Began with a balance of £230·95.

Chapter Fourteen

The Weekly Page for Pure Service Businesses

14.1 Receipts

(a) Gross Daily Takings

The takings of this type of business consist of fees received for services rendered. The sums received should be put into a till if they are numerous, and the *totals* should then be entered each day in the 'Daily Takings' columns.

(b) Debtors

Where services are given and credit is allowed to the customer, that customer becomes a debtor of your business. There are two ways of dealing with this problem (see Section 5.2). If you adopt the recommended method, which is to record the debt in a separate debtors' record book, remember to include the weekly total of 'debtors supplied during the week' in your total takings figure when you transfer it to the Weekly Summary of Takings.

(c) Other Receipts

(i) *Capital contributions.* If you put extra money into the business, for instance if you make payments out of your own pocket to keep the business going in the early days, you are in fact contributing additional capital, and this should be recorded in the 'Other Receipts' column.

(ii) *Loans from outsiders.* These should be recorded as 'Other Receipts': they become liabilities of the business.

(iii) *Debts settled.* If you have adopted the method referred to above for dealing with debtors, the cash you receive when the debt is finally paid must be treated as an 'Other Receipt'. If you were to record it under 'Daily Takings' it would be counted twice.

(iv) *Sundry earnings.* Any earnings which are not the result of normal 'services rendered' should be entered as 'Other Receipts'. Examples of sundry earnings include rent received from a sub-tenant, tax refunds, and dividends on investments held.

14.2 Paid to Bank

In this section you record any amounts paid to bank, on the day you paid them in. This helps you with your bank reconciliation statement (see Section 16.4) and also enables you to prepare your Weekly Bank Report.

14.3 Payments for Business Stock

Businesses which offer a pure service rarely if ever buy stock for resale, and do not use materials to render a service. If your business is of this 'pure service' type, you may not need to make any entries at all in the 'Payments for Busines Stock' section. If you do occasionally buy goods for resale, or to be worked into your service product in some way, enter them in date order as you make them, recording cash payments in the 'By Cash' column and cheque payments in the 'By Cheque' column.

Be careful not to enter capital purchases, such as office equipment or tools, in this section. They are recorded in the 'Payments Other than for Stock' columns.

14.4 Payments Other than for Stock

The method of recording 'Payments Other than for Stock' is exactly the same for the 'pure service' busines as for all other businesses. A detailed account of the entries to be made under this heading is given in Section 10.4.

14.5 The Weekly Cash Report

The reasons for keeping a Weekly Cash Report are explained in Section 10.5. A detailed description of how to prepare the report will be found in Section 8.3, and you should refer to this section as you make your entries. Any difference between the expected cash balance and the actual till balance as counted should be investigated.

14.6 The Weekly Bank Report

The Weekly Bank Report should be completed in accordance with the instructions given in Section 8.2.

While it is not likely that theft can occur from your bank account, cheques are easily lost or stolen. The risks of leaving cheque-books and credit cards lying about are stressed in Section 10.6.

Remember, too, that you cannot check your bank account as easily as your till. You should therefore know how to draw up a bank reconciliation statement; this is explained in Section 16.4.

14.7 What to do at the End of the Week

Various book-keeping activities have to be carried out at the end of each week's trading—although some can be postponed if necessary. Since these activities are the same for all types of business, they are discussed collectively in Chapter 15.

14.8 Exercises in Keeping the Weekly Page

1. M. Reagen is an osteopath. He uses his Simplex D Account Book to record details of his day-by-day receipts and payments. Enter the following items and total the weekly totals for Week No. 21, 23rd August-29th August 19...

Receipts Monday: Cash £35·00, cheques £160·00, credit card vouchers £64·00; Tuesday: Cash £80·00, cheques £176·00, credit cards £64·00; Wednesday: Cash £140, cheques £192·00, credit cards £84·00; Thursday: Cash £96·00, cheques £120·00, credit cards £84·00; Friday: £172 cash, cheques £164·00, credit cards £160·00.

Other Receipts: A bad debt for £37·50 was recovered, by cheque, on Wednesday.

Paid to Bank Wednesday £115 cash, cheques £336, credit cards £212; Friday £60 cash, cheques £349·50, credit card vouchers £168.

Payments for Business Stock 24th August Masseurs Ltd, cheque £49·27, Rex Pharmacy £5·50 cash.

Other Payments Rent £128·00 by cheque. Sundries £5·80 cash Wages £125·00 cash. Drawings Cash £160 Secondhand X-ray machine (capital item) £280 cheque.

Weekly Cash Report Opening balance £85·50. Cash in hand (as counted) came to £377·20.

Weekly Bank Report Opening balance £4 759·50.

2. Pat Sterling is a beauty consultant. She uses her Simplex D Account Book to record details of her day-by-day receipts and payments. Enter the following items and total the weekly totals for Week No. 24, 13th September-19th September 19...

Receipts Monday: Cash £24, cheques £42·00, credit cards £85·50; Tuesday: Cash £37·50, cheques £42·60, credit cards £80·96; Wednesday: Cash £72·50, cheques £36·20, credit cards £65·25; Thursday: Cash £48·00, cheques £92·50, credit cards £76·20; Friday: Cash £48·50, cheques £152·60, credit cards £136·35; Saturday: Cash £45; cheques £124·60, credit cards £78·50.

Paid to Bank Tuesday £40·00 cash, cheques £42·00, credit card vouchers £126·46; Friday: Cash £74·50, cheques £225·50, credit card vouchers £234·05.

Payments for Business Stock Beauty Care Ltd., cheque £103·50 on 17th September.

Other Payments Rent £50·00 by cheque. Sundries £15·80 cash. Wages £85·00 cash. Drawings cash £150; Telephone expenses £176·50 cheque.

Weekly Cash Report Opening balance £85·50. Cash in hand (as counted) came to £370·95.

Weekly Bank Report Opening balance £1 760·50.

Chapter Fifteen

Carrying the Weekly Figures to the Summaries

15.1 Detailed Instructions for the End of the Week

The activities described below will be necessary at the end of the week. If you are using the Simplex system, however, they need not *all* be performed before the next week's records can be commenced. Activities that should be carried out as soon as the business closes for the weekend are listed in Section 15.2. Activities that may be postponed if necessary until there is a slack period in the following week, or even until the following weekend, are listed in Section 15.3.

The important point is that daily and weekly records must be made at the times they occur, but the carrying of the weekly total to the summary pages at the back of the Simplex book may be postponed if necessary.

15.2 Activities that should be Carried Out at Once

On closing the business for the weekend, you should:

(a) Add up all the columns on the weekly page.

(b) Complete the Weekly Cash Report, and find the balance of cash in hand according to the book records.

(c) Check the till, and ensure that it agrees with the book-keeping balance. If it does not, discover the cause of the discrepancy—perhaps an entry in the cash payments has been overlooked. Note that any difference on books should be recorded in the space provided. There is a good reason for this. If there is a regular disparity between the two figures the Inland Revenue will feel that it indicates a general slackness either in the book-keeping or in the supervision of the tills. It may be due to the proprietor taking money which is not being recorded as drawings. They may therefore regard the total difference on the books for the year as being an extra sum to be recorded as profit—the amount having actually been extracted as drawings. It cannot be too strongly emphasised that keeping correct records is vital in establishing a sound relationship with the Inland Revenue Department.

(d) When you have reconciled these figures, carry the cash in hand (as counted) to the next week; remove the cash from the till and take it home. Leave the till open so that it will not be damaged by any burglar trying to find out if there is cash in it.

(e) Similarly complete the Weekly Bank Report. You cannot of course check this book-keeping record with your bank record unless you carry out a bank reconciliation (see Section 16.4). Carry the closing balance forward ready for the start of next week's work.

Your book-keeping system is now ready for the following week. The activities listed in Section 15.3 still remain to be performed, but you need not worry about them until a spare moment is available.

15.3 Activities that may be Postponed Until Later

These items involve carrying the weekly figures to the analysis columns at the end of the Simplex book, so that they may be used to determine the profit of the business. The stages, which are described below, take only a few minutes; it will take you longer to read this page than it will to do the actual work once you get thoroughly familiar with it. Proceed as follows:

(a) Transfer the total daily-takings figure to the 'Weekly Summary of Daily Gross Takings'. In order to find this figure you must add together the following items:

(i) the gross daily takings (cash),

(ii) the gross daily takings (cheques),

(iii) the gross daily takings (credit cards),

(iv) the debts recorded in the debtors' record book for the week, if you are using this system.

Now enter this total in the summary.

(b) Examine the 'Other Receipts' items. If they are debtors you need to record them in the weekly summary of takings if you are using the 'debtors' record book' method. If they are miscellaneous receipts or extra capital contributed or VAT repayments or Enterprise Allowance payments record them in the Summary of Other Receipts at the back of the Simplex D book. If a Loan has been received record it in the Summary of Loans and Repayments at the back of the book.

(c) Add together the totals of the 'By Cash' and 'By Cheque' columns in the 'Payments for Business Stock' section. The combined total is then carried to the 'Weekly Summary of Payments for Business Stock' page.

(d) Carry all the 'Payments Other than for Stock' to their appropriate summaries on the 'Summary of Payments for Expenses' pages. Sometimes a column has more than one item, e.g. 'Rent and Rates', and you must of course add these items together before entering them in the summary. In this summary there are several spare lines which can be used for expenses not listed on other lines, but peculiar to your business. Note that employees' National Insurance Contributions and PAYE tax deductions are really all part of wages. You can either gross up the Wages to the full figure or show the net figure in the 'Wages' column and put the total paid to Inland Revenue each month as one of the expenses of the business in the Inland Revenue column. It will then go in the Profit and Loss Account at the end of the year.

(e) Enter drawings in the 'Summary of Drawings of the Proprietor or Partners' section.

(f) Because of a House of Lords decision goods taken for own consumption have to be charged to the proprietor at selling price. Enter such items in the summary 'Goods for own Consumption' at the back of the book.

(g) Carry the capital items to the summary headed 'Capital Expenses

incurred during the Year', recording in careful detail the reference numbers of any equipment or machinery purchased.

(h) If any particular week includes a VAT Payment carry this figure to the Summary of VAT Quarterly Payments. It will be used at the end of the financial year when calculating the profits.

(i) Record any difference on books in the 'Weekly Summary of Differences on Books' at the back of the book.

15.4 Quarterly Summaries

Every thirteen weeks you will come to the end of a quarterly period. You should then add up the quarterly totals, and carry them to the annual summary if one is provided. It is always interesting to see how one quarter compares with the next, but as the years go by you can compare the Spring Quarter, for example, with the previous Spring Quarter. This is even more interesting, since you are comparing figures which really should be similar as far as sales and expenses go. You can then see how your business is expanding or contracting.

15.5 The Further Development of this Book

You now know how to keep your weekly record and carry the entries to the summaries at the back of the Simplex book. It only remains to learn how to prepare the 'final accounts' at the end of the year. These accounts enable you to find the profit you have made in the trading period. Before proceeding to this final section, there are three important matters to which we must turn our attention. These are Bank Reconciliation Statements (Chapter 16), Wages Books (Chapter 17) and Value Added Tax (Chapter 18).

Chapter Sixteen
Bank Reconciliation Statements

16.1 Introduction

The word 'reconcile' means 'to make friends again'. It frequently happens in business that two sets of figures which should agree, for some reason do not. The commonest of all such situations is the apparent discrepancy between the bank balance shown in our Weekly Bank Report, and the actual balance as shown in the bank's ledger and notified to us when the bank sends us a 'bank statement'. When we show that these two seemingly conflicting figures are in fact compatible, we are effecting a reconciliation. The major British banks now have a fully computerized system which has changed the way in which bank statements are rendered to customers, but this is unlikely to affect the need for 'bank reconciliation statements' as described in the next few pages. In order to understand why reconciliation is necessary we must consider branch banking practice.

16.2 Practical Banking

When a customer opens a current account he/she is able to make and receive payments through the cheque system. It is also possible to use many of the bank's services such as standing orders, direct debit services, bank giro credit transfers etc. Naturally one does not write to the bank and tell them every time a cheque book is used, not does the bank notify the customer every time it makes a payment on the customer's behalf. These matters have to be sorted out once a month when the bank sends the customer a bank statement. These are sent out on a 'cyclical billing' basis, in other words the work is spread out over the month, with about 5 per cent of the bank's customers getting a statement every day. If your statement arrives on the 16th day of each month that is the day you must do a Bank Reconciliation Statement.

16.3 Why a Bank Statement usually Differs from our Weekly Bank Report

In practice it will rarely be the case that the bank's statement shows the same balance as our own Weekly Bank Report. The differences are always due to a lack of knowledge of what the other person has been doing. For example, there may be

(a) differences arising from the bank's actions, about which we have not been notified, or

(b) differences arising from the time-lag which is inevitable whenever cheques are sent in payment of debts, or are received and paid into the bank for clearing through the Bankers' Clearing House, or

(c) errors, either by the bank or by ourselves. Such errors are unlikely to occur frequently, because the banks usually institute careful checks on their figures, and we naturally do our best to avoid mistakes in our own book-keeping records. Inevitably though, mistakes do occur from time to time.

Fuller explanations of the first two causes of differences are desirable at this point.

(a) Lack of Knowledge of What the Bank has Done

There are many occasions when the bank does not bother to inform us that it has taken money from, or has credited money to, our account. It sends us a statement automatically, under the 'cyclical billing' system. If you are not getting a regular statement, ask the bank to send one. Not until we receive this statement do we learn that the bank has taken certain actions. The most common items discovered on the bank statement are as follows:

   (i) Removal of sums for bank charges, or for interest on overdrafts.
  (ii) Payment of standing orders and direct debits we have arranged in the past. These reduce the balance on our account as the money is removed and paid to the organisation (for example the Building Society, or the local Council, or the Trade Association to whom we pay a subscription).
 (iii) Receipt of sums by credit transfer, otherwise known as bank giro. Numerous debtors will use the credit-transfer system as a convenient method of paying sums directly into our bank account. The only problem is that until we receive our bank statement we usually have no idea that the debt has been settled. Such items will appear on the statement as a deposit increasing the balance.

When such items are discovered on a bank statement, they must at once be entered on the weekly page of the Simplex book. Any receipts by credit transfer, either from customers or investments, should be entered in the 'Other Receipts' section. Any deductions by the bank, either for bank charges or interest on loans, should be entered in the Weekly Bank Report in the space provided. Although a cheque has not been written out, the loss has been deducted from the bank account. Any standing orders or direct debit payments must be similarly entered in the Weekly Bank Report on the line provided.

(b) Delays Inevitable in the Cheque System

   (i) Imagine that we send a cheque for £50·00 to the Betta Biscuit Company in Scotland. Before posting the letter containing the cheque, we enter the item in the 'Payments for Business Stock' section. It will probably be at least two days before the letter arrives, and when it does arrive the Betta Biscuit Company may take a day to get to the bank and pay it in. There will then be a further delay while the cheque is passed through the bank's head office in London, or the Bankers 'Clearing House if two different banks are involved. During this time-lag, our Weekly Bank Report will show that we have deducted the cheque from our available funds, but the bank will think that we still have this money. Sometimes, when a creditor puts a cheque in his pocket and forgets to pay it in, several months may pass before the bank statement and our Weekly Bank Report agree on this point. *Neither of them is wrong*, and it would be a mistake to 'correct' them or take any action—we must simply wait for the Betta Biscuit Company to put the matter right by paying the cheque into their account. Such a situation would be made clear in the **Bank Reconciliation Statement**, which as its name implies, is a written statement explaining a difference between the two records.

(ii) Now imagine that it is the last day of the month, that we are going to collect a bank statement which the bank has already prepared for us, and while we are at the bank we will pay in some cheques which arrived in the morning mail. Before setting off we record these cheques in the 'Paid to Bank' section in our Simplex book, and list them in the paying-in book. When we receive our bank statement and examine it, we find of course that it is not completely up to date, because the cheques just paid in do not appear on it. If the cashier could stop work to up-date our bank statement, there would be no problem—but this is asking too much. Instead we shall have to explain the difference between our Weekly Bank Report and the bank statement by a sentence or two in a Bank Reconciliation Statement.

16.4 How to draw up a Bank Reconciliation Statement

Consider the following bank statement as supplied by Barclays Bank to A. Ryder, on January 30th, 19... At this date the Weekly Report in Ryder's Simplex book showed a balance of £449·39.

A. Ryder—Bank Statement
In account with Barclays Bank Ltd.

Date	Details	Dr.	Cr.	Balance
		£	£	£
1.1.19..	Bal. c/fwd			508·40
3.1.19..	Cheque	14·16		494·24
5.1.19..	Sundries		62·80	557·04
12.1.19..	,,		75·00	632·04
14.1.19..	Standing Order	30·50		601·54
14.1.19..	Sundries		12·56	614·10
15.1.19..	Cheque	60·00		554·10
19.1.19..	Sundries		35·00	589·10
26.1.19..	,,		85·00	674.10
29.1.19..	Cheque	48·00		626·10
30.1.19..	Charges	4·55		621·55
30.1.19..	International Inventors (transfer)		12·80	634·35

The following points are of interest:

(a) The account is kept on a 'running-balance' method, by which the balance is shown on the account every day.

(b) Credit items are items paid in by Ryder, or credit transferred by someone who owes Ryder money (such as the transfer from International Inventors on January 30th). These items increase the balance on the account, because the bank owes Ryder more money.

(c) Debit items are cheques drawn by Ryder, and also charges deducted or standing orders paid. All these items reduce the balance on the account.

Ryder must now compare these items with his Weekly Pages for the last month. Let us imagine that he finds the following items to be a source of difficulty:

(i) On January 30th Ryder paid into the bank a cheque for £14·94 received from R. Loring. This cheque has not yet been cleared by the bank so it does not appear on this bank statement. It is a 'time-lag' item.

(ii) The £12·80 which has been transferred by International Inventors to Ryder's account is assumed to be the payment of a dividend and needs to be entered in his 'Other Receipts'. Ryder was not aware that the bank had collected this money on his account.

(iii) A cheque for £71·65 paid to T. Wilson on January 2nd has not yet been presented by him for collection through the Bankers' Clearing House. It does not appear on the bank statement at all. This is a time-lag item and will need to be explained in the Bank Reconciliation Statement.

(iv) On January 30th the bank deducted £4·55 from Ryder's account for 'bank charges'. This needs to be entered in the Weekly Bank Report section, since it is the first Ryder has heard about the bank's action.

(v) On January 31st a cheque for £120·00 was made out to Anne Employee, but has not yet been presented for payment. Like Wilson's cheque in (iii) above, this is a time-lag item.

The first thing to do to reconcile the bank statement with Ryder's Simplex book is to make entries at once in the current Simplex Weekly page to take account of the bank's actions. We must enter Bank Charges in the Weekly Bank Report, £4·55 and £12·80 in "Other Receipts" with "Dividend from International Inventors" in the particulars column. This £12·80 must also go in the Paid to Bank section. This means that our next Weekly Bank Report will take account of these differences. In the meantime we can justifiably claim that our Simplex page balance has changed from £449·39 to £457·64. This is because we have added £12·80 in 'Other Receipts' and deducted charges of £4·55, giving a new balance of £457·64. We now have to reconcile this balance of £457·64 with the Bank Statement figure of £634·35.

Special Note: Note that the entries outlined above are always made on the Weekly Page for the day the Bank Statement is received. Do not go back and try to make an entry on the date shown on the Bank Statement when the actual payment was made. Treat all events as happening on the day you received the statement, and enter them in the current weekly page.

We can now draw up a 'reconciliation statement' as shown below:

BANK RECONCILIATION STATEMENT

(as at January 31st, 19..)

		£
Balance as per Bank Report (amended)		457·64
deduct Cheque paid in, not yet cleared *(because the bank does not know we have this money)*	R. Loring	14·94
		442·70
add Cheques drawn but not yet presented for payment *(because the bank thinks we still have this money)* T. Wilson	71·65	
Anne Employee	120·00	
		191·65
Balance as per Bank Statement		£634·35

The statement above satisfactorily reconciles the Weekly Bank Report with the bank statement, and we may therefore feel confident that no errors on the bank's part or Ryder's part have occurred.

The Bank Reconciliation Statement could just as easily have been written out the opposite way, starting with the 'Balance as per Bank Statement' and ending with the 'Balance as Per Bank Report'. The explanations of course would be the other way round, as shown below:

BANK RECONCILIATION STATEMENT

(as at January 31st., 19..)

		£
Balance as per Bank Statement		634·35
deduct Cheques drawn but not yet presented for payment *(The Bank thinks we still have this money but we know we have paid it out)*		
J. Wilson	71·65	
Anne Employee	120·00	
		191·65
		442·70
add Cheques paid in but not yet cleared *(because the Bank does not yet realise we have received this money, but we know we have paid it in)*	R. Loring	14·94
Balance as per amended Bank Report		£457·64

It only takes half an hour every month to go through the bank statement and prepare this simple type of agreement between your records and the bank's. A neat copy of the bank reconciliation statement should be written out and filed away for reference purposes.

16.5 Carrying Bank Reconciliation items to the Summaries

There is one further important point about the items picked up from the Bank Statement when we do a Bank Reconciliation Statement. All these items must finish up in the Summaries at the back of the book somewhere so that they are taken into the calculations of the profit at the end of the year. The rules are as follows:

(a) Enterprise Allowance payments. These are explained more fully in Section 16.6 below, but as they are an 'Other Receipt' they must be carried to the Summary of Other Receipts where there is a special column for them.

(b) Dividends or Interest Received. These will also be entered as 'Other Receipts' and must be carried to the Summary of Other Receipts, where they are entered in the Miscellaneous Receipts column.

(c) Standing Orders. To repay loans or mortgages are carried from the Weekly Bank Report to the Summary of Loans, where they reduce the balance owing.

(d) Direct Debits. If these are to pay business rates or electricity bills, telephone bills, etc, they must be carried from the Weekly Bank Report to the Summary of Expenses and recorded in the most appropriate column. A full explanation of direct debits is given in 16.7 below.

(e) Bank Interest and Charges. These must be carried to the Summary of Payments from the Weekly Bank Report. We can open up one of the spare columns to record these entries, or they can simply be included in 'Sundries' column.

(f) Bank Interest Received. These days some banks are giving interest on Current Accounts, and if we have a Deposit Account it will certainly earn interest. All such interest must be entered in the 'Other Receipts' section on the Weekly Page. Current Account interest should be added to the Paid to Bank Section (use the line for Sunday) and will also be carried to the Summary of Other Receipts in the Miscellaneous Column. Interest on Deposit Accounts does not go in the Paid to Bank Section (it is not in the Current Account) but should be carried to the Summary of Movements In and Out of Deposit Account. It should then be recorded in the Summary of Other Receipts in the Miscellaneous Column. One special point here. Deposit Account interest should not be counted in the total of Other Receipts in the Weekly Cash Report, because of course we do not actually receive the cash, it is already in the Deposit Account. If you do add it in as cash you must take it out again in the Payments Other Than for Stock section as 'Interest Taken to Deposit Account.'

16.6 The Enterprise Allowance Scheme

This scheme is designed to help unemployed people change over to self-employment by giving them a small sum (at present £40 per week or £80 for a married couple both of whom have been unemployed and are willing to set up a partnership). The money is intended to replace the unemployment benefit for one year, by which time it is hoped the new business will be profitable. The payment is made by bank giro credit into the business bank account. The following notes will explain the entries necessary, if you are a new business under the Scheme.

(a) Your enterprise allowance of £40 per week is paid in fortnightly amounts of £80 by credit transfer into your bank account.

(b) Like all such transfers you only become aware of it when you get the monthly bank statement. Do *not* make any entries until you receive the bank statement. If you have not asked your bank for a regular monthly statement do so at once.

(c) When you get your statement go through it and find the entries for the Enterprise Allowance. They will normally come to £160 a month, but very rarely there might be three payments in the month ie £240. Enter the amount in the 'Other Receipts' column of the Receipts section and write 'Enterprise Allowance' in the 'Particulars' column. The same amount should also be entered in the 'Cheques' column of the 'Paid to Bank' section. Use the line for Sunday.

(d) Now carry the amount entered to the 'Miscellaneous Receipts' column of the 'Summary of Other Receipts' at the back of the book. This will bring the figure into the Profit and Loss Account at the end of the year because, as you will know, it has to be included as 'earnings' for income tax purposes (though it is shown separately on the Profit and Loss Account).

(e) The entry of the Enterprise Allowance is therefore really one of the things you do as part of your 'Bank Reconciliation' each month.

16.7 Direct Debits

In the last few years the 'Direct Debit' system has become more and more popular with large scale organisations who much prefer this method of collecting money due to them rather than the 'Standing Order' system or 'Credit Transfer' which has traditionally been used. It is certainly much more convenient in these inflationary times for such payments as rates and water rates, where a standing order is inappropriate because the amount payable changes every year. With a 'standing order' you will tell the Bank to pay your creditor by crediting his/her account with the sum due to him/her specified in your standing order. Your account will of course be debited. With a 'direct debit' the creditor tells the Bank to debit your account with the amount due to it, and to credit them with the money.

Certain safeguards are built into the system, for example the creditor must have your consent to the arrangement and usually asks you to sign a form agreeing to the stated system. They also should let you know in some appropriate way how much they are demanding from you before they actually do ask the bank to debit your account, so that you can protest if you do not agree. They will also usually deal sympathetically with complaints about the system.

The point traders may not be aware of is of course that in agreeing to this arrangement the trader leaves it to the creditor to pick the moment for the transfer, and gives up his/her own rights to decide when payment shall be made. It follows that if rates are payable on the first day of January you will probably pay them on that date, whether it suits you or not. Tied garages and similar organisations find that Head Office debits their full debt at the earliest possible moment, whereas the small trader very often finds it difficult to get payments from large firms, who are full of tricks to delay payment. This does not mean the system is necessarily bad. If an agreed average date is arrived at, which is fair to both parties there can be no objection to the system.

16.8 Overdrafts and the Simplex System

Some people worry about the book-keeping records needed when an overdraft is sanctioned by the bank. There is really no need to make any entry at all—though if you wish to remind yourself when it was agreed you could write at the top of the weekly page, or in some clear space on the weekly page 'Overdraft for £??? sanctioned—to be reviewed on ......19..'. There is no real impact on the business except that you may go 'into the red' on the Weekly Bank Report—see Example 2 at the front of the Simplex D Account book. Do not forget that once you go into overdraft you will not only have bank charges to pay for each cheque you write, but also you will have the interest deducted from time to time on your Bank Statement. Watch for these items when you receive a bank statement and enter them at once in the current week on your weekly page—carrying them to the Summary of Expenses at the back of the book, as explained in 16.5 above.

16.9 Bank Standing Orders and Direct Debit Mandates

The Simplex D Account Book now has a place to record the amounts of standing orders and direct debit mandates which the proprietor(s) of a business have made out. Some standing orders last many years (for example mortgages and loans) and we are liable to forget the amounts involved, so that it is wise to record them. The entries are not part of the book-keeping system, and serve only as a reminder. They need to be carried forward from one year to another, and this is a good opportunity to review them and decide whether we wish them to continue.

Note that even if this record shows an item is payable on a specific date—say the 20th of each month—it does not follow that we should enter them on that date. As has been explained above, the best time to make such entries is in the week the Bank Statement arrives, because the entry on the Bank Statement confirms that the payment has actually been made. Fig. 16.1 shows a typical set of entries.

	BANK STANDING ORDERS AND DIRECT DEBIT MANDATES							

DATE	FULL DETAILS OF PAYMENT	Frequency (wk/mth etc)	Times payable in year	Value of Payment		Total payable in year	
3.3.19..	CYTHOREAN BUILDING SOCIETY (S.O.)	MONTHLY	12	176	54	2118	48
29.6.19..	BARCLAYS BANK PLC (S.O.)	MONTHLY	12	53	34	640	08
1.8.19..	DR. BARNARDO'S (S.O.)	ANNUALLY	1	20	00	20	00
1.9.19..	MOJAVE MEATS PLC (DDR)	AS REQUIRED	AS REQUIRED	TO PAY FOR SUPPLIES		AS REQUIRED	

Note: Do not enter the payments into the Weekly Bank Report until the week in which you receive your bank statement, as this confirms that the payment has actually been made.

Fig. 16.1 *Details of standing orders and mandates agreed*

16.10 Paid Cheques as Receipts

Since the Cheques Act, 1957, declared cheques marked 'Paid' to be receipts, the customary method of giving a receipt when accounts are settled has fallen into disuse. Often the paid cheque is the only available proof that payment has been made, and it may need to be produced in support of the accounts. Few banks today, however, will return paid cheques to their customers automatically—even though it is plainly desirable that this important evidence of payments should be on hand. With the latest 'truncation' procedures it seems highly likely that cheques will not be moved to branches at all, only the electronic message will move to make the payments. To return a particular cheque banks will have to search for it wherever it was paid in. It seems best therefore if you have to make out a payment to a party whom you consider may give any difficulty, to demand a receipt, as you are entitled to do under the 1957 Act. The banks anticipate making quite high charges if asked to trace a paid cheque. (*Note:* A truncation procedure is one where the activity is shortened by avoiding any movement of paper documents, and only sending electronic data).

16.11 Exercises in Preparing Bank Reconciliation Statements

1. A. Cole's Statement reads as follows for the month of March 19..

Date	Details	Dr £	Cr £	Balance £
1.3.19..	Balance C/fwd			427·40
3.3.19..	Cheque	31·30		396·10
5.3.19..	Sundries		300·00	696·10
12.3.19..	Cheque	181·50		514·60
14.3.19..	Sundries		400·00	914·60
14.3.19..	Cheque	28·80		885·80
15.3.19..	Sundries		250·00	1135·80
19.3.19..	Sundries		350·00	1485·80
26.3.19..	Cheque	346·24		1139·56
29.3.19..	Sundries		350·00	1489·56
30.3.19..	Charges	12·50		1477·06
30.3.19..	Bank of England (transfer)		33·80	1510·86

On March 31st his Bank balance according to the Weekly Report in his Simplex D book was £1735·80. Checking through the month's records he finds the following differences between the bank statement and his Simplex D records.

The Bank charges he did not know about, and decides to enter them in the coming week.

The Bank of England transfer (dividend on Government Stock he holds) he also did not know about. He decides to enter this as an 'Other Receipt' in the coming week.

The £346·24 cheque paid out on 26th March was paid to Miller Services Ltd., for repair work. He had entirely forgotten to enter this in his Simplex D book. To save altering entries he decides to enter it in the coming week on his next Simplex Page.

Finally the payment into the bank on 19th March was recorded in error in his Simplex book as £250 like the previous entry. This error he also decides to put right by putting an extra entry of £100 in the Paid to Bank section next week.

Draw up a Bank Reconciliation Statement with suitable explanations.

2. The following statement was received from the bank indicating P. Marshall's position during January.

Bank Statement (as at January 31st 19..)

Date Jan	Details	Dr £	Cr £	Balance £
1	Balance			411·55
3	Sundries		380·00	791·55

Date	Details	Dr	Cr	Balance
Jan		£	£	£
5	Direct Debit	104·50		687·05
9	Credit Transfer (J. Jones)		38·50	725·55
10	Cheque	221·65		503·90
13	Cheque	139·25		364·65
17	Sundries		584·50	949·15
20	Standing Order	60·05		889·10
22	Cheque	48·35		840·75
25	Cheque	72·64		768·11
29	Cheque	384·26		383·85
30	Sundries		580·00	963·85

Comparing these items with his Simplex D book Marshall notes that he has to deduct the Standing Order from his books and was not aware that J. Jones had transferred £38·50 to his account. He decides to make these the first entries in his next weekly page. He also finds that a cheque paid out to British Telecom for £236·50 has not yet been presented by them. In the meantime his Weekly Bank Report shows his Bank Balance as £748·90. Do the Bank Reconciliation Statement.

3. Here are the entries made by J. Wilson in his Simplex Account book for the last week of June. Opening Balance £3621·50; Paid to Bank Tuesday £425·00; Thursday £385·55; Friday £462·85; Cheques drawn A. Summer, £26·50; B. Greystone £134·48; M. Lord £85·80; personal Drawings £300·00; Final Balance £4348·12.

The Bank statement sent to him on June 30th reads:

Date	Details	Dr	Cr	Balance
June		£	£	£
25	Balance			3621·50
26	Sundries		425·00	4046·50
27	Cheque	26·50		
	Cheque	134·48		3885·52
29	Sundries		385·55	4271·07
	Cheque	300·00		3971·07
	Direct debit (rates)	89·92		3881·15

(a) What should J. Wilson do about the direct debit for rates?
(b) Draw up a Bank Reconciliation Statement.

4. Here are the entries made by B. Senior in his Simplex Account book for the last week in July. Opening Balance £423·78; Paid to Bank Wednesday, £495·28; Friday £584·94; Cheques drawn T. Morgan £31·75; M. Rice £42·55; R. Logan £178·62; Personal Drawings £160·00; Final Balance £1091·08.

His Bank Statement sent to him on July 31st reads:

Date	Details	Dr	Cr	Balance
July		£	£	£
26	Balance			505·50
	Cheque	81·72		423·78
28	Sundries		495·28	919·06
	Cheque	31·75		
	Cheque	178·62		708·69
30	Sundries		584·94	1293·63
	Direct Debit (Rates)	89·95		1203·68

Draw up a Bank Reconciliation Statement as at July 31st 19..

Chapter Seventeen

The Wages Book

17.1 Introduction

In most countries today the employer is expected not only to pay the wages of his/her workers but also to act as an agent for the government in the collection of various forms of taxation. Welfare and social security services have grown to such an extent that it is quite impossible to finance them all by taxation on a few luxury goods, as in former times. Today every employee must pay contributions to National Health and Insurance schemes, and many must also pay income tax and pension contributions. Many also make voluntary contributions to savings schemes and to charitable organizations. These contributions are deducted from the employee's gross wages, and the employer is responsible for paying the collected totals over to the Inland Revenue Authorities, National Savings Movement, or whoever is to receive them.

17.2 The Simplex Wages System

The 'Wages Book' illustrated in Fig. 17.1 is a companion to the Simplex D Account Book. It is suitable for any small business having up to 26 employees.

The book includes a list of employees at the front, 52 weekly pages, and summary pages at the back. Since the weekly pages are cut shorter than the first page, the list of employees is visible all the year round.

Columns are provided for gross pay, statutory sick pay, statutory maternity pay and for deductions (pensions, tax, etc). These deductions are then totalled, and when deducted from the gross pay give the net wage payable. Columns are also provided for the employer's contributions, and the sub-totals provided each week give the necessary entries to go into the weekly page of the Simplex D accounts book.

For comparison with previous weeks and months, a 'Summary of Wages' is provided at the back of the wages book; the first half-year of such a summary is shown in Fig. 17.2.

17.3 Pay As You Earn

As far as employees are concerned, income tax in Britain is collected by a pay-as-you-earn' system—usually abbreviated to PAYE. This is much the most convenient system for the ordinary employee, since he/she does not have to save money in order to pay the income tax. Instead the tax, and various other deductions, are removed before the pay packet is prepared; the net 'take-home' pay is the residue which is available for the employee's own use. There are suggestions that this PAYE system will be ended shortly, but over the years it has proved an efficient and cheap method of collection.

PAYE is based on the following arrangements:

NAME	Week No.	Earnings for Week + Overtime (1)	Statutory Sick Pay (S.S.P.) (2)	Statutory Maternity Pay (S.M.P.) (3)	Total Pay for Week (Col 1+2+3) (4)	Less Allowable Charity Gifts (5)	Less Company Pension Scheme (6)	Taxable Pay (Col 4−5−6) (7)	Tax (8)	Nat. Ins. (9)	(10)	Total Deductions (Col 8+9+10) (11)	Net Cash Wage (Col 7−11) (12)	Earnings on which employee's contributions payable (1a)	Total of employee's and employer's contributions payable (1b)	Employee's contributions payable (1c)	Earnings on which employee's contributions at contracted-out rate payable included in column 1a (1d)	Employee's contributions at contracted-out rate included in column 1c (1e)
J. STOKES	1	185 80	52 10	− −	237 90	− −	12 40	225 50	31 25	21 37		52 62	172 88	237	46 19	21 37	−	− −
A. JONES	2	100 00	− −	− −	100 00	− −	4 95	95 05	8 75	7 03		15 78	79 27	100	14 06	7 03	−	− −
B. SEWELL	3	79 00	− −	− −	79 00	− −	− −	79 00	14 75	− −		14 75	64 25	−	5 56	− −	−	− −
F. SMYTH (MRS)	4	100 00	− −	36 25	136 25	− −	− −	136 25	21 50	12 28		33 78	102 47	136	24 56	12 28	−	− −
	5																	
	6																	
	7																	
	8																	
	9																	
	22																	
	23																	
	24																	
	25																	
	26																	
	27																	
Total		464 80	52 10	36 25	553 15	− −	17 35	535 80	76 25	40 68		116 93	418 87	−	90 37	40 68	− −	− −

All figures shown are merely for example purposes. Actual deductions should be made by reference to current information from the Inland Revenue and Department of Health and Social Security.

Fig. 17.1 *A page from the Simplex Wages Book*

SUMMARY

Week No.	Earnings for Week + Overtime (1)	Statutory Sick Pay (S.S.P.) (2)	Statutory Maternity Pay (S.M.P.) (3)	Total Pay for Week (Col 1+2+3) (4)	Less Allowable Charity Gifts (5)	Less Company Pension Scheme (6)	Taxable Pay (Col 4−5−6) (7)	Tax (8)	Nat. Ins. (9)	(10)	Total Deductions (Col 8+9+10) (11)	Net Cash Wage (Col 7−11) (12)	Earnings on which employee's contributions payable (1a)	Total of employee's and employer's contributions payable (1b)	Employee's contributions payable (1c)	Earnings on which employee's contributions at contracted-out rate payable included in column 1a (1d)	Employee's contributions at contracted-out rate included in column 1c (1e)
1																	
2																	
3																	
4																	
5																	
6																	
7																	
20																	
21																	
22																	
23																	
24																	
25																	
26																	
Total c/fwd																	

Fig. 17.2 *The first half-yearly summary of wages*

(a) **Code numbers.** Every employee is given a *code number,* based on the allowances to which he/she is entitled. These include *personal allowances* (for single and married persons), *additional personal allowances, pension allowances;* and other small allowances for disablements such as blindness. A person with heavy responsibilities has large allowances and hence a high code number; a person with few responsibilities has a low code number and is taxed more heavily. A change in circumstances results in a change of code number as soon as it is reported.

(b) **Tax tables.** These are prepared by the Inland Revenue and issued free to employers. They enable the employer, by consulting the tax tables, to

determine exactly how much tax should have been deducted by that week in the year. He/she can then compare this figure with the total tax paid already up to the previous week. The difference must be the amount that is to be deducted from the current week's pay packet. If a change of circumstances has resulted in an employee's code number being raised, he/she may already have paid more tax than is now due. This will be revealed by the tax tables. If a refund is due to the employee, it is put at once into the pay packet.

The total sums deducted from pay for taxation and national insurance are payable each month by the employer to the Inland Revenue authorities.

(c) **Other important tax records.** The 'P45' is a form which is given to employees who change employment. Before the new employer can deduct the correct tax, he/she must know the amount deducted by the previous employer and the total pay earned in the previous appointment. This information is suppled by the old employer on Form P45 given to the employee when he/she leaves.

The 'P60' is a form given to all employees at the end of the tax year. It shows the total pay received, the tax deducted, the National Health and other payments made, and the net pay. It is widely used as part of the social security system, and should be preserved by the employee.

Supplies of these forms are available from your local tax office.

(d) **Statutory Sick Pay and Statutory Maternity Pay (SSP and SMP).** In order to streamline payment systems for sick pay and maternity pay and enable such payments to be made in the pay packet rather than from official sources, Parliament has imposed certain duties on employers as far as these payments are concerned. Since employers have funds always available (tax and NIC revenues to be paid over to Inland Revenue after deduction from the pay packets of employees) it seems logical for the employer to pay these social security benefits out of the funds they hold, and only pay over the net amount. Despite the convenience of this from the Government's viewpoint it does place quite severe responsibilities upon employers. You will find brief explanations of the procedures in the front of the Simplex Wages Book which also gives details of the leaflets and forms you should apply for.

(e) Since 1975 when National Insurance cards were abolished, all sums due for both PAYE and National Insurance contributions (both employee's and employer's contributions) are payable monthly to the Inland Revenue Authorities. To assist the employer the Simplex Wages Book includes at the front twelve monthly 'Summaries of Payments to Inland Revenue' where the weekly sums due can be recorded and added together to give the monthly total collected, the deductions made for SSP and SMP, the balance due, the date of payment and the cheque number. One of these summaries is shown in Fig. 17.3.

17.4 Sub-contract Labour

Keeping records about employees is a tiresome and time-consuming business for employers and there has been a tendency in recent years to try to escape

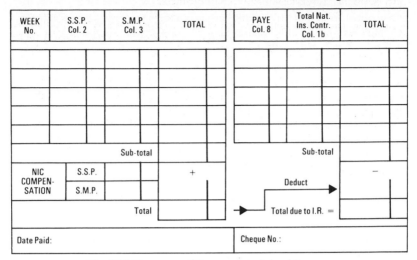

WEEK No.	S.S.P. Col. 2	S.M.P. Col. 3	TOTAL		PAYE Col. 8	Total Nat. Ins. Contr. Col. 1b	TOTAL
		Sub-total				Sub-total	
NIC COMPEN-SATION	S.S.P.		+			Deduct	−
	S.M.P.						
		Total				Total due to I.R. =	
Date Paid:					Cheque No.:		

Fig. 17.3 *Summary of Payments to Inland Revenue*

these responsibilities by making people who work for us assume self-employed status and thus become responsible for their own National Insurance contributions, tax calculations, etc. In some trades where labour has in the past been notoriously irresponsible (such as the so-called 'lump' in the building industry) steps have been taken to make firms who use the services of 'sub-contractors' deduct tax at the standard rate from all payments made, unless the sub-contractor can produce a certificate from the local tax office certifying that he/she is a bona-fide tax payer whose affairs are in proper order.

There is a difficulty in persuading an 'employee' to become a self-employed sub-contractor. The essence of sub-contract labour is that sub-contractors are self-employed, and if this proves to be only a pretence of self-employment used by an employer to reduce such 'inconveniences' as paying National Insurance contributions, taxation, etc. the Inland Revenue will reject the idea. If the Inland Revenue decides that the people are really employees not sub-contractors, it may hold the employer liable for the PAYE tax and National Insurance contributions that should have been deducted. The test is well known in law—a contractor not only decides what is to be done but the exact way of doing it, the hours for attendance to do the work, the tools to be used, etc. If the employer is deciding these things people are not truly self-employed and the Inland Revenue will hold the relationship to be an employer-employee relationship.

In that case you may find yourself having to pay the back-tax and N.I. contributions you should have deducted, since this duty is imposed upon you by law. It is therefore best to ensure that the Inland Revenue recognises any sub-contractor as a self-employed person, before you start paying them money free of tax and NIC contributions.

Another problem with persuading employees to become 'self-employed sub-contractors' is that the onerous burden of keeping records which is afflicting the employer will now afflict each of his staff. It is fairly certain that at least some of them will not wish to take on the extra worry, and the extra uncertainty, connected with self-employment. Honest, hard-working staff are hard to find, and even one or two lost may mean time, expense, losses with unreliable replacements etc. Employees can easily get into difficulties if they have to stamp their own cards for National Insurance or save up their Income Tax payments. When the 'lump' started in the building industry, and most employees became self-employed sub-contractors, the Inland Revenue lost a great deal of money. The law was changed and the Contractors had to deduct a set percentage of tax on all payments, which would be adjusted later with the 'self-employed person' if the Inland Revenue could find him/her. So the employer finished up doing the work anyway. Generally speaking the adoption of a simple system like the Simplex Wages Book will reduce the burden of these records, and the link with reliable, loyal employees of proven honesty should be preserved.

17.5 Keeping the Wages Book

The work of keeping a wages book is completed in the following stages:

(a) Enter the names of employees on the 'Record of Employees' at the front of the book.

(b) Enter the names of employees on the first page of the book.

(c) Record each employee's wages, contributions, etc each week on the line opposite his/her name. If statutory sick pay or statutory maternity pay is included this should be shown separately.

(d) Add up the columns to obtain the weekly totals; carry these totals to the summary at the end of the book.

(e) Obtain the necessary cash from the till or the bank, and make up the wages envelopes, or prepare the necessary credit slips if payment is to be made direct to a bank account.

(f) Enter in the Simplex account book the total wages paid.

(g) If it is the correct week to remit PAYE etc to the Inland Revenue Authorities, and to reclaim statutory sick pay and statutory maternity pay, complete the summary at the back of the Simplex Wages Book, make the necessary payment and enter it in the Simplex D account book.

17.6 Croner's Reference Book for Employers

Employers have many responsibilities to employees besides the payment of wages. *Croner's Reference Book for Employers,* now in its 45th year, is intended to provide an up-to-date guide to such matters.

Further information may be obtained from Croner Publications, whose address is given in the Foreword to this book.

17.7 Wages and Self-Certified Sickness Payments

Changes in United Kingdom sick pay legislation are transferring responsibility for payment of sickness benefits to employers. Since April 1983 the first eight weeks of sick pay have had to be paid by the employer. In order to reclaim this money employers must keep 'self-certified sickness' records. Forms for this purpose are available from Formecon Services Ltd, Gateway, Crewe, CW1 1YN.

17.8 Exercises in Keeping the Wages Book

Three exercises for keeping the Wages Book appear overleaf. These exercises require special ruled paper. A spare Wages Book should be purchased for training purposes in small businesses. If they wish to use these exercises in schools or colleges, teachers and lecturers should apply to George Vyner Ltd at the address shown in the front of this book.

In each of the questions below you are asked to incorporate the figures given in a Simplex Wages Book.

Name	Earning for week + Overtime (£)	Company Pension Contribution (£)	Tax (£)	Nat. Ins. (£)	Earnings on which employee's Contribution Payable (£)	Total Employer and Employee (£)	Employee's Contribution (£)
Question 1							
Mr. A.	285·50	17·15	27·50	22·47	285·50	52·30	22·47
Mr. B.	195·20	14·96	13·25	19·23	249·40	45·30	19·23
Miss C.	199·60	11·98	15·20	14·73	199·60	35·58	14·73

Mr. B. is entitled to Statutory Sick Pay of £54·20. Miss C. gives £1·50 to a charity.

Name	Earning for week + Overtime (£)	Company Pension Contribution (£)	Tax (£)	Nat. Ins. (£)	Earnings on which employee's Contribution Payable (£)	Total Employer and Employee (£)	Employee's Contribution (£)
Question 2							
Mr. G.	265·75	13·29	9·20	20·67	265·75	48·41	20·67
Mrs. H.	224·80	11·24	16·40	16·98	224·80	40·44	16·98
Mr. J.	124·60	8·05	7·50	11·31	161·00	25·84	11·31

Mr. J. is entitled to S. S. P. £36·40. Mr. G. gives £5 to charity and Mrs. H. gives £2 to charity.

Name	Earning for week + Overtime (£)	Company Pension Contribution (£)	Tax (£)	Nat. Ins. (£)	Earnings on which employee's Contribution Payable (£)	Total Employer and Employee (£)	Employee's Contribution (£)
Question 3							
Mr. P.	236·80	14·21	15·80	18·06	236·80	42·77	18·06
Mrs. Q.	195·60	16·33	12·20	21·30	272·10	49·78	21·30
Miss R.	172·60	13·26	9·50	16·71	221·00	39·86	16·71

Mrs. Q. is entitled to Statutory Maternity Pay £76·50. All three give £1·00 to charity. Miss R. is entitled to S.S.P. of £48·40.

Note: Regrettably the correctness of these figures will suffer as rates change etc. Please regard them as for demonstration purposes only.

Chapter Eighteen
Value Added Tax

(Special note re VAT changes: This book is up-dated so far as it is possible to do so whenever changes are made in the layout of our Simplex Books, but it is possible for VAT changes to occur at the whim of the Chancellor, at almost any time. In writing this description of the VAT system we must point out that it should be read with caution, and the possibility that changes have occurred should be envisaged. The only safe thing to do when dealing with VAT matters is to ask your local VAT office for their current literature on any matters that give you cause for concern (for example when purchasing a business). The author and publishers cannot be held liable for statements rendered obsolete by changes in legislation, or administrative procedures).

18.1 Introduction: How VAT Works

Value Added Tax was introduced in April 1973 as a new form of taxation, replacing Purchase Tax and Selective Employment Tax. It brings the British tax system to some extent into line with Common Market tax systems, but in truth there is no uniform system of Value Added Tax. The British system is based on a 15 per cent tax on the majority of goods and services required by ordinary consumers. Certain items are 'zero-rated', which means that in theory the consumer does not pay tax on these items. In fact there is a hidden tax item even when goods or services are exempt. This is because the exempt items, for example dental services, have to be supplied by professional people who will pay VAT on almost all supplies they use in their services. These higher costs will have to be passed on to the consumer in higher prices.

The basic idea of VAT is that tax is added at every stage of production as value is added to the product. The word 'production' is being used here in its economic meaning. Economists say that an article has not been completely 'produced' until it reaches the final consumer. Thus a typical chain of production might read as follows:

GROWER→MANUFACTURER→WHOLESALER→RETAILER→CONSUMER

Let us consider a tree cut down in a Forestry Commission plantation and made into a ladder which eventually is purchased by one Inigo Jones, a do-it-yourself enthusiast. The ladder, ignoring tax, costs Jones £60, but in fact the Forestry Commission charged £10 for the tree; the Wemakem Ladder Co. charged £30 for the ladder to Distribution Ltd., who charged Adam Smith (Do-it-Yourself trader) £45 for it. The value *added* in each stage was £10, £20, £15 and £15, respectively. VAT would be levied all the way along the 'production' line at 15 per cent of the added value. Thus the Forestry

Commission would charge the Wemakem Ladder Co. an extra £1·50 tax; Wemakem would charge Distribution Ltd. £4·50; Distribution Ltd. would charge Smith the retailer £6·75 and Smith would charge the final consumer Jones £9·00 in tax.

The tax paid by a purchaser as goods come into the business is called *input tax*. The tax collected as goods go out of the business is called *output tax*. The output tax should usually be higher than the input tax, because the trader has 'added' value to the goods—even if he/she merely adds the profit margin. Thus in the example above, the Wemakem Ladder Co. has input and output taxes as follows:

Input Tax	Output Tax
15% of £10	15% of £30
= £1·50	= £4·50

Its tax liability is therefore (£4·50—£1·50) = £3·00.

Note that the tax which the firm must pay over to HM Customs & Excise finishes up as 15 per cent of the value it has added. But the Ladder Co. has not really paid this tax; it collected it from Distribution Ltd. Distribution in turn collect it from Smith the DIY trader, and he in turn collects it from the customer. In fact the only person who really pays tax is the final consumer. The firms who pay tax over to HM Customs & Excise only do so as the agents for the Government in the collection of the tax. They are not paying it out of their own pockets. A full explanation is given in Fig. 18.1.

	Forestry Commission	Wemakem Ladder Co.	Distribution Ltd.	A. Smith (DIY Trader)	I. Jones (consumer)
Cost price without tax	£0.00 Gift of nature	£10·00	£30·00	£45·00	£60·00
Selling price without tax	£10·00	£30·00	£45·00	£60·00	—
Value added	£10·00	£20·00	£15·00	£15·00	—
Cost price with tax	—	£11·50	£34·50	£51·75	£69·00
Selling price with tax	£11·50	£34·50	£51·75	£69·00	—

(continues overleaf)

	Forestry Commission	Wemakem Ladder Co.	Distribution Ltd.	A. Smith (DIY Trader)	I. Jones (consumer)
Input tax	0	£1·50	£4·50	£6·75	£9·00
Output tax	£1·50	£4·50	£6·75	£9·00	—
VAT payable to Customs & Excise	£1·50 −£0 = £1·50	£4·50 −£1·50 = £3·00	£6·75 −£4·50 = £2·25	£9·00 −£6·75 = 2·25	—

Fig. 18.1 How Value Added Tax works. Note that the final consumer (Jones) pay £9 tax to the retailer. This £9 reaches the Customs & Excise as a succession of payments by all those businesses where value has been added, i.e.

$$as £1·50 + £3 + £2·25 + £2·25 = £9$$

18.2 Registration for VAT

Any trader who supplies goods and services which are not exempt will now have to be registered for VAT if:

(a) at the end of any month the value of the taxable supplies you have made in the past 12 months has exceeded £25 400; or

(b) at any time there are reasonable grounds for believing that the value of the taxable supplies you will make in the next 30 days will exceed £25 400.

If you are in any doubt about your need to register, a call to your local VAT office is advisable.

Deregistration is permitted, since the limits of registration were raised, if turnover is expected to be less than £24 400 in the year ahead. Persons who feel that registration will be advantageous to them, even though their turnover is less than the agreed level, are permitted to register voluntarily, but are required to remain on the register for at least two years.

Special cases, listed in Schedule 5 of the Act, are land, insurance, postal services, betting, gaming and lotteries, finance, education, health, and burial or cremation services. Firms in these fields need not register and need not keep records, but will not be able to deduct input taxes paid on goods purchased for use in the business. They are therefore effectively being treated like consumers, subject to tax. This is by no means advantageous.

To register you complete Form VAT 1, obtainable from your local office of HM Customs & Excise. Once registered you have the following duties to perform:

(a) To record your inputs.

(b) To record your outputs or keep records for an appropriate Small Retailers' Scheme.

(c) To complete your VAT return (Form VAT 100) at intervals, specifying in it which (if any) of the special retailers' schemes you are using.

(d) To keep records and accounts adequate for these purposes.

(e) To pay the tax as it falls due, if it exceeds £1. Payment by cheque, bank giro or National Giro should accompany the return form.

A trader who sells zero-rated goods to consumers will usually be entitled to a refund of tax rather than be liable to pay tax. Since this would mean positive hardship to a retailer, who had paid tax but could not obtain a refund for three months, traders selling zero-rated goods can obtain refunds of tax monthly by arrangement with their local Customs & Excise office.

18.3 Special Schemes for Retailers

'Retailers' are not necessarily shopkeepers, but anyone who supplies goods and services to the public without tax invoices. Such businesses may find it difficult to comply with the legal requirement to calculate the output tax on every supply that they make, as it takes place. Clearly this would be quite impossible for many shopkeepers at busy peak periods. Special schemes have therefore been devised to enable the retailer to calculate his/her output tax at the end of the tax period without recording every sale separately. (There are no special schemes for *input* tax; retailers will almost always be supplied by wholesalers who give tax invoices which will enable them to calculate the input tax easily). These special schemes are characterised below, (details are given later in this Chapter). In these brief descriptions reference is made to 'rates of tax'. At present there are only two rates of tax, *zero rate* (0 per cent) and *standard rate* (15 per cent). At one time a *higher rate* was also used. Any rate above zero rate is referred to as a *'positive'* rate of tax.

At the time of writing a multi-rate system is not in operation, but a multi-rate system could be introduced at any time (usually on Budget Day). If this happened users of the Simplex VAT Book would at once need columns to record the higher rate tax and possibly even a 'luxury rate' tax used in some countries. For this reason the book contains two extra columns headed Positive Rate A and Positive Rate B. These may be ignored at present, until such time as the Chancellor introduces a multi-rate system.

Scheme A. This scheme is designed for retailers who only sell goods at one rate of tax, the standard rate.

Scheme B. This scheme may be used by retailers who sell goods at two rates of tax only, but not at more than two rates. Zero counts as a separate rate. The condition is that the goods sold at the lower rate of the two, do not form more than one half (50 per cent) of the total. If they do form more than one half another scheme must be chosen. It can also be used for services provided the services are taxed at the higher of the two rates in use. This scheme cannot be used for catering establishments, unless they keep special records outside Scheme B for the catering side of their business.

There are two adaptations of Scheme B which are called Scheme B Adaptation 1 and Scheme B Adaptation 2.

Scheme B1. This scheme is based upon the trade of the retailer for a whole year. The figures are worked out for each quarter and the tax paid in the normal way but on the fourth quarter an 'annual adjustment' is made by using the figures for the whole year. If this discloses that excess tax has been paid or too little tax has been paid the excess or deficiency is included in the fourth quarter's calculation.

Scheme B2. This scheme is based on fixed mark-ups for zero-rated goods, and enables the part of a trader's supplies of zero rated goods to be calculated at a figure based on fixed mark-ups set by Customs & Excise. The scheme can only be used by traders with a turnover of less than £500 000.

Scheme C. This scheme is for retailers with a small turnover (less than £90 000 a year) whose Trade Classification is from 8 201-8 239. This number is shown on the retailers Certificate of Registration (Form VAT 4).

Scheme D. This scheme is for retailers whose taxable turnover is less than £500 000 per year. The proportion of goods bought at each rate of tax is applied to the selling price (gross takings) to find out how much output tax has to be accounted for.

Scheme E. This scheme is suitable for large scale retailers who can keep detailed records of the total amount, including VAT, which customers will be paying for goods received by the retailer, at each positive rate of tax.

Scheme E1. This adaptation of Scheme E is again a scheme for large scale retailers only and need not concern us.

Scheme F. Is suitable for retailers whose goods and services are supplied at more than one rate of tax, but who can separate the sales at each rate of tax at the point of sale.

Scheme G. This scheme is suitable for the small retailer who wants to keep his records as simple as possible. No output records are necessary except gross daily takings; the calculations of output tax are based on the cost of goods to the retailer. After the tax has been calculated by the method explained later, it has to be raised by one eighth, as experience has shown this method slightly understates the VAT payable. For businesses only concerned with two positive rates of tax the addition is only one-twelfth. This rule can be taken advantage of by retailers who sell only a tiny quantity (less than 2 per cent of turnover) of zero-rated items.

Scheme H and Scheme J. These schemes are only suitable for multiple shops and other retail outlets where exact details of the quantities of each different line can be recorded consistently. It follows that most small businessmen will not select these schemes.

Pharmacists. There are special arrangements for pharmacists. These are explained fully in Notice No 727 Retail Schemes.

Note: One final point on these schemes is that where a retailer has several departments or shops, and is able to keep separate records for them, he/she may choose to account for one field of activity on one Scheme and another field of activity on a different scheme. The rules for this are given in Notice No 727 Section 2.

18.4 Choosing a VAT Method and a Definition of Gross Takings

Before you can begin to keep your VAT records you need to decide which method you are going to use and how you are going to define your 'gross takings'.

| Sales Invoice No. | 174 | | | 18/8/87 |

From: *FOUNDATION TRADING (UK) LTD*   VAT Regd. No. 987 6543 21
      BOWMAN STREET, CHESTER

To: *A. N. OTHER LTD*
      57 NORTH ROAD, LONDON N12 5NA

Sale   Tax point *18/8/87*

Quantity	Description and Price	Amount exclusive of VAT	VAT Rate	VAT Net
		£	%	£
6	*RADIOS, SWIS @ £25.20*	151.20		
4	*RECORD PLAYERS @ £23.60*	94.40		
6	*LAMPS T77 @ £15.55*	93.30		
		338.90	15	48.29*
	DELIVERY (STRICTLY NET)	9.00	15	1.35
Terms: Cash discount of 5% if paid within 30 days		347.90		49.64

                      VAT   49.64

                TOTAL   397.54

*calculated on the discounted price

Fig. 18.2 *A tax invoice (courtesy of HM Customs & Excise)*

(a) Which Method?

The *normal* method of calculating VAT is by keeping a record of tax inputs and tax outputs, using the 'tax invoices' received from suppliers or given to customers. If you are issuing tax invoices (see Fig. 18.2) you will keep your records by this normal method. If you are not using tax invoices you will have to keep records by one of the *special schemes for retailers.*

A useful chart has now been devised by Customs and Excise about 'choosing your retail scheme'. It does not provide complete guidance because many schemes have very detailed arrangements, and in the end only the retailer can decide which scheme will suit his/her business best. This chart is reproduced on pages 128-9 by kind permission of HM Customs & Excise, as Fig. 18.3.

Fig. 18.4 tabulates the schemes and enables you to choose the one that seems best for your business. The last column of Fig. 18.4 indicates how you should use the rest of this chapter to solve your VAT problems. Whichever choice you make, you must identify the method selected in the space provided on your VAT Account when you submit it to HM Customs & Excise.

(b) Which Definition of Gross Takings?

There are two methods of calculating 'gross takings' for the period, the **standard definition** and the **optional definition.** The standard definition is based on payments received in the period and is most useful to those who do not sell on credit, and consequently have no debtors. The optional definition is based on the sales figure, both in cash and on credit. It follows that with this method the retailer pays VAT on sales even though he may never be paid by some of his debtors. Clearly this is disadvantageous to the retailer. It is now possible for retailers to claim VAT where the debtor is formally deemed to be insolvent. The rules provide that the retailer will claim as a creditor in the bankruptcy proceedings for the net amount of debt only, and claim the VAT refund in his VAT accounts. This will reduce the disadvantage of the optional definition to some extent, though it will give no relief in the large number of cases where traders do not pursue debtors as far as formal bankruptcy proceedings.

If you decide to use this alternative definition you must notify the Customs and Excise Authorities in writing before you start the scheme. A full description of these definitions is given later.

The Simplex VAT Book

The Simplex VAT book, a companion volume to the Simplex account book, has been designed to cater for any small business, of whatever type, and whatever scheme it is using. The following points are of interest:

(a) The book is intended for the sole purpose of keeping VAT records as required by the VAT regulations. It is not meant for recording financial accounts, which must still be kept separately.

(b) The records should be entered daily.

Choosing your retail scheme

This chart will help you decide which scheme best suits your business.

Although you can use any scheme that is suitable for your business, you should remember that you can use a retail scheme only for retail sales.

If you make both retail and non-retail sales you must keep completely separate sales and purchase records for your retail sales if you want to use a retail scheme for them.

If you can't keep separate records you may still be able to use either Scheme A or F for your retail sales provided you can separate the payments you get for them from your other takings.

If you supply catering, you can only use Scheme A, F or the scheme described in the VAT Leaflet *Catering and take-away food*, Section II. You will find more about all of this in the VAT leaflet.

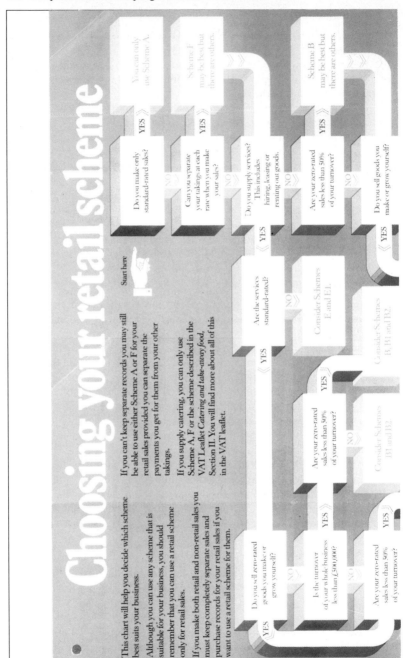

Start here

Do you make only standard-rated sales? — YES → You can only use Scheme A.

Can you separate your takings at each rate when you make your sales? — YES → Scheme F may be best but there are others.

Do you supply services? This includes hiring, leasing or renting out goods. — YES → Are the services standard-rated?

Are your zero-rated sales less than 50% of your turnover? — YES → Scheme B may be best but there are others.

Do you sell goods you make or grow yourself? — YES

Consider Schemes E and F.

Are your zero-rated sales less than 50% of your turnover? — YES

Consider Schemes B, B1 and B2.

Consider Schemes B1 and B2

Do you sell zero-rated goods you make or grow yourself? — YES

Is the turnover of your whole business less than £500,000? — YES

Are your zero-rated sales less than 50% of your turnover? — YES

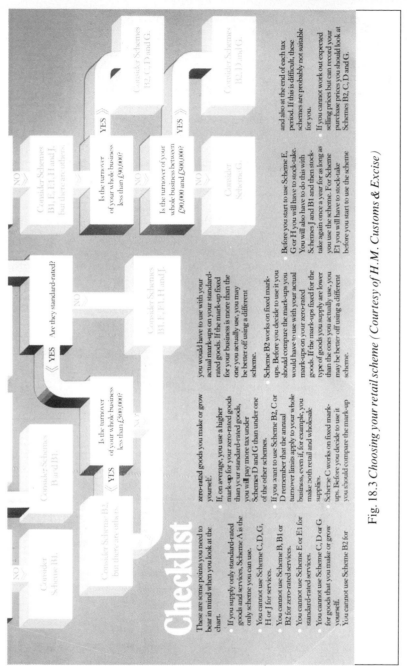

Fig. 18.3 Choosing your retail scheme (Courtesy of H.M. Customs & Excise)

(c) The book is divided into four quarters, or VAT periods.

(d) Each quarterly part contains:

(i) pages of input account, for recording 'input' tax invoices received from suppliers.

(ii) pages of output account, for recording 'output' tax invoices sent to customers, and output hire-purchase or credit-sale agreements.

(iii) One page, of which half is for recording returns sent out to suppliers and half is for recording returns by customers.

(iv) Three pages each of which is given over to one month's Daily Takings records. Thus the trader dealing chiefly in zero-rated sales who wishes to claim a VAT refund each month is able to find his monthly 'Gross Takings' total easily, while the trader who only sends in a quarterly return simply adds the three monthly totals together.

(v) Three pages each given over to calculations and a VAT Return, from which the actual VAT Return Form 100 can be prepared, either monthly or quarterly.

All these records must be preserved for six years.

You should now consult Fig. 18.4 and decide which method of VAT records is appropriate to your business. The suitability of the various schemes is given in the second column.

When you have decided which method or scheme you are going to use, you will find it helpful to study the third column, which tells you what records it is necessarily to keep. The last column then tells you which part of the text you should read for a description of your particular method Fig. 18.4 starts below.

Note: Fig. 18.4 starts here and continues on pages 131-2-3.

Method	Who is it suitable for?	Records to be kept	Remarks
Normal Method	Suppliers of goods or services, for which proper tax invoices are issued to customers.	*(a)* Figures for all taxable inputs *(b)* All taxable outputs of goods *(c)* All taxable outputs of services *(d)* Goods applied to personal use *(e)* Taxable self supplies *(f)* Credits for returns in or out	Read Section 18.5 in the main text. This method can be used for services, hirings etc.

Method	Who is it suitable for?	Records to be kept	Remarks
Scheme A	*Suppliers of goods and/or services at the standard rate of tax*	*(a)* Daily gross takings	Read Section 18.6 and 18.7 in the main text. Also obtain the leaflet 'How to work Scheme A' from your VAT office.
Scheme B	Firms which supply goods without tax invoices at two rates of tax only. Services may be included if they are at the higher rate of the two. The goods sold at the lower rate must not be more than half (50 per cent) of taxable turnover.	*(a)* Gross daily takings for all goods (lower rate goods need not be recorded separately) *(b)* Cost price plus profit margin and VAT (if any) of all goods at the lower rate of the two *(c)* Sales figures for HP (etc.) goods	Read Sections 18.5, 18.6 and 18.8 in the main text See first column about services under this Scheme Obtain the brochure 'How to work Scheme B' from your local VAT office
Scheme B1	As for Scheme B, but you must be able to work out your zero-rated stock on hand when you start the scheme.	As for Scheme B, but the scheme is based on your trade over a full year.	Read sections 18.5, 18.6 and 18.9 in the main text Obtain the brochure 'How to work Scheme B1 from your local VAT office.

Method	Who is it suitable for?	Records to be kept	Remarks
Scheme B2	As for Scheme B, but you cannot use Scheme B2 if your total sales exceed £500 000 per annum.	As for Scheme B, but you have to use fixed mark-ups specified by Customs & Excise to work out the figures for *(b)* above.	Read sections 18.5, 18.6 and 18.10 in the main text. Obtain the brochure 'How to work Scheme B2 from your local tax office.
Scheme C	Firms in trades 8201-8239 and whose taxable turnover is less than £90 000. Not to be used for goods grown or manufactured, or for services.	*(a)* the *cost* to you (including VAT) of all the things bought at a positive rate of tax *(b)* The cost to you of all zero rated items *(c)* If growing or manufacturing you must use some other scheme for these items and keep records accordingly—or use the normal method.	Read Section 18.11 in the main text. For *(c)* read Section 18.5 in the main text or see other schemes
Scheme D	Firms where sales at different rates cannot easily be distinguished; and where total turnover is less than £500 000 per year. This scheme may not be used for services.	*(a)* Gross daily takings *(b)* Cost (including VAT) of all goods purchased *(c)* Sales figures for HP (etc) goods *(d)* All goods applied to personal use.	The scheme calls for an annual scheme adjustment. Read Sections 18.5, 18.6 and 18.12 Not to be used for goods grown or manufactured, or for services.

Method	Who is it suitable for?	Records to be kept	Remarks
Scheme E and Scheme E1	Multiple shops and other retailers who can consistently record all types of goods at selling price	Details of these schemes may be obtained from your local VAT office	Not described in this text
Scheme F	Firms which supply the following without tax invoices: (a) services, and/or (b) goods, where sales at standard and zero rates can be clearly distinguished.	(a) Separate gross daily takings for all standard-rated, and zero-rated goods or services (b) Sales figures for HP (etc) goods (c) All goods applied to personal use.	Read Sections 18.5. 18.6 and 18.13 in the main text Can be used for services, hirings etc.
Scheme G	Same as D above but this scheme is for businesses whose turnover exceeds £500 000. Cannot be used for services or for goods grown or manufactured.	(a) Cost (inc. VAT) of stock in hand at start, with a separate total for each rate of tax (b) Cost of goods purchased (including VAT) for each rate of tax (c) Gross daily takings (d) Sales figures for HP (etc) goods (e) Taxable outputs of services (f) All goods applied to personal use	Read Sections 18.5, 18.6 and 18.14 in the main text
Schemes H and J	See E above	See E above	see E above

Fig. 18.4 *Choosing the most appropriate method of VAT for your business*

18.5 VAT by the Normal Method

(a) The Input Account

You should record in the Input Account details of all invoices in respect of purchases of goods or services made by you. It is to your advantage to record such invoices immediately they are received, even if you do not pay them immediately. You are obliged to identify separately (i) goods for retailing and (ii) services (your general business overheads, including business stationery, etc.), taxable at different rates. Columns have therefore been provided in the Simplex VAT book to enable this to be done (see Fig. 18.5). For convenience we have imagined a multiple rate system using Standard Rate 15%, Positive Rate A 25%, Positive Rate B 40% and zero rated items. Until a multiple-rate system is introduced columns A and B should be left blank.

The totals at the end of each page can be carried forward to the next page, but if your monthly or quarterly records finish the carry-forward line is ignored and you complete the section at the foot of the page to obtain your 'VAT Return' figures. Sufficient pages are provided to be adequate for most small businesses.

In completing the final lines in any tax period 'Returns' should be deducted by taking away the totals carried from the 'Input Returns' account. The final total in the 'Deductable VAT Input Tax' column labelled 'Carry this total to the VAT Account' is then ready to be carried to the VAT account, either monthly or quarterly.

INPUT ACCOUNT—PURCHASES OF GOODS. SERVICES AND CAPITAL ITEMS

Invoice Date	Invoice Number	From whom purchased	Invoice Total	Cost of Goods (excluding VAT) Standard Rate	Positive Rate 'A'	Positive Rate 'B'	Zero rated Goods	Input Services	Deductible VAT Input Tax	Exempt and non deductible (inc. VAT)
APL.3.	00214	SMITH & JONES.	252 50	50 00	40 00	100 00	5 00		57 50	
Totals for accounting period			51807 08	13450 00	4017 50	5268 00	3757 50		5129 08	185 00
Less totals from 'Input returns (Credits) account'			506 48	108 00	44 70	221 00	17 00		115 78	
Grand totals for accounting period			31300 60	13342 00	3972 80	5047 00	3740 50		5013 30	185 00

Carry this total to the VAT Account ➔

INPUT RETURNS—(CREDITS) ON GOODS. CAPITAL ITEMS AND SERVICES PURCHASED

Invoice Date	Invoice Number	From whom received	Credit Note Total	Cost of Goods (excluding VAT) Standard Rate	Positive Rate 'A'	Positive Rate 'B'	Zero Rated Goods	Input Services	Deductible VAT Input Tax	Exempt and non deductible (incl. VAT)
APL.7.	00310	SMITH & JONES	6 90	6 00					90	
Totals to be carried to 'Input Account'			506 48	108 00	44 70	221 00	17 00		115 78	

Fig. 18.5 *The Simplex VAT input records*

Input records are used in some of the Special Schemes of Retailers as the basis for output tax. For example, if a retailer cannot separate off the amounts sold at different rates of tax himself, the Customs & Excise will assume that what he sells must be what he buys. Therefore, if they can tell from the Input Records what he buys at Standard Rate and Zero Rate it is fairly easy to work out what he sells at these rates. This is explained more fully in Section 18.11, 18.12 and 18.14 below.

(b) The Output Account

If you are recording VAT by the normal method, details of all VAT invoices issued by you during the account period have to be entered in the Output Account section of the VAT book. The details should be recorded in the columns shown in Fig. 18.6, according to the column headings. If you are using one of the small retailer's schemes you should only record in the Output Account invoices issued in respect of goods or services that fall *outside* the scheme. The invoices should be numbered and recorded consecutively.

OUTPUT ACCOUNT—INVOICED SALES, SERVICES, WRITTEN HP & CREDIT SALE TRANSACTIONS

Invoice Date	Invoice Number	To whom sold	Gross Invoice Total	Standard Rate	Positive Rate 'A'	Positive Rate 'B'	Liable at Zero Rate	Exempt	VAT Output Tax	Export Sales
APL. 1.	0001	R.T. BROWN.	317 00	80 00	60 00	100 00	10 00		67 00	
Totals for accounting period			58016 06	26146 00	8211 41	9765 00	4012 90		9880 75	
Less totals from 'Output returns (Credits) account'			669 15	325 00	48 00	160 00	11 40		124 75	
Grand totals for accounting period			57346 91	25821 00	8163 41	9605 00	4001 50		9756 00	

Carry this total to the VAT Account ➤

OUTPUT RETURNS—(CREDITS) ON GOODS SOLD AND SERVICES SUPPLIED.

Invoice Date	Invoice Number	To whom given	Credit Note Total	Standard Rate	Positive Rate 'A'	Positive Rate 'B'	Liable at Zero Rate	Exempt	VAT Output Tax	Export Sales
APL. 7.	0012	R.T. BROWN	11 50	10 00					1 50	
Totals to be carried to 'Output Account'			669 15	325 00	48 00	160 00	11 40		124 75	

Fig. 18.6 *The Simplex VAT output records*

Numbered copy invoices should be kept. Two spare columns for Positive Rate A and B have been provided for use if the Chancellor should introduce a multi-rate system; until then they should be left blank.

If you sell goods under written hire-purchase or credit-sale agreements, appropriate documents must be issued and the details recorded in the relevant columns of the Output Account. The totals at the end of each page are to be carried forward to the next page.

(c) The VAT Account

At the end of each VAT period the figures of input tax and output tax are carried from the Input and Output Accounts to the VAT Account, and are then used to complete the VAT Return which you will receive from HM Customs & Excise. A 'normal' VAT Account is shown in Fig. 18.7. It is also possible to submit a VAT Account only once a year. The details are given in section 18.17.

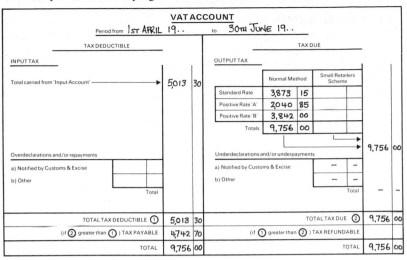

Fig. 18.7 *A VAT Account by the normal method*

18.6 Gross Daily Takings

The whole idea of the small retailer's schemes is to enable small businesses, which do not give their customers tax invoices, to account for VAT in a relatively simple way. All these schemes require proprietors to know their quarterly total of gross daily takings. There are two methods of calculating this: *(a)* the 'Standard Method', based on the payments actually received from customers in the tax period, and *(b)* the optional method which is based on supplies made during the tax period whether payment was received or not.

(a) The Standard Method

Gross daily takings for the purpose of VAT special schemes means the total value of all the supplies made by the retailer *inside* the scheme. Any items sold on hire-purchase, credit-sale or conditional-sale terms, having completed a proper agreement under the Consumer Credit Act, are *outside the scheme* and should be accounted for by the 'normal' method (see Section 18.5). Any services (as opposed to goods) are outside Schemes C, D, E, G, H and J, and if they are at lower rate they are outside Scheme B as well and must be accounted for either by the normal VAT method or by Schemes A or F. Goods applied to your own use are inside the scheme, and should be included in the gross daily takings at selling price, including tax. So are any goods sold against Barclaycard, Access and other credit cards. You must also include the face value of all trading checks, coupons, vouchers, book tokens, record tokens and gift tokens which you exchange for goods. If you run your own trading-stamp scheme and exchange stamps for goods, you do not include these in takings.

Add all these items together on the 'Daily Takings' page of your VAT book, as shown in Fig. 18.8, and then deduct from the total figure all items which reduce your takings, for example cash refunds to customers who return goods or present trading stamps for redemption *in cash*. (If they redeem trading stamps in goods, you have already disregarded these in working out your takings). You also deduct takings on written HP agreements, payments to trading-stamp companies for stamps supplied, and all the services supplied unless you are using Schemes A or F or Scheme B in certain circumstances.

When you have subtracted the total of these deductions from the total takings, you are left with your 'Gross Daily Takings' figure.

(b) The Optional Method

The calculation is the same as in the standard method already described except that sales made on credit must be included (+ VAT) in the daily takings figure. This means that later on, when they actually pay, the settlement payments are left out of the calculation. Also left out of the calculation are payments received in the trading period for goods supplied before the trader starts to use the optional method.

Other Points of Interest

The records of gross daily takings must be made every day. Many of the columns will only require an entry occasionally, and some retailers may never require to make entries in certain of the columns.

At the end of the month, or the quarter, according to the length of your trading period for VAT, all columns must be totalled. A retailer who wishes to simplify this addition should consider the purchase of a printing calculator. These are appreciably more expensive than an ordinary calculator, but they do give a printout of your entries which you can use to compare with your VAT book.

The final total in Column 11 of the VAT book is the figure to be used for calculation of the output tax. This calculation will have to be in accordance with your Scheme leaflet, obtainable from your tax office; specimen calculations are given in Sections 18.7, 18.11, 18.12, 18.13 and 18.14.

All calculations and records must be kept for six years, together with all documents relating thereto, unless a Customs & Excise official has authorised their destruction, permission for which must be sought well in advance.

VAT fractions

When output tax is calculated from Gross Daily Takings we have to use a VAT fraction. It is interesting to know how the fractions are arrived at. Here is a short explanation.

Standard-rate Goods—VAT Fraction = 3/23

When we sell goods at standard rate, we add on 15 per cent VAT. The goods therefore sell at:

$$\text{Selling Price} + 15\% = 100\% + 15\% = 115\%$$

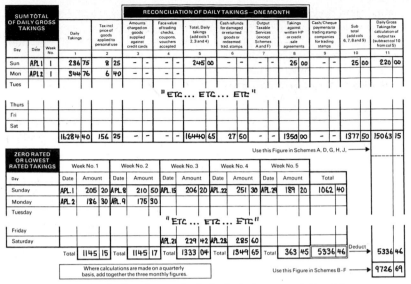

Fig. 18.8 *The Simplex method of calculating gross daily takings*

If we now want to find out how much VAT is included in the gross takings total for standard-rated goods it is not 15/100, but 15/115ths of the total. 15/115 cancels down to 3/23 and that is why the VAT fraction for standard-rated goods is 3/23.

Other positive-rated goods. At present there are no goods sold at higher rates of VAT than the standard rate. It is however quite easy to find a VAT fraction for any rate of VAT using the following formula:

$$\frac{\text{Rate of VAT}}{100 + \text{Rate of VAT}}$$

e.g. If rates of 25% and 30% were introduced, the VAT fractions would be

$$\frac{25}{100 + 25} = \frac{25}{125} = \frac{1}{5}\text{th}$$

$$\frac{30}{100 + 30} = \frac{30}{130} = \frac{3}{13}\text{ths}$$

Adding VAT to Cost Price Totals

In certain Retailers Special Schemes the Output Tax is calculated by using the tax inclusive price of goods purchased for retailing. The simplest way to get this tax inclusive figure is to take the total of each positive rated column in the Input Records and add on the VAT at the correct rate. It would be a great waste of time to add back the VAT on each item, it is only necessary to add it to the final total. Since at the time of writing the Standard Rate is 15 per cent, all that is necessary is to increase the Cost Price column by 15 per cent.

(Note: In the schemes described below reference has been made to an imaginary 'higher rate' of 25%).

18.7 Retailers: Special Scheme A

This scheme, as explained in Fig. 18.4 is for traders who only supply goods or services (or both) at one positive rate of tax. This means that you need only keep records of the goods or services (a hiring, lease or rental of goods is deemed to be a service) supplied at this rate. If you also supply goods at zero-rate disregard these for the purpose of Scheme A.

Records. For Scheme A you must keep a full record of your daily gross takings for the supplies covered by the scheme, according to whether you use the Standard Method or the Optional Method (see Section 18.6). For this record you will use the Simplex Daily Takings page. If you are concerned with any special types of transactions, such as the sale of book tokens, make sure you deal with them correctly as shown in booklet 727, Sections 10-18, which your local VAT office will supply.

Calculations of VAT by Scheme A

Under this scheme the calculation is as follows:

Step 1. Find the *gross takings total* from your records by adding them up for the complete trading period. Suppose this comes to £23 756·00.

Step 2. Multiply this figure by the VAT fraction for the rate of tax which applies to your goods and services. For standard-rate (15%) items of VAT the fraction is 3/23rds, for higher rate (25%)items it is one fifth. Let us imagine we are dealing with standard rate items. Then £23 756·00 × 3/23 = £3 098·61. To do this quickly and easily it is obviously best to use an electronic calculator.

(Check: the best way to check this is to deduct the VAT from the gross takings total. This gives us £20 657·39. Now this must be the real selling price, and the VAT on this figure is 15%. If we find 15 per cent of £20 657·39 it should come to £3 098 61. On the calculator £20 657 39 × ·15 = £3 098·61. Our calculation of Output Tax is therefore correct).

You should now be able to complete your VAT account, as shown in Fig. 18.7. A scheme leaflet about calculations is available free of charge from George Vyner Ltd.

18.8 Retailers: Special Scheme B

Scheme B, as explained in Fig. 18.4 is for retailers who supply goods at *only two* rates of tax. Services may also be included provided that they are sold at the higher rate of the two. There is a condition for the use of this Scheme, that the takings of the lower rated goods must not amount to more than one half (50 per cent) of the taxable turnover. Taxable turnover is defined as the total value, including VAT of all the supplies made under the scheme.

Traders who sell goods at standard rate and zero rate can use this scheme, and can include services if they are taxed at the higher rate.

The idea of the scheme is this. Some retailers cannot separate off their daily takings at the different rates and simply finish up with a total takings figure for the period. Let us suppose this figure is £44 000. How much of it is tax? Since this scheme is for people who only sell at two rates of tax, we can work out how much is tax by finding out from the input records how much of the takings was at the lower rate. Suppose the input records show that lower rate goods were bought worth £10 000. The retailer knows what profit margin he adds on—let us say 20 per cent. This means that the lower rate goods bought for £10 000 were sold for £12 000 + VAT. If zero rated tax applies they were sold for £12,000, but if the lower rate in this case was standard rate they would be sold for £12 000 + 15% = £12 000 + £1 800 = £13 800. Now if we take these figures from the grand total of £44 000 it means that the rest was the goods sold at the higher of his two rates. So a trader selling at zero rate and standard rate must have sold:

Zero Rate + Standard Rate = Total
£12 000 + £32 000 = £44 000

A trader selling at standard-rate and higher-rate must have sold:

Standard Rate + Higher Rate = Total
£13 800 + £30 200 = £44 000

From this, by applying the correct VAT fractions, we can find out the Output Tax owed to Customs & Excise Department.

Calculations of VAT by Scheme B

Step 1. Find the gross takings total from your Simplex records by adding the daily takings together for the whole tax period.

Step 2. Find out the cost to you of the goods you bought at the lower of your two rates during the period. This means that you must go back to your purchases invoices and find the cost prices paid by you for the goods supplied. Add on your usual profit margin to this, and if your lower rate is the standard rate add 15 per cent tax as well.

Step 3. Take the total of Step 2 from the total of Step 1. The result is your estimated takings including VAT at the higher of your two rates.

Step 4. Now apply the proper VAT fraction to these totals. If your two rates are Zero and Standard Rate there will be no tax on the Zero Rate and 3/23rds on the standard rate. If your two rates are standard and higher rate (25% imagined) there will be 3/23rds of the standard rate total and 1/5th of the higher rate total to account for.

Step 5. Now write up your VAT account as shown in Fig. 18.7. A scheme leaflet about the calculation is available free of charge from George Vyner Ltd.

18.9 Retailers: Special Scheme B1

This scheme is very similar to Scheme B above, but the actual figures are taken into account for the whole tax 'year'—a 'year' running for four quarters from the date you start the scheme. The first three quarters you keep your records in the usual way, but in the fourth quarter output tax you then repeat the calculation for the whole tax year, using the whole year's figures. If the tax due on the whole year's figures is less than the four quarterly total you will have paid too much if you send in the full amount of the 4th quarter's tax. You are therefore allowed to set down the amount overpaid on the 'deductible' side, and you need only send in the balance payable. If the annual adjustment shows that you have underpaid VAT you must increase the amount due in the fourth quarter. The leaflet from your local VAT office. 'How to work Scheme B; Adaptation One' has a very clear layout of the calculation.

18.10 Retailers: Special Scheme B2

This scheme is very similar to Scheme B except that when you work out the value of your zero-rated goods received for re-sale you have to add on a fixed mark-up specified by H.M. Customs instead of the mark-up you usually use. The mark-up rates are:

Food = 20%
Children's clothing and footwear = 35%
Books, booklets, maps, etc. = 40%
Newspapers, magazines ,etc. = 33%
Other goods = 15%

The scheme was introduced to meet certain problems with mark-ups being claimed by some traders, where—perhaps by manipulating the mark up rate—they could reduce the amount of tax payable below what was actually being collected. The leaflet 'How to Work Scheme B Adaptation 2' explains exactly how to do the calculation.

18.11 Retailers: Special Scheme C

This scheme is for retailers in trades 8 201-8 239, whose taxable turnover is less than £90 000 per year. It cannot be used for services, which must be accounted for seperately outside the Scheme. Since it bases the output VAT on the goods purchased for re-sale, it cannot be used by growers and manufacturers who are adding value to their products other than their profit margin.

The principle of the scheme is that Output Tax is calculated on the basis of input records, because for most trades what you sell is only what you buy with a profit margin added. The VAT authorities have laid down 8 bands of margins which are usual in the various trades, and the trader adds on the correct margin to his cost prices to find his selling prices. The VAT is then calculated on these selling prices.

Calculating VAT under Scheme C

Step 1. Add up the cost to you, including VAT, of all the things you buy to sell again at a *positive rate of tax*. You need a separate total for each positive rate you are dealing with.

Step 2. Add on the correct profit margin for your trade, which is given in the Scheme C leaflet issued by the VAT office. For example, at the time of writing, June 1990, Grocers add on 20 per cent and Jewellers 75 per cent.

Step 3. Now multiply this total (with the profit margin added on) by its correct VAT fraction (3/23 for standard rate; 1/5 for our imagined higher rate of 25%). The result is the Output Tax due under the Scheme, for that class of goods. If you have both standard rate and higher rate goods add the two lots of output tax together to get your total tax due to Customs and Excise. You should now be able to complete your VAT account. A scheme leaflet about the calculation is available free of charge from George Vyner Ltd.

18.12 Retailers: Scheme D

Scheme D is for retailers whose turnover is less than £500 000 per year and who cannot conveniently distinguish sales at different rates of tax. They keep a record of daily gross takings either by the standard or the optional method, but the Output Tax on these takings is calculated from the input records. Because there must be a close link between what you buy and what you actually sell eventually, it is possible to calculate the output tax by working out the proportion of things bought at each rate of tax. Thus if one third of your purchases are standard rate presumably one third of your total takings will also be at standard rate, and by using the VAT fraction 3/23 on that one third the Output Tax can be calculated.

One point about Scheme D is that it may result in an overpayment or underpayment of tax. For example, retailers stocking up with Higher Rate goods which are to be sold in the Christmas season may find themselves paying high output tax in the quarter concerned, when in fact sales of the highly taxed lines have barely started. For this reason there is a *Scheme Adjustment* annually. The calculation explained below, which is carried out in every tax period is repeated once a year with the whole year's figures. This will enable the retailer to discover whether tax has been overpaid or underpaid. Any overpayment will be reclaimed at once out of the next VAT payment. Any under-payment must be accounted for.

As explained in Fig. 18.4 Scheme D cannot be used for manufacturing, or for farms and smallholdings etc., who raise stock or grow produce. It cannot be used for services either, since it depends upon finding Output Tax from the input records of goods bought for re-sale.

The step-by-step procedure for using Scheme D is quite long and to assist you the Scheme D leaflet obtainable from your local VAT office includes a worksheet at the back, which can be used to help you. The details are give in the next section. Once again an imaginary 'higher rate' of 25% has been used.

Calculating VAT under Scheme D

Step 1. Find the gross takings total for the tax period, using your Simplex VAT 'Reconciliation of Daily Takings' pages; say £210 000. Call this Total (1).

Step 2. We are going to find out how much VAT output Tax we must pay on the total in Step 1, by finding how much the various types of goods cost us. We therefore need to find the cost, including VAT, of all the goods received for retailing at:

(a) the standard rate (at 15%)—say £40 000 = Total (2)
(b) the higher rate (at 25%)—say £50 000 = Total (3)
(c) the zero rate (at 0%)—say £10 000 = Total (4)

          Grand total £100 000 = Total (5)

Step 3. The Output Tax payable is therefore as follows:

$$\text{Tax on Standard Rate items} = \frac{\text{Total (2)} \times \text{Total (1)} \times 3}{\text{Total (5)} \qquad\qquad 23}$$

$$= \frac{£40\,000 \times £210\,000 \times 3}{£100\,000 \qquad\qquad 23}$$

$$= £10\,956 \cdot 52 \ \text{Output tax}$$

$$\text{Tax on Higher Rate items} = \frac{\text{Total (3)} \times \text{Total (1)} \times 1}{\text{Total (5)} \qquad\qquad 5}$$

$$= \frac{£50\,000 \times £210\,000 \times 1}{£100\,000 \qquad\qquad 5}$$

$$= £21\,000 \ \text{Output tax}$$

For zero-rated items there is no need to do a calculation since there is no tax. Total output tax is therefore found by adding these two items together.

Output tax = £10 956·52 + £21 000 = £31 956 52

Once a year the *Scheme Adjustment* referred to above must also be made. You should now be able to complete your VAT Account. A scheme leaflet about the calculation is available free of charge from George Vyner Ltd.

18.13 Retailers: Special Scheme F

As explained in Fig. 18.3 Scheme F is a very straightforward scheme for retailers who can distinguish clearly their sales at each rate of tax. In such a case there is no problem at all in knowing the Output Tax to be accounted for.

Calculating VAT under Scheme F

Step 1. Keep separate daily gross takings record for supplies at each positive rate of tax.

Step 2. Multiply each total by the correct VAT fraction to find the Output Tax. You should now be able to complete your VAT Account. A scheme leaflet on this calculation is available free of charge from George Vyner Ltd.

18.14 Retailers: Special Scheme G

Scheme G is very similar to Scheme D, except that there is no limit of £500 000 turnover. Because the Scheme tends to understate the VAT payable, the final total has to be increased by one eighth ($\frac{1}{8}$) but for those who sell no zero rated goods at all, or whose zero rated goods are very small in number (less than 2 per cent of total sales) the uplift is reduced to one twelfth (1/12).

The rules for calculating output tax are a little complicated, and the best thing to do is to ask for a current scheme leaflet from your local VAT office. Not only does the cost (including VAT) of all goods received for retailing have to be used in the calculation but also the cost (including VAT) of the stock in hand at the start of the trading period. This leads to fairly complex rules in the calculation, which the leaflet makes clear. There is no Scheme Adjustment for Scheme G.

The scheme is very similar to Scheme D. Again a 25% Higher Rate has been used.

Calculating VAT under Scheme G

Step 1. Find the 'Gross Takings' total for the tax period—say £800 000. Call this Total (1).

Step 2. Find the cost including VAT, of goods *in stock* at the start of the period, and *received for retailing* during the tax period:

(a) at the standard rate (at 15%)—say £150 000 = Total (2)
(b) at the higher rate (at 25%)—say £250 000 = Total (3)
(c) at the zero rate (at 0%)—say £50 000 = Total (4)

Grand total £450 000 = Total (5)

Step 3. The output tax is now calculated as follows:

$$\text{Tax on Standard Rate items} = \frac{\text{Total (2)}}{\text{Total (5)}} \times \text{Total (1)} \times \frac{3}{23}$$

$$= \frac{£150\,000}{£450\,000} \times £800\,000 \times \frac{3}{23}$$

$$= £34\,782 \cdot 61 \text{ Output tax}$$

$$\text{Tax on Higher Rate items} = \frac{\text{Total (3)}}{\text{Total (5)}} \times \text{Total (1)} \times \frac{1}{5}$$

$$= \frac{£250\,000}{£450\,000} \times £800\,000 \times \frac{1}{5}$$

$$= £88\,888 \cdot 89 \text{ Output tax}$$

Once again there is no need for any calculation on the zero rate items. Total output tax is found by adding these two answers together.

Output tax = £34 782·61 + £88 888·89 = £123 671·50

You should now be able to complete your VAT Account. A scheme leaflet on this calculation is available free of charge from George Vyner Ltd.

18.15 Cautionary Note

It is almost impossible to describe these schemes fully without reproducing the whole 'Scheme Leaflet'. I have attempted—at the expense of some detail—to convey to the reader the general ideas behind the Schemes, which are in fact quite ingenious as ways of finding the tax payable. They are simple schemes, yet they do not read very easily, and the detail is often very important. A retailer who has decided upon one scheme has only to familiarise himself/herself with that one scheme. Phone your local VAT office if in difficulty with the details.

18.16 Special Note: VAT on Capital Items

A special difficulty arises with VAT on capital items, except for the purchase of motor cars (not vans) on which VAT is not recoverable. Since the VAT element is not a long-term asset, but is only paid and refunded within three months, it must be recorded as a business expense for the current year in the Profit and Loss Account at the end of the year. If this is not done the profits will be overstated, and tax will be paid on the inflated profit figure.

The rules for this are as follows:

(a) Enter the purchase of the capital item in the VAT book in the ordinary way, as explained in 18.5 above.

(b) When entering the capital item in the weekly page put the figure in inclusive of VAT in either 'cash' or 'bank' column.

(c) When carrying this capital item to the Summary of Capital Expenses at the back of the book enter the net value only in the Amount column, and enter the VAT alongside, as shown below.

(d) At the end of the year enter the £600 VAT on the Profit and Loss Account, on the line provided, so that this will read 'VAT on capital items £600.' This will reduce the profits you have made to the correct figure. The correct figure for the asset on the Balance Sheet is the 'Net Value'. (Remember that VAT cannot be reclaimed on motor cars even if they are for business use, but it can be reclaimed on vans and lorries).

CAPITAL EXPENSES INCURRED DURING THE YEAR						
DATE	NATURE AND FULL DETAILS OF EXPENSE	INVOICE VALUE		NET VALUE OF ASSET		VAT
21·7·19..	PURCHASE OF MACHINE No XYZ 7184	4600	00	4000	00	600	00

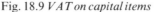

Fig. 18.9 *VAT on capital items*

Remember also that if you are not VAT registered you cannot reclaim this VAT and must ignore the VAT lines on your Profit and Loss Account at the end of the Simplex book.

18.17 Cash Accounting for VAT

There is now an optional scheme of 'Cash Accounting for VAT' open to all businesses with turnovers below £250 000—who account for VAT by the normal invoice method. It is *not* available to those using Small Retailers Schemes.

Businesses wishing to change over to this scheme must first apply to H.M. Customs & Excise and if approved must remain in that scheme for 2 years.

Cash Accounting
The Simplex VAT Record Book can be still be used for this scheme. It does not alter the general method of recording invoices.

The only change is that all invoices which you receive for goods or services provided to you (Inputs) should only be entered in the Simplex VAT Record Book when those invoices are paid and not before payment is made.

Similarly all invoices which you issue to your customers (Outputs) should only be entered in the Simplex VAT Record Book when payment is received from the customer, and not before payment is received.

Annual VAT Return
Businesses with an annual turnover of less than £250 000, who have been in business for more than one year and approved by H.M. Customs & Excise will be permitted to submit an annual VAT Return.

Based on the previous years VAT payments an agreed assessment of the expected VAT liability will be raised.

The figure will be divided by 10, and 9 monthly payments will be made by direct debit, starting 4 months after the beginning of the year. The tenth payment accompanied by the Annual VAT Return, will balance the account.

An annual VAT Return will not be compulsory. You can still use the present system of quarterly accounting. However, if you wish to make an annual VAT Return we still recommend use of the Simplex VAT Record Book to maintain quarterly records (without calculating the VAT liability) and to summarise the 4 quarters at the end of the VAT year.

It will then be an easy matter to determine the total VAT liability for the whole year. When this figure has been established, subtract the total of the 9 payments already made and the difference will be the 10th payment. The Annual VAT Return should be submitted with the 10th payment.

18.18 The transfer of going concerns

Special rules apply to the transfer of a business, or part of a business as a going concern. Basically, the transfer of a going concern is not a supply of goods or services for VAT purposes, and the vendor is not therefore entitled to charge output tax on the transfer. Nor is the new proprietor entitled to deduct any sum paid as input tax. If it is deducted the VAT authorities will disallow it and claim an immediate refund—leaving the new proprietor with a debt to pay to them, and only a right to re-claim from the vendor (if the vendor can be found, or has funds to pay). If the vendor is still in business he/she could issue the purchaser with a credit note. The VAT authorities recommend that a prior ruling from Customs and Excise should be requested in any case where there is doubt as to whether a business transfer counts as the transfer of a going concern.

18.19 VAT and the Simplex D Account Book

We sometimes get accountants who complain about the way VAT is done in the Simplex D Account Book and it is true that we have adopted a simpler system than most accountants use. The reason is that many users of the Simplex System are busy traders and don't make out VAT invoices for outputs and there is little point in analysing VAT out of each day's takings.

The way VAT works in the Simplex D Account Book is as follows:

(a) Sales (Daily Takings) and Purchases (Payments for Business Stock) are recorded gross.

(b) When these figures are entered in the Trading Account they give a Gross Profit which is larger than it should be (Gross profit + VAT).

(c) When taken into the Profit and Loss Account this Gross Profit is set against.

(i) The expenses (inclusive of VAT)

(ii) The payment to the VAT man (Output Tax—Input Tax)

(iii) The VAT on capital items

This removes all the VAT that is in the Gross Profit and reduces it to a Net Profit free of VAT.

Chapter Nineteen

The Simplex Licensees Account Book

19.1 Introduction

Some years ago George Vyner Ltd., were asked by a major brewery if they would devise a simple record book for licensees which would meet the special needs of the licensing trade. The result of this enquiry was the 'Simplex Licensees' Book, which incorporates both the ordinary financial records and the VAT records in one book. It follows exactly the same principles as the Simplex D Account Book and the VAT Record Book. Certain of the rulings have been altered to make them more appropriate for the licensees trade. Readers of Simplified Book-keeping for Small Businesses who are in this trade, or thinking of becoming managers or owners of a public house, should certainly obtain a copy of the Licensees Book and study it in conjunction with the present volume. If copies are not available at your local stationer write to George Vyner Ltd., at the address shown at the front of this book.

19.2 Layout of the Licensees Book

The layout of the licensees book follows the general pattern of the Simplex System but is adapted to meet the needs of the trade. The chief features of the book may be listed as follows:

(a) The 53 weekly pages provided follow the usual patterns but the rulings have been adapted to assist the licensee to analyse his receipts under various headings, liquor, tobacco, catering etc.

(b) The VAT input records are achieved in a special Invoice Register at the front of the book which gives room to record the invoices from suppliers and to draw up quarterly totals. These are then carried to a summary at the back of the book.

(c) The VAT output records are extracted from the weekly pages (see (a) above) and carried to summaries at the back of the book and thence to VAT accounts for each quarterly period.

It is difficult to imagine a more simple and comprehensive system.

The weekly page of the Simplex Licensee's book is illustrated on page 149.

RECEIPTS

Week ending :

Week No.

Day/Date	Standard Rate Takings (incl. Credit Card Sales)				Zero Rate Takings (incl. Credit Card Sales)		Exempt Takings	Total Takings	Particulars of Other Receipts	Paid to Bank
	Tobacco	Liquor	Catering	Other	Food	Other				
Sun. :										
Mon. :										
Tues. :										
Wed. :										
Thurs. :										
Fri. :										
Sat. :										
Personal Use										
Totals									(E)	

PAYMENTS – TAXABLE INPUTS

Invoice Date	Ref No	Details per Invoice Register	By Cash	By Cheque
		Totals		
			(A)	(C)

PAYMENTS – EXEMPT INPUTS ONLY

Nature of Payment	By Cash	By Cheque
Wages – Net Amount Paid		
NIC Stamps – Self		
Inl. Rev. – PAYE & NIC		
Insurances		
Licences		
Rent		
Rates		
Postages		
Sundries		
Bank Charges		
V.A.T. Paid to Customs & Excise		
Personal Amounts Withdrawn		
Personal Goods Not Paid For (see Takings)		
Totals		
	(B)	(D)

WEEKLY BANK RECONCILIATION

Add	Balance at Bank from Last Week	
	Payments to Bank During Week (E)	
	Credit Card Receipts	
	Total	
Deduct	Cheque Payments (C)	
	Cheque Payments (D)	
	Cash Withdrawn from Bank	
	Bank Standing Order	
	Total	
	Balance at Bank at End of Week	

WEEKLY CASH RECONCILIATION

Add	Cash in Hand (as counted) br/fwd	
	Totals Takings for Week	
	Cash Withdrawn from Bank	
	Total	
Deduct	Cash Payments (A)	
	Cash Payments (B)	
	Credit Card Sales	
	Payments to Bank	
	Total	
	Cash balance carr. fwd	
	Cash in Hand (as counted) at weekend	

© George Vyner Ltd.

Fig. 19.1 *The Simplex Licensee's Weekly page.*

Chapter Twenty
The Simplex Everall Farm Account Book

20.1 Introduction

The Simplex Everall Farm Account Book is a convenient analysis book for farmers and smallholders which has been widely used for many years. It is in three sections, Receipts, Payments and Livestock.

20.2 The Receipts Section

This is an analysis of receipts under various headings, which enables the farmer to see what his receipts are over the course of the trading period in such areas as cattle, sheep, pigs, poultry, wool, potatoes etc. There are columns for VAT repayments, and other receipts of various kinds.

20.3 The Payments Section

Analysed in a similar way to the Receipts Section described above, the payments section permits the farmer to collect costs related to the care of particular animals, or incurred in raising various crops. At the end of the year this permits him to assess their relative profitability.

20.4 The Livestock Section

This section enables the farmer to keep a record month by month of changes in flocks, poultry, etc., whether by births or deaths, purchase or sale.

Although the Farm Account Book does not at present incorporate a full Simplex system of accounts it is a very useful record to be compiled in association with a Simplex D Account Book for the financial results of an agricultural holding.

Chapter Twenty-one

Discovering your Profit

21.1 Introduction

Those who undertake the organization and risks of a business venture are entitled to some reward for their efforts. This reward may assume many forms, but the financial part is the profit made on the venture; in other words, it is the amount by which the receipts of the venture exceed the outgoings.

Profits are usually worked out in two parts. The first part is called the *gross profit*, or the total profit made. It is the profit on the trading activities of the firm, and hence the name *Trading Account* is applied to the section of the accounts where we find this gross profit. Some firms are not trading firms, so they do not have a Trading Account, or a gross profit. Instead they calculate all their profits in the *Profit and Loss Account*. This is the second half of the profit calculation with a trading firm. In the Profit and Loss Account we take all our overhead expenses and running expenses away from the gross profit, to which we also add any miscellaneous profits that are not trading profits, such as fees received, commission received, rent received, etc. This gives us the *net profit*, or 'clear' profit. This profit belongs to the person or persons who showed enterprise in setting up and running the risks of the business, in other words it belongs to the proprietor or proprietors. Based on this profit the Inland Revenue Department will have to assess how much tax is payable by the entrepreneur concerned, so there have to be a few rules about how the net profit is calculated. Fortunately in the Simplex System we have a very simple system which conforms to these rules.

Before looking at this system in detail, one or two words of warning are necessary. These are:

(a) Manufacturing Accounts. Some firms that use the Simplex System are manufacturers. This means that before they can trade they have to make the goods they hope to sell. This means that they need an extra layer of calculations *before* they come to the Trading Account and Profit and Loss Account. The publishers of the Simplex System now issue a simple set of Final Accounts for Manufacturers. If you are a manufacturer you will find these explained in Chapter Twenty-two. Please send for a set of our Final Accounts for Manufacturers as you get near the end of your financial year. There is no charge.

(b) Partnerships. There is a problem with partnerships in that the profit at the end of the year has to be shared up between the partners. Here again we provide a free set of Partnership Final Accounts to those who run their businesses as a partnership. Please send for a set as you get near the end of your financial year. They are fully explained in Chapter Twenty-two.

(c) Limited companies. There are a few differences in keeping the accounts of

a limited company, but as companies must have their books audited by professional accountants it is usual for the accountants to prepare the final accounts. For those trading as limited companies who do wish to prepare their own accounts, before submitting them to an accountant we again supply a set of helpful notes, free of charge. Those wishing to receive a set should apply a few weeks before the end of their financial year.

Calculating your profits at the end of the year is a process known as the 'preparation of final accounts'. In many small businesses this process is left entirely to professional accountants. We will assume that you, however, are reading this because you wish to learn how to prepare your own final accounts. There are three parts to the exercise: we have to draw up

(a) the Trading Account, in which we find the gross profit;
(b) the Profit and Loss Account, in which we find the net profit, and
(c) the Balance Sheet, in which we list the assets and liabilities of the business.

From these final accounts you should be able to gauge the progress of your business and detect any weaknesses.

21.2 Drawing up the Trading Account

Users of the Simplex system can easily prepare a Trading Account at the end of the year, from the summary sheets which you have drawn up week by week. Before considering this in detail, we shall look at some very simple Trading Accounts which illustrate the underlying principles. Let us turn for a moment to Fig. 21.1.

Trading Account
(for year ending December 31st, 19. .)

	£		£
Purchases	80	Sales	100
Gross Profit	20		
	£100		£100

Fig. 21.1 *The simplest Trading Account possible: the cost price of the goods is set against the selling price, and the difference is the gross profit*

Stock Valuation

Unfortunately the Trading Account shown in Fig. 21.1 is not very sensible, because in real life we rarely sell out completely, so there is always 'stock in hand' to worry about. Clearly we shall need to know how much of our stock remains unsold if we are going to work out the profits of the business. We shall have to count stock and then value it, and add up all the different items to give us a grand total which is the 'closing stock' figure. What value shall we place on the items? Shall we value them at cost price or at selling price? What about a shop-soiled item that will not fetch its original price?

The answers to these problems are now laid down in an official Statement of Standard Accounting Practice from the accountancy bodies: *Stock is valued at the lower of cost, or net realisable value.* If an item will sell above cost price you must value it at cost price; if it is shop-soiled or in some way unsatisfactory so that you will lose money on it, you must value it at net realisable value. Net realisable value means you value it at what you think you could get for it if you dispose of it, *less* any costs of disposal (for example auctioneer's charges). This rule is based upon a very important concept in accounting the *prudence concept.* This rule says that a prudent trader never takes a profit until he/she actually knows he/she has made it, but always takes a loss as soon as it is pretty certain that a loss will be made. If we valued things above cost we would be taking a profit before we had made it, but if an item has deteriorated and is worth *less* than cost price we take that loss at once.

When we have valued our stock we can draw up a slightly more realistic Trading Account by including opening- and closing-stock figures, as shown in Fig. 21.2.

Trading Account
(for year ending December 31st, 19..)

	£		£
Opening Stock	15	Sales	100
Purchases	80		
	95		
less Closing Stock	27		
	68		
Gross Profit	32		
	£100		£100

Fig. 21.2 *A slightly more realistic Trading Account*

According to Fig. 21.2 the profit has now increased to £32. This is because some of the goods purchased have not been sold (£27 worth in fact) but we have sold the rest of the £80 worth, and also £15 worth that were in hand at the start of the year. We have thus sold £15 + (£80 − £27) = £68 worth of goods for £100, giving a profit of £32.

Note that if you tried to tell the inspector of taxes that your profit was only £20, as revealed in Fig. 21.1, he would doubtless remind you that unsold stock has to be taken into account before you can find your true profit.

We will now look at the Trading Account as it appears at the back of the Simplex Account Book (Fig. 21.3).

		TRADING ACCOUNT for year ending 31st DECEMBER 19..								
LAST YEAR			19..		**LAST YEAR**			19..		
5420	90	Opening Stock at	7295	45	67259	80	Sales or Work completed	98250	50	
45525	60	Purchases of Business Stock during year	62355	00	1011	20	Value of goods taken for own consumption	1249	50	
50946	50	Total	69650	45	68271	00	Total turnover	99500	00	
7295	45	Less Closing Stock at 31st DEC.	11214	60						
43651	05	Cost of Sales Total	58435	85						
24619	95	Gross Profit (Carried to Profit & Loss Account)	41064	15						
68271	00	TOTAL	99500	00	68271	00	TOTAL	99500	00	

Fig. 21.3 *A Trading Account from the Simplex account book*

Notes:

(a) A Trading Account always indicates by a date at the top the period which it covers in the lifetime of the business.

(b) The goods taken for own consumption are added at selling price to the 'Sales' figure *(see note (e) below)*.

(c) The gross profit figure of £41 064·15 is carried to the Profit and Loss Account.

(d) The previous year's figures, for comparison purposes, are given alongside those of the current year. This meets the requirements of the Companies Act 1985. It is not strictly necessary for small businesses which are not trading as companies.

(e) The rule that goods taken for own consumption must be valued at selling price and appear as 'sales' was given in a case called 'Sharkey v Wernher' some years ago. It has been challenged (because it is really rather silly to talk of someone making a profit out of himself). The Inland Revenue has listened to some extent to this argument (for example caterers who sell food left over to staff at cost price are allowed to do so—otherwise, it would just go bad). If your business is one of those special cases you can deduct goods taken for own consumption, at cost price, from purchases. For the vast majority of firms the position shown in Fig. 21.3 is correct.

We have now discovered the true gross profit of the business, and have completed the first part of our 'final accounts'.

21.3 Drawing up the Profit and Loss Account

The Profit and Loss Account is opened with the entry of the gross profit, transferred from the Profit and Loss Account. To this gross profit are added any miscellaneous receipts which have been collected in the columns of the 'Summary of Other Receipts'? VAT refunds will also be added if the trader has received any. Of course VAT is normally only refunded to traders dealing in zero-rated goods.

A word about enterprise allowances is also needed. From the start the Government has always held that the enterprise allowance must be regarded as income of the business, and therefore must become part of the 'profits' of the business and included in the assessment for tax purposes. Really this amounts to little more than a claim by the Government that if a business it has helped to start proves to be successful it is entitled to claim back some of its contribution in the tax net. Since this money is not really 'profit' in the normal sense of that word it is actually collected under a different part of the Schedule D tax arrangements, and for that reason it is shown separately on the profits side (the right-hand side) of the Profit and Loss Account. Of course this allowance is only paid for the first 12 months of a new business, so after that time the line can simply be ignored.

The expenses to be charged against the profits are listed on the left-hand side of the Profit and Loss Account. They are the total carried from the 'Summary of Payments for Expenses' pages.

Two other items which appear on the 'expenses' side (the left-hand side) of the Profit and Loss Account are the payments made to Customs and Excise for VAT, both on goods for re-sale and capital items. The explanation for these has already been given (see Section 18.19). However one important point is that these entries *must not be included by traders who are not registered for VAT.* If you are not registered for VAT because your trading turnover is less than the prescribed figure, and you have not agreed to register voluntarily then there is no entitlement to deduct VAT from your profit figure, since your Trading Account figures do not include any VAT element other than VAT which falls upon you personally. The non-registered trader is in the same position as a consumer and pays the VAT personally.

The grand total of these expenses when deducted from the profits available, as shown in Fig. 21.4, reveals the net profit.

The net profit is the clear profit made by the business. It is the profit figure on which tax is calculated, and forms the starting point for the inspector of taxes in assessing the tax payable. This is discussed in Chapter 24.

21.4 The Balance Sheet of the Business

A Balance Sheet may be described as a 'snapshot' picture of the affairs of the business, at a given moment in time. It is only true for that particular moment, which is shown by the date which is always written at the top. Strictly speaking even the time ought to be stated, but we usually take for granted that the Balance Sheet applies to the close of business on the date shown.

A tremendous amount of information can be gathered from a Balance Sheet by the astute trader, and the reader will find in Section 23.6 of this book a guide to interpreting the evidence displayed. A few introductory points may be mentioned here.

(a) Marshalling the Assets

It is a principle of modern accounting that the accounts should be arranged in such a way that anyone (provided he/she has some basic understanding of the subject) will be able to appreciate immediately the important aspects of the business, and be able to assess the firm's true position. In former times

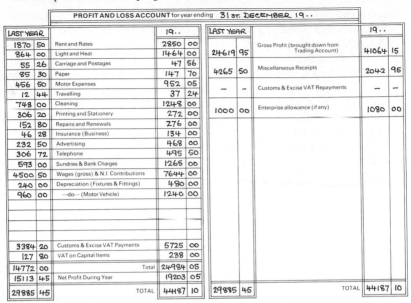

LAST YEAR		Description	19..		LAST YEAR		Description	19..	
		PROFIT AND LOSS ACCOUNT for year ending 31 ST. DECEMBER 19..							
1870	50	Rent and Rates	2850	00	24619	95	Gross Profit (brought down from Trading Account)	41064	15
864	00	Light and Heat	1464	00					
55	26	Carriage and Postages	47	56	4265	50	Miscellaneous Receipts	2042	95
85	30	Paper	147	70					
456	50	Motor Expenses	952	05	—	—	Customs & Excise VAT Repayments	—	—
12	44	Travelling	37	24					
748	00	Cleaning	1248	00	1000	00	Enterprise allowance (if any)	1080	00
306	20	Printing and Stationery	272	00					
152	80	Repairs and Renewals	276	00					
46	28	Insurance (Business)	134	00					
232	50	Advertising	468	00					
306	72	Telephone	495	50					
593	00	Sundries & Bank Charges	1265	00					
4500	50	Wages (gross) & N.I. Contributions	7644	00					
240	00	Depreciation (Fixtures & Fittings)	480	00					
960	00	—do— (Motor Vehicle)	1240	00					
3384	20	Customs & Excise VAT Payments	5725	00					
127	80	VAT on Capital Items	238	00					
14772	00	Total	24984	05					
15113	45	Net Profit During Year	19203	05					
29885	45	TOTAL	44187	10	29885	45	TOTAL	44187	10

Fig. 21.4 *Finding the net profit in the Profit and Loss Account*

accounts were sometimes drawn up deliberately in such a way as to hide the true state of affairs from interested parties. This was particularly undesirable with limited companies, since innocent shareholders, unable to discover weaknesses in the business until too late, were often left with worthless shares on their hands. Today the Companies Act 1985 requires auditors to report whether, in their opinion, the accounts do give a 'true and fair view' of the affairs of the company.

One of the ways in which a clear picture can be presented is to divide up the assets into separate classes. There are about about four types of asset, but here we shall only consider the two chief types: *current assets* and *fixed assets*.

Current Assets. Current assets, sometimes called *circulating assets,* are assets which are continually being turned over. The word 'current', like the French word *courant,* means 'running'. Fig. 21.5 illustrates the way in which current assets 'run round' from cash to stock and back to cash, or from cash to stock, to debtors, and back to cash again. Stock which has been manufactured or purchased for resale is marketed and sold, either for cash or on credit terms. The cash received (or eventually received) is then used to purchase further stock for resale.

These current assets may be seen listed in the Balance Sheet of Fig. 21.6; the most liquid assets 'Cash in hand' and 'Payments in Advance' being placed at the bottom of the list below the more permanent items. Payments in advance is so liquid you have actually spent it.

Fixed Assets. Fixed assets are assets which are not 'turned over' and sold at a profit, but are 'fixed' in the business and retained for a very long period. They

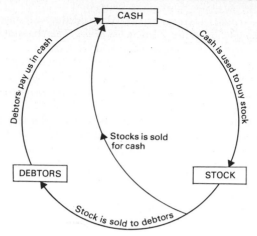

Fig. 21.5 'Circulating' or current assets

are often called *capital assets,* since they form part of the permanent capital equipment in use. The longest-lasting item is land, which may be said to be eternal. Fixtures are expected to last for several years, while assets like motor vehicles are written off after only a few years.

All assets are obtained in order to carry on the affairs of the business, but fixed assets serve their purpose for many years, and may be defined as *assets which permanently increase the profit-making capacity of the business.*

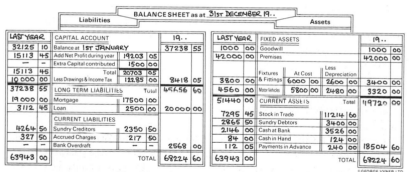

Fig. 21.6 The Simplex Balance Sheet

(b) Marshalling the Liabilities

Just as the separation of current assets from fixed assets on the Balance Sheet is helpful in presenting a simple picture to the businessman, so is a clear division of the liabilities. The liabilities of any business are the funds it owes. The people to whom these funds are owed are the creditors of the business, and they may be listed under three headings:

(i) *Short-term creditors* who may expect to be paid almost at once. The funds owed to these people are called *current liabilities*. The commonest Balance Sheet items of this sort are 'sundry creditors' and bank overdrafts.

(ii) *Long-term creditors*. These will usually have made a special contract with the owner of the business, and their repayment terms will be specified in that contract. The funds owed to these creditors are known as *long-term liabilities*. Examples are mortgages and personal loans.

(iii) *The proprietor*. The owner of a business expects eventually to be repaid the capital originally contributed, plus any profits retained in the business over the course of the years. The amounts owing to the owner are contained in a Capital Account. By convention it is usual to display on the Balance Sheet the capital at the start of the trading period, plus any extra capital contributed during the year, as recorded in the 'Summary of Other Receipts'. We then add the net profit after deducting drawings (as shown in Fig. 21.6). This enables anyone studying the Balance Sheet to see the profits earned in the trading period, and how much of them has already been drawn by the proprietor. Remember that both the drawings and any sums paid to Inland Revenue for the owner's *personal* tax liability have to be deducted from the profits earned, since payment of personal tax is just another form of drawings.

In Fig. 21.6 there are two long-term liabilities, the mortgage and a loan. Details of these would be found in the Summary of Loan/Mortgage Repayments.

Remember also that if VAT liabilities to the Customs & Excise exist, they should be included under 'Accrued Charges' as a current liability; any VAT refunds owed to you by the Customs & Excise should be included under 'Payments in Advance' as a current asset.

With the final clear picture of your business you have completed your set of Final Accounts, which may now be submitted to the inspector of taxes as a true record of your profits for the year.

21.5 Submission of Accounts to the Inland Revenue

This is a very simple procedure under the Simplex System and may either be done directly by the trader, or you may prefer to submit them through your accountant. The procedure is made very straightforward because the Trading Account, Profit and Loss Account and Balance Sheet are repeated at the back of the book. On the first copy you work out your Final Accounts and on the back of this copy is a page headed 'NOTES' where you can make a note of any points you wish to explain to the Inspector of Taxes. For example if you have changed motor vehicles in the year you need to give the full details of the trade-in value of the old vehicle and the purchase price of the new vehicle. You would need to give details of the purchase of any other assets, and ask to be given appropriate capital allowances.

When you have your figures fully completed you make a fair copy of it on the second set of Final Accounts provided. This set has a declaration at the bottom, to the effect that you certify the accounts to be a true copy which can be checked from your actual records.

You then turn over that page and use the ruled lines on it to write a letter to explain any points you have made a note about. It is customary to conclude this letter by offering to present your books for inspection if required. The inspector may ask you to do this, especially in the first year, if he/she has any reservations about your figures. If your accounts are submitted by your accountant this will not be necessary as the accountant will confirm that your records are in reasonable order.

21.6 Some Problem Areas in Final Accounts

One does not want to over-emphasise the problem areas in Final Accounts for it is simple enough to prepare one's own Final Accounts, especially if the Simplex System is being used. As has already been mentioned there are special arrangements needed for manufacturing, and for partnerships and limited companies. These are dealt with in Chapter 22.

There are a few other problems which may arise, which are referred to below, and a number of other problems not specifically related to Final Accounts are dealt with in the final chapter headed 'Sundry Other Matters'. Here we will explain a few of the problems to do with Final Accounts that Simplex users have raised with the Simplex Advice Bureau over the years. Remember that this free advice service exists to give you help with any difficulty, and most matters which appear to be of general interest eventually appear in revised editions of this book. We always welcome correspondence from anyone facing a difficulty in book-keeping (but we are not able to act as tax consultants or financial, advisers). These are the true functions of accountants and other professionals in the financial field.

(a) Adjustments in Final Accounts

One of the most difficult problems met by the owners of small businesses who are keeping their own accounts is the question of 'adjustments'. For many small businesses the Inland Revenue department disregards adjustments altogether and allows the accounts to be kept on a 'Receipts and Payments' basis. This means that the moneys actually received during the trading period are counted in as income as far as profits are concerned, while the payments actually made during the year are allowed as expenses against the profits earned. Strictly speaking this is not correct, for I might pay out money this year (for example for a stock of advertising brochures) which I do not intend to give away until next year. Strictly speaking this expense should be deducted from next year's profits, not this year's and I ought to do an adjustment for it.

Adjustment No. 1: Payments in Advance
Let us take an example to illustrate the adjustment. In Fig. 21.4 there is an entry for Advertising £468·00 in the Profit and Loss Account. This is my payment for advertising brochures delivered to the houses in the town every

four weeks, giving details of Special Offers etc. In fact the total of my advertising column in the summary of expenses totalled £708·00, but it included an amount I had just paid on December 30th for the January leaflets which the printer sent round on that date. The cheque was for £240·00.

The adjustment looks like this:

$$
\begin{array}{lrr}
& & £ \\
\text{Total of advertising column} & = & 708\cdot00 \\
\text{Deduct item for January} & = & 240\cdot00 \\
\hline
& & £468\cdot00 \\
\hline
\end{array}
$$

Therefore the amount I must enter in the Profit and Loss Account is £468·00 for the year, and the £240·00 must be carried forward to the next year. As I am going to carry it forward it must appear on the Balance Sheet. Is it an asset or liability? Clearly it is an asset, for I have this stock of brochures ready to send out, which I have paid for in advance.

The item appears on the assets side of the Balance Sheet, as a temporary asset, Payments in Advance.

Current Assets: Payments in Advance £240·00

The effect of the adjustment in this case is to reduce the amount written off the Profit and Loss Account—the balance being carried forward as an asset for use next year. As soon as the new year comes this asset will be used up in the January distribution, and will become an expense of the business next year.

Adjustment No. 2: Accrued Charges
Of course adjustments might be necessary in the opposite direction. In Fig. 21.4 again there is an entry of Light and Heat £1 464·00. As a matter of fact, the total of my Light and Heat column in the Summary of Expenses in my Simplex D Account Book shows that I have paid £1 246·50 in the year, but a large electricity bill for for £217·50 has just come in, although I have not yet paid it. Clearly the adjustment required is as follows:

$$
\begin{array}{lrr}
& & £ \\
\text{Total of Light and Heat column} & = & 1\ 246\cdot50 \\
\text{Add electricity bill due} & = & 217\cdot50 \\
\hline
& & £1\ 464\cdot00 \\
\hline
\end{array}
$$

I must now enter the figure of £1 464·00 in my Profit and Loss Account—since that is the true loss for the year, and carry the overdue bill into the Balance Sheet as a current liability—Accrued Charges £217·50.

Keeping accounts in this way—using adjustments—is called keeping accounts on an 'accruals basis'. This means that the Trading Account, and the Profit and Loss Account, are adjusted so that they include every penny of loss suffered during the year, and every penny of profit earned in the year, but they do not include anything that applies to the next trading period or the previous trading period. Such accounts are more accurate than the simpler accounts kept on a 'receipts and payments' basis.

A full description of adjustments is not possible here, but those who wish to pursue the matter further should purchase a copy of *'Success in Principles of Accounting'* by Geoffrey Whitehead (published by John Murray Ltd.). This book also has a complete answer book to help students check their work.

Adjustment No 3—Work in progress. We shall see when we consider Manufacturing Accounts that work-in-progress requires manufacturers to make allowance for work that was not completed at the beginning and end of the year. There are similar problems for people who do contract work. You have to decide what proportion of the work has been done and that is the proportion of the contract price which has to be included. Suppose you have a £5 000 job of which two fifths has been completed, then £2 000 of the final price has to be included as if it was actually taken. It might be a good idea to make out an invoice for this amount and ask the customer to pay it for the proportion of the work done.

If they are unwilling to pay for part performance in this way at least you have them on your books as a debtor for that amount. Of course set against this 'income' you will have included the expenses incurred so far, so that the profit you will have made will only be the difference between the two figures. However, even if this increases your profit figure to show your benefit from the part of the work done you will not be able to draw out this profit in cash form, unless the debtor actually pays up. The profit made, which will appear on your Balance Sheet as a liability to you as owner, will be represented not by an asset cash, but by an asset 'debtor'—which you hope will one day finish up as cash.

(b) Depreciating assets at the end of the financial year. Every asset wears out in the course of time and depreciates in value over the years. The amount of the depreciation on the asset is therefore a legitimate charge against the profits of the business, which can be written off in the Profit and Loss account. However, this process need not really concern business people today, since whatever we deduct for depreciation is completely disregarded by the Inland Revenue, which adds it back on again as if we had never deducted it. Instead it gives us a 'capital allowance'. The reason for this behaviour is quite simple. Suppose a firm making good profits disliked paying taxes, and thought it would benefit the business if it reduced its liability to tax by buying plenty of assets and depreciating them by 100% in the first year. This would seriously reduce the revenues. To ensure reasonable behaviour the Government lays down standard rates of depreciation called 'capital allowances' and if a firm uses some other rate of depreciation it disregards the reduction the firm makes (ie it

adds the money back to the profit figure) and only gives the firm the allowance it is entitled to. At the time of writing this is 25% but it can vary from year to year and you need to consult a book like 'Income Tax Simplified' (see the address at the front of this book) to be quite sure you have the correct figures for any particular year.

It follows that if we imagine that we purchase a £2 000 machine we get a 25% capital allowance in the first year (£500) and the rest goes into a 'pool' of assets not yet depreciated. In the next year we shall get 25% of what is in the 'pool', which is 25% of £1 500 (not 25% of the original price). We thus get depreciation on what is called the 'diminishing balance' of our assets.

If you have your accounts prepared by a firm of accountants they will usually do your capital allowance computations for you. If you send in your own accounts to the Inland Revenue and point out in a covering letter the various capital items you have purchased during the year and ask the Inspector to give you the allowances to which you are entitled he will usually oblige. However, sometimes an Inspector who wishes to put you under pressure (because perhaps he does not believe you are keeping proper accounts) may ask you to send in your capital allowance computations. The probable aim is to force you to take accountancy advice, and this might indeed be the best thing to do.

However, recently the system of capital allowances has been greatly simplified (and become much less generous). We can't go into the Government's motives in reducing these allowances to 25%, but basically it is something to do with the fact that if we make it too easy for firms to buy machines (many of which are imported) they will replace labour with machinery and make unemployment worse.

The basic situation is this. Since 31st March 1986 the initial allowance (first year allowance) on any asset purchased for use in the business is 25%, and the balance goes into a 'pool' of assets, which means 75% goes into the pool. Next year you get 25% allowance on any new items and 25% of the pool, so you get 25% of the 75% in the pool (which actually comes to $18\frac{3}{4}$% of the original price in the second year). In this way there is a statutory amount of depreciation to which we are entitled each year.

Of course when we do our final accounts we deduct a figure for depreciation from our assets. It is up to us what we write off, but the snag is some people would write 100% off as depreciation if there were no rules—and thus save a lot of tax. To make it fair to everyone the Inland Revenue says 'You deduct what you like, but we will not take any notice of it. We shall add your depreciation back to your profit figure, and then we will give you the Capital Allowance Parliament says you may have.' This is at present for most items 25% of any new item and 25% of what is in your pool. Of course if you buy a machine for £2 000 and get a £500 allowance on it the £1 500 that goes in the pool cannot get a 'writing down' allowance (ie ordinary 'pool' allowance) until next year. You cannot have a 'pool' allowance on an item in the year you took the initial allowance.

Generally speaking if the Inland Revenue queries what you are doing about capital allowances it means that in their opinion the deductions you have made are not correct, and if you don't want to turn to an accountant it is best to go to the Tax Office and discuss the matter with them—when you will usually find them absolutely fair, and very helpful.

More usually, when you put in your depreciation on your Profit and Loss Account make it 25% of any new item and 25% of last year's pool which you will find the Inspector of Taxes usually mentions when he/she approves your accounts at the end of the previous year. Tell the Inspector what you have done and show how you worked it out on your various assets. Explain what new items you bought this year and what you got for any assets you disposed of (for example if you traded in an old vehicle for a new one). The Inspector needs to know that because he/she has to do a 'balancing allowance' (or make a balancing charge if you have had too much of an allowance on the old item now disposed of).

Note: For some short-life assets the Inland Revenue has now decided to leave them out of the pool and leave it to the trader to depreciate them at 25% in the first year and 25% *on the diminishing balance* in subsequent years. At the end of the asset's life the trader may deduct any outstanding balance, after any realisation value on disposal has been taken into account, as the depreciation in the final year. This saves the Inland Revenue work, and makes no difference to traders.

(c) Depreciating Goodwill. Goodwill has been explained earlier (see page 24) but the question of depreciating goodwill was left until this point. *Remember* goodwill is an intangible asset—we cannot touch it like a typewriter or a motor vehicle—it is an idea in the heads of our customers, who like our business because they used it when the previous owner was in charge of it, and they keep coming back. We paid good money for this 'goodwill' but it is not really a physical asset at all. It is usual to write this value off over the first few years (usually 25% per year for 4 years). However, this is depreciation of a special type. It is not like fair wear and tear on a machine or a piece of furniture. We are writing it down in value because we want to clear it from our Balance Sheet. This is therefore not a revenue expense, a loss of the business, but a management decision to sacrifice some of our profits in order to remove this 'asset' from our books. Therefore the reduction in value of Goodwill has to be matched by a reduction in our capital (in other words we treat the amount we are writing off as extra 'Drawings'. We do not draw any money out, we reduce the amount the business owes to the proprietor because the proprietor now owns less 'assets'; some of the goodwill has been written off.

Suppose the original value of the Goodwill was £2 000 and we are now writing off £500. The fact is that when we purchased the business we lost £2 000 to the seller—which we didn't recognise as a real loss—we took it on as an intangible asset. When we write down that asset by £500 we are really saying 'I am now well enough off to recognise some part of that loss as a loss'. By the time four years is up we will have written it all off out of our profits.

The main point to understand here is that written-off Goodwill cannot be shown as a business expense in the Profit and Loss account. It is *not* a business expense—it is a proprietor's decision to tidy up his/her affairs by clearing off an asset that is not a real asset at all, but an intangible item.

(d) Stock losses and 'Final Accounts'. Some traders find it difficult to understand why they are not allowed to write off stock losses in the Final Accounts of the business. They feel that as these goods have definitely been lost, they should appear as separate item in either the Trading Account or the Profit and Loss Account. The explanation is that as the Trading Account includes an item 'Closing Stock' which is the result of stock-taking done on the last day of the financial year, the loss will be taken into account there—because when you count the stock the missing items are not there. This means that the Closing Stock Figure is less than it ought to be. If you were to deduct Stock Losses again you would be taking the loss twice over, and the Inland Revenue would not approve.

(e) Balance Sheets that won't Balance. One of the commonest complaints by businessmen using the Simplex, or any other system is that they cannot get their Balance Sheet to balance. Goethe, one of the greatest minds of his age and one of the supreme geniuses of all time once described book-keeping as the sublimest creation of the human mind for the Balance Sheet will only agree if the book-keeping has been perfect. It is a fact though that the Balance Sheet is a comparatively recent invention, and many businessmen did not bother at all about it. For the first thirty years of its use the Simplex System did not even have a Balance Sheet in it. Today the Inland Revenue is more interested than formerly in seeing a Balance Sheet, and it is certainly desirable that one should be prepared each year.

The preparation of the Balance Sheet in this edition has been fully described in two places, Section 4.4 and Section 21.4. It is hoped that the explanations given there will enable the reader to prepare his/her Balance Sheet properly and thus join Goethe in appreciating the finest point in book-keeping. If you have done your Balance Sheet at Dawn on Day One correctly, and have kept careful records, your Balance Sheet should balance. If you find it is not balancing, and have genuinely searched for any possible error, we usually tell people if the amount is not great, to treat any difference (if this will solve the problem) as extra drawings. This means you are accepting the loss as 'undeclared drawings' (which the tax man may feel is satisfactory—since you are not trying to say the missing amount is a business expense). It can never be satisfactory to have a Balance Sheet that does not work out—there is a mistake somewhere—but we do meet occasions when we can't get it right. The strictly correct way is to open up a Suspense Account—but the Simplex System does not really have accounts.

(f) Taking-stock at the end of the year. At the end of any trading period it is necessary to value the stock in hand so that the final accounts can be worked out. It is also a good idea to hold unscheduled and surprise stock-taking sessions to check the availability of both stock and capital assets—particularly if such things as tools etc, are likely to be pilfered. The method in both cases is to draw up an inventory of stock—a list of every stock item, preferably in some sensible order (such as the order in which they appear on the shelves). This is a

chore the first time it is done, but on subsequent occasions it can simply be photocopied and any extra items added at the end. It is best if the items can be on loose leaf sheets retained in a lever arch file, for easy extraction and photo copying. There should be a place at the top of the page to record the date of the stock check and columns for recording the actual stock as counted. Personal supervision, or the supervision of a reliable person, is always advisable on any sort of stock-taking and random checks are desirable. Thus if there is a record on the sheet of pocket calculators—counted as being 15—ask to see the 15 and count them as a random check. Managers frequently exaggerate stock counts—leaving the losses (or thefts) to be discovered next time around.

(g) Loss (or profit) on sale of an asset (or disposal in some other way). Users of the Simplex System sometimes write to the Advice Bureau and say they cannot understand what they need to do when they dispose of an asset either by selling it, or throwing it away, etc, etc. The answer is really very simple. Any asset is on our books at a stated value (see the last Balance Sheet you drew up for that value). If we take an example of a second hand car valued at £800 on our last Balance Sheet, but now traded in for a newer vehicle costing £3 500. Suppose the trade-in value of the old car was £500. These are the points to recognise:

   (i) The old car is completely removed from our books and we were allowed £500 for it.

  (ii) That means we made a 'loss on sale of motor vehicle' £300. This is a legitimate expense of the business and should appear on the Profit and Loss Account at the end of the year 'loss on sale of vehicle'. Put it temporarily in the Summary of Expenses but write it in very small £300 (loss).

 (iii) Go to the Summary of Capital Expenses and write in red ball point pen, sale of vehicle £800 for trade in value £500, loss £300. This wipes the old vehicle off our list of assets.

  (iv) In the Weekly Page on the week you traded in the vehicle on the 'capital items line' enter new vehicle £3 000—but when you carry this to the Summary of Capital Expenses enter the vehicle at its full price of £3 500—because of course the trade-in value of the old vehicle becomes part of the value of the new car.

   Although this gets your books straight you must tell the Inland Revenue about it so they can get you 'pool' right. They may not have the same value of the asset as you have, and they may amend your profits figue to get the 'loss' correct according to their figures.

   (v) Of course—you might not sell the car at a loss. You might sell it for more than its book value. In that case you must include the 'profit on sale of motor vehicle' in your Profit and Loss Account. What it means is that you have over-depreciated in earlier years, and the tax authorities expect you to declare this over-depreciation—so they recoup a bit of tax you underpaid in years gone by.

(h) Bad Debts. The aim in Final Accounts is to achieve two results, a perfectly accurate profit figure and a perfectly honest Balance Sheet which does state truthfully what the assets and the liabilities of the business are. If we allow bad

debts to continue unrecognised we defeat both these objects. The loss suffered by bad debts is not included in the Profit and Loss Account—so that profits are overstated—while the debtors which appear on the Balance Sheet include some who are never going to pay. Our assets are therefore overstated.

The best way to prevent this situation is to appraise the Debtors at regular intervals. Business specialists like Kalamazoo Ltd., do offer simple check-up systems for keeping debtors constantly under review.

Once a month take the Debtors' Record Book and consider the debts still outstanding. Bad debtors should be approached for payment and certainly should not be allowed any further credit. If a debtor cannot pay it may help to offer to accept less than the full debt—i.e. cut your losses. If the debtor is unable to pay anything, the question is whether to accept the loss and take no further action or to pursue the matter through the legal process of bankruptcy. It depends very much on our assessement of the situation as to what action we take. Generally the best principle is to pursue an unprincipled debtor relentlessly, in the general interests of the business community, while taking no action against hard-luck cases.

As far as book-keeping is concerned, the bad debt is written off in the Profit and Loss Account, and removed from the list of debtors so that the figure of Debtors on the Balance Sheet is reduced to the correct figure of known, reliable debtors.

21.7 Simple Tax Accounts for Businesses with Turnover less than £10 000

Very small businesses (those with a *turnover* of less than £10 000) can now submit their accounts to the Inspector of Taxes in a very simple 3 line form. However the Inland Revenue specify in their pamphlet IR104 that such traders must still keep proper records of account for their businesses, and it is only the submission of their accounts to the Inland Revenue which is simplied. It is therefore not of very much interest to a user of the Simplex D Account Book who already has a full set of Final Accounts available which may be submitted.

If you do decide to submit three line accounts there is a special form in the pamphlet IR104 from your local tax office. It is reproduced below by kind permission of the Inland Revenue Department. *(See pages 167-8.)*

21.8 Exercises in the Preparation of Final Accounts

1. Using the figures given below for Tom Price's business taken from the summary pages of his Simplex Account book draw up the Trading Account and Profit and Loss Account for the year ending December 31st, 19.. and the Balance Sheet as at that date.

Trading Account: Opening Stock £1 200·00; Purchases £26 000·00; Sales £42 000·00; Closing Stock £1 450·00; Goods taken for own consumption £250·00.

Profit and Loss Account: Miscellaneous Receipts £350·00; Customs and Excise Repayments £148·50; Rent and Rates £682·00; Light and Heat

**Inland Revenue
Income Tax**

Summary of profits from _____ **to** _____

You can use this form to give the information the Tax Office will need .
Make sure you read this leaflet before you start to fill in the form and you will know exactly what to do.

To_____ District   Reference _from your Tax Return or Assessment_ _____

Your National Insurance no

Please use CAPITALS

My name is

The nature of my business is

My business address is

_____ Postcode _____

Turnover   £ _____ show your total business earnings before expenses

Expenses   £ _____ show your total business expenses

Profit   £ _____ take your expenses from your turnover to give your profit

To the best of my knowledge and belief the information I have given above is correct and complete.

Signature   Date

If you bought or sold any vehicles or machinery which you use in your business please give details over the page.

41K

Fig. 21.7 _Simple 3-line Tax Accounts_
(Courtesy of the Inland Revenue Department)

£420·00; Carriage and Postages £186·00; Paper £124·00; Motor Expenses £372·00; Travelling £56·00; Cleaning £284·00; Printing and Stationery £130·00; Telephone £285·00; Repairs and Renewals £176·00; Insurance £125·00; Advertising £230·00; Wages £2 756·00; National Insurance Contributions £525·00; Bank Charges £60·00; Sundries £124·00; Depreciation (fixtures) £250·00; Depreciation (Motor Car) £500·00.

Balance Sheet: Premises £12 000·00; Fixtures £750·00; Motor Vehicles £950·00; Debtors £24·85; Cash at Bank £796·50; Cash in Hand £23·15; Capital at Start £8 008·00; Drawings during year £1 865·00; Creditors £138·00.

2. Using the figures given below for Brian Wood's business taken from the summary pages of his Simplex Account Book draw up the Trading Account and Profit and Loss Account for the year ending December 31st, 19.. and the Balance Sheet as at that date.

The details are:

Trading Account: Opening Stock £1 350·00; Purchases £27 550·00; Sales £37 700; Closing Stock £1 850·00; Goods taken for own consumption £1 250·00.

Capital allowances

Before you give the details below you may find it useful to read leaflet IR106 ' Capital Allowances for Vehicles and Machinery '. You can get a copy from any Tax Office.

Items bought in the period of the summary shown over the page

Enter the total cost, including any part exchange allowance. Do not include finance charges if you buy the item on credit or any part of the cost covered by a grant or subsidy.

Date bought	Items bought	Cost	*Business use
		£_____	
		£_____	
		£_____	

* Enter here the fraction or the percentage of business use (for example 1/2 or 50%)

Items sold or part - exchanged in the period of the summary shown over the page

Date sold	Items sold	Sale price or part - exchange value	*Business use
		£_____	
		£_____	
		£_____	

* Enter here the fraction or the percentage of business use (for example 1/2 or 50%)

Fig. 21.8 *Reverse side of Fig. 21.7*
(Courtesy of the Inland Revenue Department)

Profit and Loss Account: Miscellaneous Receipts £250·00; Customs and Excise repayments £249·00; Rent and Rates £600·00; Light and Heat £501·50; Carriage and Postages £176·00; Paper £84·00; Motor Expenses £422·00; Travelling £50·00; Cleaning £300·00; Printing and Stationery £120·00; Telephone £145·00; Repairs and renewals £166·00; Insurance £95·00; Advertising £190·00; Wages £3 000·00; National Insurance Contributions £531·00; Bank Charges £10·00; Sundries £130·00; Depreciation (Fixtures) £200·00; Depreciation (Motor Car) £556·00.

Balance Sheet: Premises £10 000·00; Fixtures £1 000·00; Motor Vehicles £1 950·00; Debtors £525·50; Cash at Bank £850·35; Cash in Hand £85·00; Capital at Start £12 865·35; Drawings during year £2 500·00; Creditors £773·00.

3. Using the figures given below, and taking into account the adjustments given at the end of the question, draw up the Trading Account and Profit and Loss Account of the business of A. Fashionable and her Balance Sheet as at 31st December, 19..

Trading Account: Opening Stock £1 550·00; Purchases £25 250·00; Sales £39 750·00; Goods taken for own consumption £725·00.

Profit and Loss Account: Miscellaneous Receipts £725·00; Rent and Rates £450·00; Light and Heat £386·00; Carriage and Postages £275·00; Paper

£284·60; Motor Expenses £725·55; Travelling £178·50; Cleaning £728·50; Printing and Stationery £165·50; Telephone Expenses £184·00; Repairs and Renewals £1 318·00; Insurance £258·00; Advertising £425·00; Wages £4 728·50; National Insurance Contributions £482·50; Bank Charges £42·60; Sundries £427·50.

Balance Sheet: Premises £20 000·00; Fixtures £1 800·00; Motor Vehicles £2 000·00; Debtors £147·50; Cash at Bank £1 585·65; Cash in Hand £13·72; Capital at start £25 560·00; Drawings £3 500·00; Creditors £146·62.

The Adjustments are as follows:
(a) Closing Stock is found at stocktaking to be £1 750·00.
(b) You are asked to depreciate fixtures by £360·00 and motor vehicles by £500·00.
(c) A bill for outstanding Light and Heat is due (£14·00) and is to be included in the sums paid under this expense and carried forward as an accrued charge.

4. Using the figures given below, and taking into account the adjustments given at the end of the question, draw up the Trading Account and Profit and Loss Account of Julia Browne's business and her Balance Sheet at 31st December, 19..

Trading Account: Opening Stock £1 470·00; Purchases £31 350·00; Sales £49 840·00; Goods taken for own consumption £285·00.

Profit and Loss Account: Miscellaneous Receipts £262·50; Rent and Rates £1 400·00; Light and Heat £478·00; Carriage and Postages £138·75; Paper £186·50; Motor Expenses £824·65; Travelling £290·00; Cleaning £485·00; Printing and Stationery £378·50; Telephone Expenses £295·65; Repairs and Renewals £1 460·00; Insurance £148·00; Advertising £869·70; Wages £5 358·60; National Insurance Contributions £428·70; Bank Charges £38·50; Sundries £217·00.

Balance Sheet: Premises £18 000·00; Fixtures £3 600; Motor Vehicles £1 800; Debtors £155·50; Cash at Bank £1 725·60; Cash in Hand £23·30; Capital at Start £23 438·95; Drawings £4 000·00; Creditors £1 295·50.

The Adjustments are as follows:
(a) Closing Stock is found at stocktaking to be £1650·00.
(b) You are asked to depreciate fixtures by 10% and motor vehicles by 20%.
(c) A bill for outstanding Motor Expenses is due (£48·50) and is to be included in the sums paid under this expense and carried forward as an accrued charge.

Chapter Twenty-two

Special cases of Final Accounts; Manufacturing Accounts, Partnership Accounts and Limited Company Accounts

22.1 The Simplex System and Manufacturing Accounts

If your business is a manufacturing business you may find it is a little difficult to see how to prepare your Final Accounts using the ordinary Simplex D book. For this reason we have drawn up a special set of Final Accounts for Manufacturing Businesses which we are prepared to supply free of charge to users of the Simplex D Account Book who are manufacturers. If you are one of those who requires a set of these special notes please write in for a set about two months before you reach the end of your financial year. These notes are fully explanatory when you receive them, and show that a set of Final Accounts for manufacturers consists of:

(i) A Manufacturing Account in two parts, A Prime Cost Section and a Cost of Manufactured Goods Section.
(ii) A Trading Account.
(iii) A Profit and Loss Account.
(iv) A Balance Sheet.

These are outlined in the pages that follow, to explain the main points about Manufacturing Accounts. These are:

(a) Before a Manufacturer can begin to trade the goods have to be made up from raw materials! You cannot begin trading until some goods have been made to trade with, so that a manufacturing business has to start by buying whatever raw materials it requires and making them up into finished goods. The purchases of raw materials, and perhaps semi-manufactured goods made by sub-contractors, are recorded in the usual way in the Payments for Business Stock Section.

You now have to work on these goods to turn them into a finished product and this requires us to keep a record of the wages paid for the production staff since these expenses have to be recovered when we fix the price of the goods. It may be a good idea to keep a separate Simplex Wages book for production staff so that the total wages paid to them can be easily arrived at. If we only have a few staff it may be possible to use the upper half of the Wages Book for the production staff and the lower part for other staff. We call these direct costs (raw materials, production wages and other costs directly involved in production—for example power for machines) prime costs. The word 'prime' means first, and prime costs are the first costs we incur in manufacturing. Other costs, not directly related to the output are called 'overheads'.

We have now gone far enough to look at the first part of a Manufacturing Account, which is called the Prime Cost Section. All that we do in the Prime Cost Section is to list the costs incurred in actually manufacturing the product, as shown in Fig. 22.1 below:

**Manufacturing Account for
year ending 31 December, 19..**

Prime Cost Section

Raw materials		£	Prime costs (carried to	£
Stock at start		37 256	Cost of Manufactured	
Purchases	48 214		Goods Section)	94 300
Less returns	—			
		48 214		
Total stock available		85 470		
Less closing stock		41 360		
Cost of raw materials used		44 110		
Wages		45 265		
Power for machines		4 925		
		£94 300		£94 300

Fig. 22.1 *The Prime Cost Section*

Notes (i) The raw materials in stock at the start together with the raw materials purchased, come to £85 470. As stocks are still available at the end of the year these are deducted, giving the value of the raw materials used as £44 110.

(ii) Besides this expense, labour and power for machines bring the total prime costs to £94 300. These are carried into the second part of the Manufacturing Account, as shown in Fig. 22.2.

(b) Overheads. Besides the prime costs of the manufactured goods there are a great many overhead expenses which have to be added to the prime costs to get the total cost of manufacture. Since all these expenses have to be recovered from the customer we must build them into the 'cost of manufactured goods' before we work out a selling price. Typical overheads are management salaries, factory rent, lighting, repairs, depreciation on machinery and maintenance costs.

(c) Work in progress. Just as we know that at the end of the year any trader will have stocks of goods unsold on the shelves, and these stocks must be taken into account when working out the Trading Account, it is obvious that any manufacturer will have partly finished goods going through the manufacturing

process, and they will be at all sorts of stages. Some will be practically raw materials, having only just entered production, and some will be almost complete. If we are going to take these stocks of work-in-progress into account we have to value them at some fair figure and this usually means we value them all as if they were half-finished (i.e. we take an average value). We can therefore say that work-in-progress is an adjustment made in the second half of the Manufacturing Account to take account of goods going through the manufacturing process, which are as yet incomplete. This second part of the Manufacturing Account is called 'The Cost of Manufactured Goods Section' and is shown in Fig. 22.2.

Cost of Manufactured Goods Section

		£			£
Prime costs (from Prime Cost Section)		94 300	Cost of manufactured goods (transferred to Trading Account)		124 493
Overheads:					
Salaries	15 252				
Rent	4 680				
Lighting	1 452				
Repairs	3 165				
Depreciation	7 928				
		32 477			
		126 777			
Work-in-progress					
Stock at start	2 216				
Less Closing Stock	4 500				
		− 2 284			
		£124 493			£124 493

Fig. 22.2 *The Cost of Manufactured Goods Section*

Notes: (i) The prime costs are transferred in from the Prime Cost Section.

(ii) The overhead expenses are then added. These figures would come from the Summary of Expenses, but there might need to be a bit of analysis of the figures to ensure that the manufacturing costs (for example lighting) were separated from office lighting expenses (which would of course go in the Profit and Loss Account).

(iii) The work-in-progress is a little difficult to understand. At the start of the year there were stocks of partly manufactured goods worth £2 216. On the first few days of the present year these stocks would have finished their journey through the manufacturing process, but at the end of the year stocks still in production were worth £4 500, and these will be finished off in the coming year. As the £4 500 is bigger than £2 216, it means that the total manufactured output has to be reduced by £2 284, because more was held back at the end of the year than was pushed through in the first few days of the year.

(iv) The total cost of the finished goods made available for sale to the Trading Account was £124 493.

(d) The Trading Account of the Manufacturer. We can now see how the Trading Account of a manufacturer differs from the Trading Account of an ordinary trader who buys goods to sell them again. Instead of purchases coming in on the Trading Account on the left hand side they have already come in on the Prime Cost Section as 'Purchases of raw materials'. What we now have instead is the 'Cost of Manufactured Goods' coming in from the Manufacturing Account. The figures will appear as shown in Fig. 22.3 below. When you receive your free set of pages for Manufacturing Accounts from our Huddersfield Office you will find they enable you to prepare a set of Final Accounts perfectly.

**Trading Account
for year ending 31 December 19..**

	£		£
Opening stock of		Sales	388 560
finished goods	38 247	Less returns in	4 560
Cost of manufactured			
goods	124 493	Net turnover	384 000
	————	Good taken for own use	150
	162 740		————
Less closing stock	44 265		384 150
	————		
Cost of stock sold	118 475		
Warehouse wages	9 752		
Warehouse expenses	3 256		
	————		
Cost of sales	131 483		
Gross profit	252 667		
	————		————
	£384 150		£384 150

(Continues overleaf)

**Profit and Loss Account
for year ending 31 December 19..**

	£
Gross profit	252 667

Fig. 22.3 *The Trading Account of a manufacturer*

Notes: (i) As may be seen, the Trading Account is very similar to the Trading Account in the Simplex D book, except that there are no purchases. Instead the manufactured goods supplied by the factory replace the purchases.

(ii) One or two warehouse expenses are also incurred as goods are warehoused in the period between manufacture and sale.

(iii) The final figure of gross profit is carried through to the Profit and Loss Account in the normal way.

22.2 Exercises on Manufacturing Accounts

1. P. Hawksmoor is a manufacturer. You are asked to prepare his Manufacturing Account and Trading Account for year ending 31 December 19..

	£
Stock at 1 January, 19..	
Raw materials	28 824
Work-in-progress (value at factory cost)	8 259
Finished goods	38 297
Purchases of raw materials	66 358
Sales	388 566
Returns in	1 566
Factory:	
Wages (prime cost)	24 268
Power (prime cost)	1 896
Factory:	
Salaries (overhead)	28 258
Rent (overhead)	5 960
Lighting (overhead)	4 265
Repairs (overhead)	2 792

(Continues opposite)

	£
Depreciation (overhead)	2 160
Warehouse: (Trading Account)	
Wages	29 284
Business Rates	3 786
Stocks at 31 December 19..	

Raw Materials	29 964
Work-in-progress (valued at factory cost)	14 416
Finished goods	29 348

2. T. Jones is a manufacturer. Prepare his Manufacturing Account and Trading Account for year ending 31 December 19..

	£
Stock at 1 January, 19..	
Raw materials	22 400·50
Work in Progress (value at Factory cost)	18 800·75
Finished Goods	37 200·25
Purchases of Raw Materials	128 750·00

Sales	366 300·00
Returns In	5 300·00
Factory:	
Wages (variable)	47 800·50
Power (variable)	5 600·50

Salaries (fixed)	32 800·00
Rent and Rates (fixed)	18 300·00
Lighting (fixed)	4 400·75
Repairs (fixed)	4 600·25

Depreciation (fixed)	12 300·00
Warehouse:	
Wages	23 600·50
Rates	2 600·00
Stocks at December 31, 19..	

Raw Materials	22 800·50
Work in Progress (valued at Factory Cost)	16 800·25
Finished Goods	58 000·50

22.3 Partnerships

There are many circumstances in which a partnership seems to be the best type of business unit. For example, in family businesses it is sometimes helpful to recognize the merits of various interested parties by designating them as partners in the business. Names such as Harrison Bros., Sorrell & Son, and Scammell & Nephew are common. In the professions, such as medicine and law, a partnership is often the only satisfactory form of business unit, for limited companies are not permitted by some professional bodies. Moreover a single person rarely has all the expertise required to offer a fully comprehensive service.

The chief reasons for forming partnerships may be listed as follows:

(a) In order to bring more capital into an enterprise, so that improved machinery, equipment and buildings may be obtained.

(b) In order to broaden the knowledge and experience available, and thus to offer a more comprehensive service to the public. Thus lawyers who specialize respectively in divorce, motor-accident, criminal and conveyancing law may form a partnership to pool their knowledge and experience in these fields.

(c) In order to unite wisdom and experience with youth and vitality. A doctor of mature years may seek a young and active partner who will take on the more strenuous part of the practice; the younger person will benefit by having the senior colleague's greater knowledge put at his/her disposal.

(d) In order to reduce the onerous responsibilities of a sole trader business, where it is often impossible to take time off, and where sickness can endanger the very existence of the business.

Agreements between Partners

Early partnerships were often called 'common ventures' or 'joint ventures', which conveys the idea that all business is to some extent an adventure in the way of trade, and no doubt many were inaugurated with a mere handshake. There is in fact no legal requirement to have an agreement in writing. Partnerships may be held to have existed by the courts if either partner can prove:

(a) an oral agreement (proved by witnesses), or

(b) a systematic course of dealing together by way of engaging in trade or the provision of professional services, or

(c) a written agreement, whether formal (drawn up by a solicitor in deed form) or informal (a mere undertaking in writing), to be associated with one another.

Clearly the formal Partnership Deed is most desirable, since a lawyer experienced in these matters will bring to the partners' attention many points that have caused controversy in similar situations in the past. Even where people agree to work together at the start of a partnership, there is no guarantee that disagreement will not arise at a later date.

Matters to be included in a Partnership Deed

The following major points should be included in any partnership agreement:

(a) The amount of capital to be contributed by each partner.

(b) Whether this capital is to earn interest for the partner, and if so at what rate per cent. Usually it is desirable to give interest on capital if the amounts contributed are unequal. This prevents the partner contributing the greater sum from developing a sense of grievance.

(c) Whether any partner is to receive a salary, and if so how much. It often happens that a young person contributes very little to a partnership in capital, but a great deal in health, strength and energy. This contribution should be recognized as one entitling the younger partner to a reward in the form of a basic salary.

(d) The ratio for sharing profits and losses. Simple fractions are usually adopted, such as half and half, two-thirds to one-third, or three-fifths to two-fifths.

(e) The date the partnership shall commence, and the duration of the partnership. Where the duration is to be 'at will', i.e. indefinitely, some mention should be made of what is to happen if one of the partners dies. The heirs of the deceased partner will be anxious to obtain their rightful share of his estate, and so perhaps will the Inland Revenue authorities. If assets have to be sold to realize funds to meet such demands, the whole enterprise may collapse. It is therefore a wise precaution to insure your partner's life (and he/she yours), so that if one partner dies the business will receive a sum of money which can be used to settle any claims on the business.

(f) How much each partner is permitted to take as 'drawings' each month or week, and whether interest is to be paid on these drawings.

(g) In the event of disputes, how the dispute shall be resolved. Some partners specify a particular person to act as arbitrator; others simply agree on how an arbitrator should be chosen if and when the need arises, perhaps a bank manager for financial issues and a solicitor for legal points.

The Partnership Act of 1890

Partnership law was codified in 1890, that is to say the legal cases on which the law had formerly depended were enacted as a formal set of rules by Parliament, and modified in line with current thought at that time. It was an age when legislators still believed that controls in business affairs were largely undesirable. The Act therefore established rules to which reference could be made as a last resort, when partners had failed to agree on how the particular point in question was to be settled. It should be emphasized that the rules stated below are only used in the rare cases where partners have entered into no clear arrangements with one another on the point concerned, and then only as a last resort. Any original agreement, however informal, to behave differently from what was suggested in the Act will always be upheld by the courts.

(a) All partners are entitled to contribute equally to the capital of the firm. They must share equally in the profits and contribute equally to the losses.

(b) No partner may have a salary.

(c) No partner may have interest on capital.

(d) A partner loaning money to the firm, over and above his/her capital contribution, is entitled to interest at an official rate per annum.

(e) Any partner may see and copy the books of the firm, which must be kept at the ordinary place of business.

(f) No new partner may be introduced without the general consent or all the partners.

Nowadays the vast majority of partnerships include clauses in their agreements which replace some or all of these rules.

22.4 The Simplex System and Partnership Accounts

The Simplex system is entirely adequate for keeping the records of partnership businesses but the 'final accounts' pages at the back of the book are not appropriate. It has not been possible to include sufficient pages to provide a full description of partnership accounts in the Simplex D book and for this reason we offer a set of notes about Partnership Accounts and two copies of special pages for the Final Accounts of Partners. When completed one copy should be sent to the Inland Revenue inspector, the other should be kept for reference. Please send for a set of notes if you operate as a partnership when you get close to the time for preparing your final accounts.

A full set of Partnership Accounts requires:

(a) A Trading Account.

(b) A Profit and Loss Account.

(c) An Appropriaton Section of the Profit and Loss Account in which the partnership profits are appropriated in the way agreed.

(d) A Capital Account for each partner.

(e) A Current Account for each partner.

(f) A Balance Sheet.

Parts (a) and (b) The Trading Account and the Profit and Loss Account

These are exactly the same as for sole traders and can be kept in the same way as in the Simplex D Account Book at the back of the book. They need no special explanations, but the important point about Partnership Accounts is that when we have found the net profit we cannot give it straight to the proprietor, because there are now two or more of them. The profit has to be shared between them, or among them, in the Appropriation Account.

Part (c) The Appropriation Account

The word 'appropriate' means 'allocate to a particular use'. When the Net Profit has been found in the Profit and Loss Account is has to be allocated to the partners in the way they have agreed. This is done in the Appropriation Account which is illustrated in Fig. 22.4 opposite.

LAST YEAR		APPROPRIATION ACCOUNT for year ending 31 ST DECEMBER 19··	THIS YEAR		LAST YEAR			THIS YEAR	
1,000	00	GOODWILL (WRITTEN OFF)	1,000	00	27,625	00	NET PROFIT (brought down	39,750	00
4,000	00	SALARY (MRS. A)	5,000	00			from Profit and Loss A/c)		
2,500	00	INTEREST ON CAPITAL MR. B.	2,500	00					
200	00	" " " MRS. A.	200	00					
13,283	33	SHARE OF RESIDUE MR. B. ⅔	20,700	00					
6,641	67	" " " MRS. A. ⅓	10,350	00					
27,625	00	TOTAL	39,750	00	27,625	00	TOTAL	39,750	00

Fig. 22.4 *The Appropriation of Profits in a partnership business*

Notes:

(i) First the partners decide to reduce Goodwill on the Balance Sheet by £1 000·00. Remember writing off goodwill in this way has to be done out of profit, it cannot be charged to Profit and Loss Account as a business expense.

(ii) Mrs. A. (the younger partner) is given her agreed salary, which reflects the fact that she is doing a good deal of the day-to-day work of the partnership.

(iii) Each partner is then given interest on his/her capital at the agreed rate (here we are imaging 10 per cent). Note that Mr. B. the senior partner, has much more capital in the business than Mrs. A. If it is decided to do so partners can give interest on the balance left in Current Accounts at the start of the year, and can charge interest on overdrawn Current Accounts at the start of the year and also interest on drawings made during the course of the year. They then charge the agreed rate pro rata for the number of months to run until the end of the year, from the time of the drawing. An explanation of Current Accounts is given later.

(iv) The residue of the profit is shared up one third to Mrs. A.; two-thirds to Mr. B.

(v) Each of the sums appropriated to the partners is taken on the partners' Current Accounts, as shown above.

The Capital Accounts of Partners

It is usual for the Capital of partners to remain fixed during the years of the partnership unless a firm arrangement to increase capital in some agreed way is made. This would be a fairly rare event. The 'fixed' nature of partnership capital means that at the end of the year we do not (as with sole traders) add on profits and take away drawings, with the capital that results changing year by year. As shown in the Partnership Balance Sheet (see Fig. 22.7), Capital Accounts remain unchanged. Instead the fluctuations connected with profit making and drawings are carried in a Current Account as shown in Fig. 22.6. The Capital Accounts (see Fig. 22.5) only contain the original capital contributions.

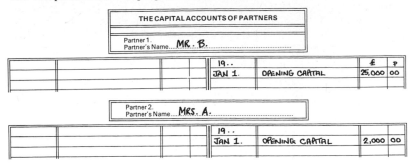

Fig. 22.5 *The Capital Accounts of the Partners*

The Current Account of Partners

The Current Accounts of partners must not be confused with the Bank Account, which is a Current Account at the bank. The name is the same, because like a Bank Account, the partners' Current Accounts are credited with any appropriations due to the partner and debited with any amounts drawn out by the partner (Drawings).

The use of the Current Account is made clear in Fig. 22.6 and explained in the notes below it. The final total on the Current Account of each partner will then appear on the Balance Sheet (Fig. 22.7).

THE CURRENT ACCOUNTS OF PARTNERS

Partner 1.
Partner's Name...... **MR. B.**

19..			£	P.	19..			£	P.
DEC. 31	DRAWINGS FOR YEAR		15,680	00	JAN. 1	BALANCE	B/FWD.	2,600	00
" 31	BALANCE	C/D.	10,120	00	DEC. 31	INTEREST ON CAPITAL		2,500	00
					" 31	SHARE OF RESIDUE		20,700	00
			25,800	00				25,800	00
					JAN. 1	BALANCE	B/D	10,120	00

Partner 2.
Partner's Name...... **MRS. A.**

19..			£	P.	19..			£	P.
JAN. 1	BALANCE	B/FWD.	800	00	DEC. 31	SALARY		5,000	00
DEC. 31	DRAWINGS FOR YEAR		12,240	00	" 31	INTEREST ON CAPITAL		200	00
" 31	BALANCE	C/D	2,510	00	" 31	SHARE OF RESIDUE		10,350	00
			15,550	00				15,550	00
					JAN. 1	BALANCE	B/D	2,510	00

Fig. 22.6 *The Current Accounts of the Partners*

Notes:

(i) Notice that at the start of a year the Current Account can have either a credit balance or a debit balance. Mr. B. had a credit balance on January 1st. This means that the business besides owing him his capital also owed him £2 600 on his Current Account. Mrs. A. on the contrary—had drawn out so much drawings in the previous year that she was in debt to the business for £800.

(ii) The various appropriations of profit are carried from the Appropriation Account to the credit side of the partners's Current Accounts. Mrs. A. has her salary, interest on capital and one third share of the residue of the profit Mr. B. of course was not given a salary.

(iii) The total drawings for the year is debited to the account since the partners have already had this money in expectation of profits made. The figures are in the Summary of Drawings. In both cases the total drawn is less than the total earned so that both accounts finish up with credit balances. This means that the business owes both partners a balance of profits earned, which they can draw out if they wish. In the meantime, these balances must appear on the Balance Sheet.

The Balance Sheet

The chief difference between the Balance Sheet of a partnership and that of a sole trader is that the capital of the partners remain fixed, as explained above. The two capitals are shown in Fig. 22.7. The Current Accounts, which have been shown in Fig. 22.6 appear also on the Balance Sheet, and if they are both credit balances appear as liabilities. Where a partner has drawn more in Drawings than he/she earned in profits the debit balance would appear on the asset side; the partner would then be temporarily a debtor of the business for that moment. The rest of the Balance Sheet is exactly the same as the sole trader's Balance Sheet.

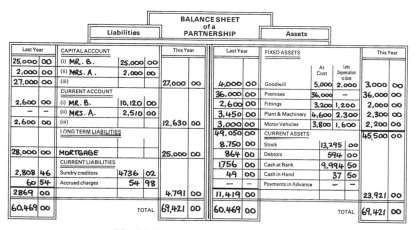

Fig. 22.7 *A Partnership Balance Sheet*

You should now use one of the sets of Partnership Final Accounts provided on request by George Vyner Ltd to draw up your final accounts for your business. When you are satisfied that it is correct, copy it out and sign the declaration at the foot of the copy before submitting it to the Inland Revenue Department (or your accountant for professional approval of your records).

22.5 Exercises in Partnership Accounts

1. The following trial balance was extracted from the books of the partnership of Smith and Jones at December 31st 19.., after the profit for the year had been ascertained:

	Dr.	Cr.
Capital Accounts (January 1st, 19..):		
Smith		14 000·00
Jones		5 000·00
Current Accounts (January 1st, 19..):		
Smith		1 000·00
Jones	800·00	
Drawings during year:		
Smith	2 800·00	
Jones	1 600·00	
Profit for year		9 300·00
Cash in Hand	125·00	
Balance at Bank	1 750·00	
Goodwill	500·00	
Furniture and Fittings	1 500·00	
Sundry Debtors and Creditors	635·00	285·50
Rent due to landlord		200·00
Stock	4 950·00	
Premises	15 000·00	
Insurance Prepaid	125·50	
	£29 785·50	£29 785·50

You are required to draw up the Balance Sheet of the partnership as at December 31st, 19.., having regard to the following notes:

(a) Goodwill is to be written down to zero this year.

(b) Jones is to have a salary of £1 500 for his extra activity as a junior partner.

(c) Interest on capital at 10 per cent is to be allocated to both partners (No intereest will be given or charged on Current Accounts).

(d) The residue of profit after making these arrangements is to be shared two thirds to Smith and one third to Jones.

(e) In preparing the Balance Sheet, you are to group the assets and liabilities so that the total can be clearly seen of (i) the fixed assets, (ii) the current asset, and (iii) the current liabilities.

2. Brewer and Stillman conduct a merchanting business in partnership on the following terms:

(a) Interest is to be allowed on partners' Capital Accounts at 10 per cent annum.

(b) Stillman is to be credited with a partnership salary of £2 000·00 per annum.

(c) The balance of profit in any year is to be shared by the partners in the ratio ¾ to Brewer ¼ to Stillman.

After preparing their Trading and Profit and Loss Account for the year ended March 31st, 19.., but before making any provision for interest on capital or for partnership salary, the following balances remained on the books:

	Dr.	Cr.
Capital Accounts:		
Brewers (as on April 1st previous year)		15 000·00
Stillman (as on April 1st previous year)		5 000·00
Current Accounts:		
Brewer (as on April 1st previous year)		500·00
Stillman (as on April 1st previous year)	1 000·00	
Drawing Accounts:		
Brewer	3 850·00	
Stillman	2 500·00	
Profit and Loss Account—Net Profit for year		8 650·00
Stock at end of year	8 450·00	
Goodwill Account	1 000·00	
Plant and Machinery, at cost	7 700·00	
Plant and Machinery, depreciation		1 700·00
Fixtures and Fittings, at cost	9 250·00	
Fixtures and Fittings, Depreciation		1 250·00
Trade Debtors and Creditors	942·00	825·75
Loan from H. Smith		3 000·00
Rent accrued due at March 31st, 19..		200·00
Insurance unexpired at March 31st, 19..	258·50	
Cash at Bank, Current Account	1 175·25	
	£36 125·75	£36 125·75

It is agreed by the partners to reduce the book value of goodwill by writing off £250·00 at March 31st, 19.. (to be charged to the Appropriation section of the Profit and Loss Account).

(*Continues overleaf*)

You are asked to prepare the Appropriation section of the firm's Profit and Loss Account and the partners' Current Accounts for the year ended March 31st, 19.., together with the Balance Sheet as on that date.

22.6 Private Limited Companies

Limited companies carry out the vast majority of business activities in the free-enterprise countries of the world. There are over half a million 'private' limited companies and about 3 000 'public' limited companies in the United Kingdom alone. The popularity of companies is explained by the *limited liability* which the shareholder has. Whereas a sole trader, or a partner, is liable to the full extent of his/her personal wealth for all the obligations of the business, the liability of the shareholder is limited to the value of his/her shareholding. A shareholder cannot be held personally liable for the debts of the business in excess of the nominal value of the shares he/she has purchased, or agreed to purchase. Before this concession was made by Parliament in 1855, the liability of shareholders was unlimited and, if their company collapsed, they were held fully liable for the debts of the company even though they were not directors of the company and had no change of influencing personally the conduct of its affairs. Small investors could find themselves thrown into the debtors' prisons just because they owned a share in a company which had failed.

If the shareholders are now freed from liability for the debts of the business, who can be held liable? The answer is—no one. Creditors can only hope for repayment to the extent that the contributed capital will allow. This is plainly a position that creditors would wish to avoid, and so Parliament enacted that every company must display, immediately after its name, the word *Limited*. This is a warning to suppliers to check on the financial soundness of a company before doing business with it. Readers may think that a Limited Company is a sound and reliable organization. Of course the majority are, but many have only £100 or less as the capital to which creditors may look should the company get into difficulties. It is unwise to supply goods in large quantities to companies where the capital is insufficient to cover the order. The registered share capital of a limited company can be discovered from the records which are open to examination (for a nominal fee) at Company House in London, and Cardiff. The company's current Balance Sheet merits careful study in this context, for there is always a risk that losses over the years have eroded the initial capital almost entirely. Today the larger companies are Public Limited Companies and their names must end with these words (often abbreviated in conversation to PLC).

Forming a Company

The chief advantage of forming a company is the one explained above—limited liability. If the business gets into difficulties you are only liable to the extent of the capital you have contributed, and not to the full extent of your personal wealth.

Forming a company is a fairly simple process which in theory anyone can perform. In practice it is better to use the services of an expert. Some firms specialise in registering companies to meet the exact needs of the businessman/woman. They also usually have a stock of companies already registered, 'ready-made' companies, which by a simple transfer process can be made available to any one requiring a company. You will find a number of such firms in your local Yellow Pages under 'Company Registration Agents'. Alternatively your local accountant will advise you on these matters.

Limited companies have to operate within a much tighter framework of law than that which governs the sole-trader or partnership enterprise. This means that the book-keeping requirements are considerably stricter. If you are running your business as a company, you may find it helpful to make a careful study of the Companies Acts, 1985-9. However, for most small companies, since your accounts must be audited by professional accountants you can safely leave it to your accountant to ensure that your accounts comply with the Companies Acts 1985-9.

22.7 The Simplex System and the Final Accounts of a Company

A considerable number of Simplex users operate as companies, and the system is adequate for their needs except that the pages at the end of the Simplex D Account Book are not satisfactory because it is necessary to have an Appropriation Account (sometimes called an Appropriation Section of the Profit and Loss Account) before we get to the Balance Sheet. Also the Balance Sheet itself is different because the capital is provided by many people (called shareholders). It is often presented in vertical style—which needs some explanation.

The main points about company Final Accounts are these:

(a) A company is a separate business entity—an incorporation set up by registration under the Companies Acts 1985-89. The word incorporation means 'to create a body' and this legal body is quite separate from all other legal persons, and certainly separate from the shareholders, directors and other officials. A company can do all the things other legal persons can do—own property, employ labour, manufacture, trade, etc., etc. However it cannot get married, have children or do the personal things ordinary people do. It can't be sent to prison—we have to send the directors instead if offences are committed.

(b) The profit a company makes are worked out in the normal way with a Trading Account and a Profit and Loss Account. If it is a manufacturing company it starts with a Manufacturing Account, of course.

(c) The profits it earns belong to the company. Whether any of the profits are passed on to the shareholders depends upon whether the directors recommend a 'dividend'. They usually recommend a dividend large enough to keep the shareholders quiet, but they rarely divide up all the profits, as is usual with partnerships. All profits that are not distributed become 'reserves' and are used to expand the business. Profits ploughed back in this way are called 'revenue reserves'. There is another kind of reserve called a 'capital reserve' which has not been made in the ordinary way, by the company's trading activities, but in some other way—for example profits made by revaluing premises to take account of rises in property values become capital reserves. They are not allowed to be distributed to shareholders, but they can be given to the shareholders as bonus shares.

(d) All the profits made go into an Appropriation Account, very similar to the Appropriation Account used in partnerships. So the full system of Final Accounts for a limited company consist of:

(a) A Manufacturing Account (if the company manufactures)
(b) A Trading Account
(c) A Profit and Loss Account
(d) An Appropriation Account
(e) A Balance Sheet

Since the Manufacturing Account, Trading Account and Profit and Loss Account are exactly the same as those for sole traders and partners we begin with Fig. 22.8, the Appropriation Account. The facts are as follows:

Prosperous Ltd. made profits in the year 19.. of £179 269. At the start of that year there was a balance on the Appropriation Account of undistributed profits from earlier years, totalling £14 331. The directors decided:

(a) To set up a Reserve for Corporation Tax of £65 000.
(b) To set up a Plant Replacement Reserve of £30 000 and a Computer Renewals Reserve of £25 000.
(c) To put £30 000 in General Reserve A/C.
(d) To pay the Preference Shareholders a 9% dividend on their shares (100 000 shares of £1).
(e) To pay the Ordinary Shareholders a 25% dividend on their shares (50 000 shares of £1).

These decisions are shown in Fig. 22.8 (last year's figures have been ignored).

APPROPRIATION ACCOUNT for year ending 31st December 19..						
LAST YEAR		THIS YEAR	LAST YEAR			THIS YEAR
CORPORATION TAX RESERVE		65,000 00		BALANCE AT 1st JAN		14,331 00
PLANT REPLACEMENT RESERVE		30,000 00		NET PROFIT (FROM PROFIT & LOSS A/C)		179,269 00
COMPUTER RENEWALS RESERVE		25,000 00				193,600 00
GENERAL RESERVE ACCOUNT		30,000 00				
PREFERENCE DIVIDEND		9,000 00				
ORDINARY DIVIDEND		12,500 00				
		171,500 00				
BALANCE CARRIED DOWN		22,100 00				
TOTAL		193,600 00		TOTAL		193,600 00
				BALANCE (TO NEXT YEAR) B/D		22,100 00

Fig. 22.8 *The Appropriation Account of a Company*

Notes:
(a) The balance of undistributed profit from last year starts the account on 1 January.

(b) The profits made during the year are brought in to give a total available for distribution of £193 600.

(c) Very little of this is actually distributed to the shareholders. About 35% of it is put away for Corporation Tax. The vast majority of the rest is used to increase the reserves for various purposes. The chief purpose of a General Reserve is to equalise the dividend over the years. For example if we have a bad year next year and make no profit these reserves can be used to pay a dividend next year.

(d) Preference Shareholders are shareholders who wish to have a regular dividend even if it is not large. They settle for a steady dividend at a fixed rate—in this case 9%. Ordinary shareholders are more interested in a good dividend, even if there is some risk that in a bad year they will get nothing (because when profits are scarce the preference shareholders have preference).

(e) Any balance left over is carried forward to next year.

(f) All the figures which appear in the Appropriation Account will also appear in the Balance Sheet somewhere, because, like the net profit of an ordinary trader, they are balances in hand available for some purpose or other.

The Balance Sheet of a Limited Company. The Balance Sheet of a limited company is similar in many ways to other Balance Sheets in that it has the assets set against the liabilities and the two sides should balance. However, limited companies are controlled by the Companies Acts 1985-9 which sets out in Schedule 4 two alternative presentations of the Balance Sheet which companies are to use. One of these presentations is in continuous style, which means it is a Balance Sheet in vertical style. The other is in horizontal style like the ordinary Simplex Balance Sheet. Since most accountants present the Balance Sheet in vertical style this is the method used in the special sets of Final Accounts paper provided by George Vyner Ltd. An example is shown in Fig. 22.9 on pages 188-9. Last year's figures have been ignored.

22.8 Exercises on Company Accounts

1. A limited company has an authorized capital of 150 000 Ordinary Shares of £1, of which 100 000 are issued and 50 000 9% Preference Shares of £1 of which 30 000 are issued. On March 31st 19.. it was found that the Net Profit was £98 420 for the year. There was also a balance on the Appropriation Account of £6 450 from 1 April the previous year. The directors resolved:
– to put £25 000 to a new General Reserve and £18 500 to a new Plant Replacement Reserve.
– to reserve £25 000 for Corporation Tax.
– to pay the 9% Preference Dividend.
– to recommend a 20% dividend on the Ordinary shares.
  Show the Appropriation Account and the Balance Sheet. In addition to the current liabilities resulting from the Appropriation Account there were £2 300 of debts to creditors outstanding. Fixed assets totalled £178 000 and current assets £59 170.

Balance Sheet of Prosperous Ltd. as at 31 December 19..

Last Year
(Last year's figures have been omitted in this illustration)

Fixed Assets	At Cost £	Less Depreciation to date £	Net Value £
Land & Buildings	160 000	—	160 000
Plant & Machinery	88 000	12 000	76 000
Fixtures & Fittings	8 540	3 360	5 180
Motor Vehicles	17 295	6 918	10 377
	273 835	22 278	251 557
Current Assets			
Stock	67 285		
Debtors	4 962		
Cash at Bank	57 295		
Cash in Hand	176		
			129 718
			£381 275

Financed by:

Preference Shareholders Interest in the Co

		Issued
8% Preference Shares of £1	Authorised £60 000	50 000

Ordinary Shareholders Interest in the Co

Ordinary Shares of £1	Authorised 100 000	100 000

Revenue Reserves

Plant Replacement Reserve	20 000	
Additions	30 000	
	50 000	

Computer Renewals Reserve		25 000	
General Reserve	15 000		
Additions	30 000		
Balance on Appropriation A/C	45 000		
	22 100		142 100
Ordinary Shareholders' Equity		242 100	
		292 100	
		65 000	
Corporation Tax Reserve			
Current Liabilities			
Pref Dividend	9 000		
Ord Dividend	12 500		
Creditors	2 675		
		24 175	
		£381 275	

Fig. 22.9 *The Balance Sheet of a Limited Company, in vertical style*

Notes:

(a) The Companies Acts require that fixed assets are shown at cost, less the depreciation to date.

(b) The total of the assets £381 275 is followed by the words 'Financed by' to show how these assets were financed.

(c) The chief sources of finance were the contributions by the Ordinary Shareholders, plus the Preference Shareholders (if any), but a lot of the finance was provided by profits ploughed back into the business as reserves. Notice that all reserves belong to the Ordinary Shareholders—all the preference shareholders get is the dividend they have contracted to receive.

(d) The total of the Ordinary Shareholders' interest in the company is called the 'equity'—because it will be shared equally among them. It is one of the things that decides the value of the shares on the market—the 100 000 shares are worth £2.42 each (but market expectations also influence the market price—which may be above or below £2.42 per share).

(e) The rest of the finance was provided by the unpaid Corporation Tax and the creditors.

(f) You should now use the pages provided by George Vyner Ltd. to work out the Final Accounts of your company.

Fig. 22.9 *The Balance Sheet of a Limited Company, in vertical style*

2. The following Trial Balance was extracted from the books of Robespierre Ltd, as at December 31st 19..

Trial Balance

	£	£
Share Capital (authorized and issued)		
80 000 Ordinary Shares of £1 fully paid		80 000
20 000 7 per cent Preference Shares of £1 fully paid		20 000
Motor Vans at costs	14 460	
Freehold Property at cost	95 200	
General Reserve		10 000
Premium on Preference-Shares A/C		2 000
Provision for Depreciation of Motor Vans		10 142
Stock-in-Trade at December 31st 19..	17 754	
Provisions for Bad Debts at December 31st 19..		400
Profit and Loss Account Balance at January 1st 19..		10 680
Balance at Bank	14 170	
Trade Debtors and Creditors	28 325	24 150
Rates and Insurance in advance	272	
Wages Due		944
Net Profit for year		11 865
	£170 181	£170 181

You are told that the directors propose
  (a) To place a further £5 000 to General Reserve A/C.
  (b) To pay the 7 per cent preference dividend.
  (c) To pay a 10 per cent dividend on the ordinary shares.
  Draw up an Appropriation Account, and a Balance Sheet as at December 31st 19..

Chapter Twenty-three

How to Control Your Business

23.1 Introduction

When a business has been running for some time it becomes possible to compare the current trading period with earlier periods. Such comparisons are almost always interesting, especially if attention is paid to *relative* changes rather than *absolute* changes. For example, a manager who tells you that sales have increased by £100 per week is giving you the actual figure of the increase, i.e. the absolute change that has taken place. It sounds very impressive, but you should inquire what relative change the increase represents, i.e. what percentage change. If sales have been running at £10 000 per week, the £100 increase is only a 1 per cent change and no one would think it miraculous. The success of an advertising campaign or similar activity is always best judged in percentage terms.

Even if the business has only been running a short time, it is possible to compare it with similar businesses; statistics are usually available from trade associations and similar bodies which analyse the activities of enterprises in their particular field. It is also possible, if a certain amount of planning is undertaken, to make estimates of future performance in selling, expenditure, cash turnover and so on. These budgets may then be compared with actual performance as the weeks go by. This is the system known as *budgetary control*.

The most useful control figures which can be derived from the final accounts are as follows:

(a) From the Trading Account
- (i) the gross profit percentage
- (ii) the rate of stock turnover

(b) From the Profit and Loss Account
- (i) the net profit percentage
- (ii) the expense ratios

(c) From the Balance Sheet
- (i) the working capital ratio
- (ii) the acid test ratio
- (iii) the debtors-to-sales ratio
- (iv) the return on capital employed
- (v) the return on capital invested

As we consider these control figures we shall learn the meaning of several technical terms, such as 'turnover', 'average stock', 'fixed capital', 'floating capital', 'working capital', 'liquid capital', 'overtrading', 'insolvency', 'opportunity cost' and other useful pieces of account vocabulary. The more important control figures are listed in Fig. 23.1 and Fig. 23.2 along with the methods of calculation and the uses to which they may be put.

Background figure	Formula	Ratios derived (see Fig. 23.2)
Turnover	Total sales − Returns by customers	Gross profit percentage Net profit percentage Expense ratios Debtors-to-sales ratio
Average stock at cost price	$$\frac{\text{Opening stock at start of year} + \text{Closing stock at end of year}}{2}$$	Rate of stock turnover
Average stock at selling price	$$\frac{\left[\text{Opening stock} + \text{profit margin}\right] + \left[\text{Closing stock} + \text{margin}\right]}{2}$$	Rate of stock turnover
Working capital	Current assets − Current liabilities	Working-capital ratio
Liquid capital	$\left[\text{Current assets} - \text{Stock}\right] -$ Current liabilities	Acid-test ratio (Liquidity ratio)
Capital employed	*For ordinary firms:* Capital at the start of the year + profits retained in the business + long-term loans and mortgages from outsiders *For companies* Capital from ordinary and preference shares + Reserves at start of year + Debentures + other long-term loans	Return on capital employed
Capital invested	*For ordinary firms:* Capital at start of year *For companies:* Capital at start of year + Reserves at start of year	Return on capital invested
Opportunity cost	The earnings you could expect in some other form of employment	Return on capital invested

Fig. 23.1 *Background figures required to calculate control ratios*

Before preparing any control figures it is essential to have a set of 'final accounts' in good style, prepared in the way suggested throughout this book. It is not easy to analyse the affairs of a business whose accounts have been prepared poorly: first you must rearrange the accounts in good style, then most of the control figures may be readily determined.

23.2 Controlling Trading—a Trading Account for Analysis

Let us consider the Trading Account shown in Fig. 23.3. We will assume that the gross profit in the previous year was £13 700 on sales of £32 000, so both the turnover and the profit have increased.

The points to consider in analysing the results shown by a Trading Account are, first, the gross profit expressed as a percentage of turnover and, secondly, the rate of stock turnover.

Control ratio	Formula	Purpose	Remarks
Gross profit percentage	$\dfrac{\text{Gross profit}}{\text{Turnover}} \times 100$	To check on trading profitability and detect trouble in trading areas	Commonly in range 25-40%
Rates of stock turnover	*either* $\dfrac{\text{Cost of stock sold}}{\substack{\text{Average stock at} \\ \text{cost price}}}$ *or* $\dfrac{\text{Turnover}}{\substack{\text{Average stock at} \\ \text{selling price}}}$	To detect rapidity of turnover with a view to increasing profitability	Varies with product; e.g. 360 for newspapers, 1 or 2 for grand pianos
Net profit percentage	$\dfrac{\text{Net profit}}{\text{Turnover}} \times 100$	To check on overall profitability	Commonly about 10–25%; lower for groceries, etc.
Expense ratios	$\dfrac{\text{Expense item}}{\text{Turnover}} \times 100$	To detect areas where expenses are rising, with a view to control	Useful in diagnosing possible inefficiency
Working capital ratio	$\dfrac{\text{Current assets}}{\text{Current liabilities}}$	To detect risk of failing to meet current liabilities	Should be about 2:1

(Continues overleaf)

Control ratio	Formula	Purpose	Remarks
Acid test (or liquidity) ratio	$\dfrac{\text{Current assets} - \text{Stock}}{\text{Current liabilities}}$	To detect really serious trouble in being able to meet current liabilities	Should be about 1:1
Debtors-to-sales ratio	$\dfrac{\text{Debtors}}{\text{Sales}} \times 12$	To discover the average credit period in months	Normally about one month, i.e. 30 days' credit
Return on capital employed	$\dfrac{\text{Net profit} + \text{Interest paid out}}{\text{capital employed}}$ (see Fig. 23.1)	To compare this firm's use of funds with similar firms so far as figures are available	Should be about 5% above bank interest rates – otherwise why be in business
Return on capital invested	$\dfrac{\text{Net profit} - \text{Opportunity Cost}}{\text{Capital at start}} \times 100$	To discover whether being in business is worth while	Should be at least 10%

Fig. 23.2 *Control ratios to help you evaluate and control your business*

23.3 The Gross profit Percentage on Turnover

The gross profit percentage on turnover is found by the formula

$$\frac{\text{Gross profit}}{\text{Turnover}} \times 100$$

Turnover is the net sales of the business, i.e. the sales less returns inwards.

$$\text{In Fig. 23.3 the percentage is } \frac{£16\ 500}{£42\ 000} \times 100$$

$$= \frac{275}{7}$$

$$= \underline{39 \cdot 3\%}$$

Sunshine Boutique (E. Rawlinson)
Trading Account
(for year ending December 31st 19..)

19..		£	19..	£
Dec. 31 Opening Stock		2 564	Dec. 31 Sales	42 240
Purchases	29 860		*less* Returns	
less Returns			(if any)	240
(if any)	424			
			Net Turnover	42 000
		29 436		
Total Stock				
Available		32 000		
less Closing Stock		6 500		
Cost of Stock Sold		25 500		
Gross Profit		16 500		
		£42 000		£42 000

Fig. 23.3 *A Trading Account to be appraised*

Constancy of the Gross profit Percentage

One of the interesting things about the gross profit percentage is that *it will tend to be constant,* i.e. the same from year to year, if business trends are steady. For example, supposing business doubled in the following year. Sales would be twice as great and purchases would be twice as great; profits ought therefore to double as well. When we come to work out the gross profit percentage we find that

$$\frac{\text{Gross profit}}{\text{Turnover}} \times 100$$

$$= \frac{£33\ 000}{£84\ 000} \times 100$$

$$= \underline{39 \cdot 3\% \text{ as before}}$$

So the percentage tends to remain the same even if everything has doubled. The usefulness of the gross profit percentage is that it shows the *relative* profitability of the business, this year compared with the previous year. If business conditions are steady the gross profit percentage will be steady too.

Returning to Fig. 23.3, it is possible to compare this figure of 39·3 per cent with last year's gross profits percentage. Last year the figure were gross profit £13 700 and sales £32 000.

$$\therefore \quad \frac{\text{Gross profit} \ = \ \text{£13 700}}{\text{Turnover} \ = \ \text{£32 000}} \times 100$$

$$= \underline{42\cdot8\%}$$

Clearly the gross profit percentage has fallen from 42·8 per cent to 39·3 per cent. This is a significant fall and, although it may have occurred for perfectly good reasons, it certainly detracts to some extent from the apparent performance of the business. Let us examine the possible causes of a decline in gross profit percentage.

Causes of a Decline in Gross profit Percentage

(a) **Cash losses.** If the manager takes money out of the till before cashing up the daily takings, the 'Sales' figure will be reduced; this in turn will reduce the gross profit, and hence the gross profit percentage. It would be unwise, on this evidence alone, to accuse the manager of theft, but if his/her way of life suggests that he/she is living beyond his/her earnings it may be necessary to take some corrective action. If the manager is not at fault it may be that someone else is the culprit. Where there are several cash registers it is possible for staff to steal money by incorrect ringing up of receipts. A trader should be suspicious if a till has been deliberately placed so that the customer cannot see the amount being rung. Modern tills do much to overcome this type of theft by keeping an automatic record of each sum as it is rung up. The practice of giving customers till receipts for every purchase also reduces the chances of embezzlement.

(b) **Stock losses.** If the takings are being properly recorded, the cause of a fall in gross profit percentage may be theft of stock. Regular losses of small quantities of stock by theft will reduce the stock in hand at the end of the trading period. This will increase the 'Cost of Stock Sold' and reduce the gross profit and hence the gross profit percentage. The two common forms of theft are *passing out* (deliberate handing over by staff of stock without payment to friends or accomplices) and *shoplifting*. Shoplifting is believed to cost at least £10 billion each year to shops in the United Kingdom. The provision of store detectives, two-way mirrors and other devices helps reduce this activity— especially when it leads to a successful prosecution.

Other forms of stock losses include *breakages* in departments where fragile goods are sold. Some assistants are naturally clumsy and should be transferred from departments where this is a disadvantage. Skylarking and tomfoolery should be discouraged and action taken against offenders. The *spoiling* of perishable commodities usually indicates bad buying. Poor storage may lead to stock losses due to evaporation, blowing away of powdery commodities like meal and flour, and the contamination of foods by other substances, or by insects.

(c) **Clearance items.** Sometimes stock has to be disposed of at reduced prices because it is shop-soiled, or selling too slowly. This is another indication of bad

buying. Some buyers may be out of touch with what is fashionable and readily saleable. Products which for some reason do not achieve expected sales figures may have to be marked down, thus reducing the gross profit and the gross profit percentage. An appraisal of such 'clearance items' may reveal that a particular buyer is responsible for a high proportion of them, and the remedy is then fairly obvious.

(d) **Increased purchase prices.** Fluctuations in world prices of raw materials often result in higher purchase prices for goods. Increased purchase prices should be passed on to the consumer as increased selling prices. Sometimes this is not possible because of competition, and the result is falling profit margins and a lower gross profit percentage. At least a proprietor who is aware of these falling profit margins can be ready, when circumstances are less competitive, to recoup past losses. He/she may also vary the mixture of goods to include more items where competition is less fierce, reducing those where rivals are particularly efficient and are able to undercut him/her.

(e) **Incorrect stock valuation.** An overvalued stock overstates the profit and gives an artificially high percentage of gross profit. As this stock then becomes the 'Opening Stock' of the next period, it will artificially inflate the 'Cost of Stock Sold' and lower the percentage of gross profit in the following year. The consequent difference between the two successive years is a symptom of bad stock-taking rather than of bad management. Undervalued stock understates the profits this year and overstates it next year.

Securing a Rise in Gross profit Percentage

Whilst a fall in gross profit percentage signals that something is wrong with our business we must always seek wherever possible to *raise* the gross profit percentage. The chief ways to achieve this are by better buying—buying what the customer wants so that slow-moving 'shelf-warmers' and other clearance items are avoided; the protection of stock both from inherent vices (decay, desiccation, fading of material, etc) and protecting stock from theft, accidental damage, etc. Careful supervision of staff, stock levels, cash handling and use of materials may do much to assist the gross profit percentage.

23.4 The Rate of Stock Turnover

The rate of stock turnover (also called rate of stockturn) is a figure which can be calculated to show how many times the stock turns over in a year. It is significant because every time the stock turns over it yields a profit, so a rapid turnover will increase the total profit earned in the year. Turnover must be rapid with some merchandise; perishable foods and newspapers, for example, should turn over every day if possible. At least one chain of supermarkets throws away all cut meat products unsold at the end of the day. Overstocking in such circumstances can be very expensive.

Two formulae are available for finding the rate of stock turnover. The easier to use is:

$$\text{Rate of stock turnover} = \frac{\text{Cost of stock sold}}{\text{Average stock at cost price}}$$

The other is:

$$\text{Rate of stock turnover} = \frac{\text{Turnover}}{\text{Average stock at selling price}}$$

Applying the first formula to the Trading Account in Fig. 23.3, we have

$$\text{Rate of stock turnover} = \frac{\text{Cost of stock sold}}{\text{Average stock at cost price}}$$

$$= \frac{25\,500}{(2\,564 + 6\,500) \div 2}$$

$$= \frac{25\,500}{4\,532}$$

$$\text{Rate of stock turnover} = 5\cdot6 \text{ times}$$

Is this is a satisfactory rate of turnover? The answer depends on what the product is. It would be satisfactory for grand pianos but quite inadequate for groceries. It would perhaps do well enough for antiques, but not for sweets or tobacco.

The rate of stock turnover tells us how many times the stock turns over in a year. If we divide the 52 weeks of the year by the rate of stock turnover we find how long the average item is in stock. In the example above it is clearly $52 \div 5\cdot6 = 9\cdot3$ weeks. Rather too long for bread or bacon, but perfectly satisfactory for furniture or ironmongery.

Improving the Rate of Stock Turnover

Since the point of turnover is the point at which profit is made, it follows that all businesses should try to improve the rate of stock turnover. In implementing any plans to effect such an improvement we must watch the situation carefully, for the policy may prove to be less profitable than we hoped. Many firms have gone in for unlimited expansion of turnover only to find that they have saturated the market, or increased costs to the point where profitability of the enterprise declined. Expansion achieved by offering bonus schemes to salesmen will be marginally less profitable. This means that the extra business (the marginal sales) will contribute less to profit than the earlier sales did.

The rate of stock turnover may be increased by:

(a) Extending opening hours, within the limits set by law.
(b) Improving goodwill by courtesy, efficiency, honesty and service.
(c) Advertising selectively in local and national newspapers.

(d) Tightening stock control. This attempts to reduce 'average stock' by eliminating slow-moving items. It may conflict with *(b)* above, since customers who know that you are likely to have the less common items in stock may call more frequently; but in general reduction of average stock is a desirable thing since it reduces the capital tied up in stock and releases space on shelves and counters for more saleable items.

23.5 Controlling Expenses—the Profit and Loss Account

The gross profit is carried forward to the Profit and Loss Account where other profits are added to it and losses are deducted. The resulting net profit can be used as the basis for a *net profit percentage,* which is found by the formula

$$\text{Net profit percentage} = \frac{\text{Net profit}}{\text{Turnover}} \times 100$$

Once again there is a tendency (though it is less clear cut than with gross profit percentage) for this to be constant from year to year. If it is not we should seek for an explanation. For example, in Fig. 23.3 the gross profit to be carried forward is £16 500.

Sunshine Boutique (E. Rawlinson)
Profit and Loss Account
(for year ending December 31st 19..)

19..	£	19..	£
Dec. 31 Wages	5 500	Dec. 31 Gross Profit	16 500
Salaries	1 500	Discount Received	750
Administration		Commissions	
Expenses	420	Earned	1 550
Light and Heat	680		
Rent and Rates	1 650		18 800
Insurance	450		
Advertising	1 240		
Carriage Out	100		
	11 540		
Net Profit	7 260		
	£18 800		£18 800

Fig. 23.4 *A Profit and Loss Account to be appraised*

The Profit and Loss Account may be imagined to be as shown in Fig. 23.4 Calculating the net profit percentage, we have

$$\text{Net profit percentage} = \frac{\text{Net profit}}{\text{Turnover}} \times 100$$

$$= \frac{7\ 260}{42\ 000} \times 100$$

$$= 17\cdot3\%$$

Analysing the Net Profit Percentage

The net profit percentage will never be as constant as the gross profit percentage, for many of the expenses do not vary with turnover. For example, rent and rates are not linked to turnover, nor are administration expenses and insurance. The chief advantage of the ratio is that it enables us to compare one trading period with another. Let us imagine that last year the net profit percentage of Sunshine Boutique was 20 per cent. Evidently there has been a fall of 2·7 per cent over the past twelve months. What can have been the cause of this decline? If the *gross profit* percentage has remained constant we may assume that the reason has nothing to do with the trading activities of the firm. There can only be two explanations:

(a) The expenses have increased for some reason.

(b) The 'other profits' may have declined for some reason.

(a) Increasing Expenses

A useful method of diagnosis here is to prepare *expense ratios*. Expense ratios enable the accountant to compare every expense with its counterpart from the previous year to see which, if any, has risen abnormally. The formula is

$$\text{Expense ratio} = \frac{\text{Expense item}}{\text{Turnover}} \times 100$$

By way of example, let us apply the formula to the salaries paid by Sunshine Boutique.

$$\text{Salaries ratio} = \frac{1\ 500}{42\ 000} \times 100$$

$$= 3\cdot57\%$$

Suppose that last year the salaries were £1 000 and turnover was £32 000. Then

$$\text{Salaries ratio (previous year)} = \frac{1\ 000}{32\ 000} \times 100$$

$$= 3\cdot13\%$$

There has been quite a large increase in the salaries figure relative to the volume of trade alone, and this seems to indicate some inefficiency somewhere.

(b) **Falling 'Other Profits'**

If the decline in net profit percentage cannot be attributed to an increase in expenses, it may have been caused by a decrease in 'other profits' such as commission received or rent received. Perhaps a sub-tenant has been given notice to quit because his share of the building was required for expansion. In such a case there is nothing we can do about the lost rent. Perhaps commission previously earned has not been forthcoming for some reason. Here we can do something: we must determine that this type of earnings is pursued more vigorously in the following year.

Regular analysis of changes in the gross profit percentage and net profit percentage between successive trading periods is extremely useful in revealing the trends (both favourable and unfavourable) that are taking place in the business. Many firms prepare quarterly *interim* final accounts so that they can check the profitability of their enterprises at three-monthly intervals.

23.6 The Condition of a Business—a Balance Sheet for Interpretation

Fig. 23.5 shows the Balance Sheet of Sunshine Boutique as a basis for discussion. The reader will recall that it is a 'snapshot' of the affairs of the business at a moment in time.

Sunshine Boutique (E. Rawlinson)
Balance Sheet
(as at December 31st 19..)

Capital		£	*Fixed assets*		£
At Start		58 080	Goodwill		14 000
add Net Profit	7 260		Land and Buildings		28 000
less Drawings	3 600		Fixtures and Fittings		3 600
		3 660	Motor Vehicles		1 000
		61 740			46 600
Long-term Liabilities			*Current Assets*		
Mortgage		15 000	Stock	32 540	
Current Liabilities			Debtors	2 240	
Creditors	12 350		Cash at Bank	7 800	
Wages Due	150		Cash in Hand	60	
		12 500			42 640
		£89 240			£89 240

Fig. 23.5 *A Balance Sheet to be appraised*

We have already met in Chapter 21 the main terms used in drawing up a Balance Sheet, including Fixed Assets, Current Assets, Long-term Liabilities and Current Liabilities. We now have to extend our vocabulary with a further array of book-keeping terms, many of which are simply alternative phrases for those with which you are already familiar. The others extend your knowledge and increase your ability to appraise a Balance Sheet.

In appraising a Balance Sheet we want to know as a matter of course the total value of the business, and who 'owns' it. To say that it all belongs to the proprietor(s) or to the shareholders would be too simple a view. Let us now consider the question in relation to the ownership of Sunshine Boutique.

(a) The 'Capital Employed'

In the Balance Sheet of Sunshine Boutique (Fig. 23.5), the owner's capital at start is given at £58 080; yet the business is worth £89 240, as the total of the Balance Sheet shows. It follows that the capital employed in the business is greater than £58 080, and must have been provided in some other way than by the original contribution of the proprietor, E. Rawlinson. It is easy to see where these extra funds came from. A mortgage provided £15 500, creditors supplied goods worth £12 350 without payment, employees are waiting for their wages and to this small extent are providing funds for the business, while £3 660 was ploughed back out of profits over the year. The capital employed in this business has therefore been provided in five different ways.

There are various ways of defining capital employed, but the one in commonest use is to take the figure of long term capital used—which implies the Capital of the proprietor, plus profits retained in the business, and the long-term liabilities. With a company it would be usual to take the capital contributed by the shareholders, plus the reserves, plus the debentures and any long-term loans. In this particular case we have:

$$\text{Capital employed} = £61\ 740 + £15\ 000$$
$$= £76\ 740$$

(b) Fixed Capital and Circulating Capital

The 'capital employed' above is being used to provide two classes of asset: fixed assets and current assets. Capital used to provide fixed assets is called *fixed capital,* and that used to provide current assets is called *circulating capital* or *floating capital.* In other words, fixed capital is tied up in fixed assets, which are in permanent use in the business and form the framework for running its affairs, while circulating (or floating) capital is tied up in current assets, which are in the process of turning over, or circulating, in the manner shown in Fig. 21.5.

For Sunshine Boutique the figures are

$$\text{Fixed capital} = \text{Total of fixes assets} = £46\ 600$$
$$\text{Circulating capital} = \text{Total of current assets} = £42\ 640$$

(c) Working Capital

The most important guiding figure when appraising a Balance Sheet is the 'working' capital. This is that portion of the capital employed which is not tied up in fixed assets (fixed capital) but is available to 'work' the business; in other words, it is available to *meet revenue expenditure*. The figure is found by the formula

$$\text{Working capital} = \text{Current assets} - \text{Current liabilities}$$

Applying this formula to Sunshine Boutique, which has current assets of £42 640 and current liabilities of £12 500,

$$
\begin{aligned}
\text{Working Capital} &= £42\,640 - £12\,500 \\
&= £30\,140
\end{aligned}
$$

(d) Liquid Capital

'Liquid' capital is the name given to capital tied up in liquid assets, which may be described as cash and 'near-cash' items. Liquid assets are cash in hand, cash at the bank, debtors (who have a legal obligation to pay) and any investments which are readily marketable. The best definition is:

$$\text{Liquid capital} = (\text{Current asssets}—\text{Stock})—\text{Current Liabilities}$$

For Sunshine Boutique the current assets total is £42 640, including £32 540 worth of stock. Hence

$$
\begin{aligned}
\text{Liquid capital} &= (£42\,640—£32\,540)—£12\,500 \\
&= -£2\,400
\end{aligned}
$$

We see that this gives a minus quality, showing how very short Sunshine Boutique is of ready cash.

(e) Working Capital Ratio and Acid Test (or Liquidity) Ratio

The *working capital ratio* is an important figure which tells us the ratio between the saleable part of a firm's assets and its current liabilities. It is defined by the formula

$$\text{Working capital ratio} = \frac{\text{Current assets}}{\text{Current liabilities}}$$

The figure for Sunshine Boutique is

$$
\begin{aligned}
\text{Working capital ratio} &= \frac{£42\,640}{£12\,500} \\[2mm]
&= 3{\cdot}4
\end{aligned}
$$

As a general rule it is agreed that 2:1 is a satisfactory working-capital ratio, so Sunshine's result appears to be quite good. However, we shall now apply a more crucial test.

The *acid test ratio* (or liquidity ratio) tells us the ratio between a firm's readily available cash or near-cash assets (i.e. its liquid assets) and its current liabilities (due for payment in one month). It is defined by the formula

$$\text{Acid test ratio} = \frac{\text{Liquid assets}}{\text{Current liabilities}}$$

For Sunshine Boutique the figure is

$$\frac{\text{Liquid assets}}{\text{Current liabilities}} = \frac{\text{Current assets—Stock}}{\text{Current liabilities}}$$

$$= \frac{£42\ 640—£32\ 540}{£12\ 500}$$
$$= \frac{£10\ 100}{£12\ 500}$$
$$= \underline{\underline{0{\cdot}8}}$$

The acid-test ratio should never be less than 1:1, except in a temporary situation which the management has anticipated and for which suitable provision (e.g. an overdraft) has been made. Sunshine Boutique is clearly too short of liquid capital; it could not meet its short-term liabilities and would need to borrow to pay them.

To the investor considering the purchase of shares, the acid test ratio offers a particularly valuable means of comparing the liquidity position of one firm with another.

(f) Debtors-to-Sales Ratio

The chief cause of liquidity in any firm is the failure of debtors to pay promptly for goods supplied. If you allow debtors to become slip-shod over payments, your volume of debtors will increase and bad-debt losses will be suffered. The *debtors-to-sales ratio* will assist in evaluating your debtors' position. Its formula is

$$\frac{\text{Debtors}}{\text{Sales}} \times 12 = \text{Average debt (in months)}$$

Applying this ratio to Sunshine Boutique, we find that the average debt is

$$\frac{\text{Debtors}}{\text{Sales}} \times 12 = \frac{2\ 240}{42\ 000} \times 12$$
$$= \underline{0{\cdot}64\ \text{months}}$$

This is less than a month, and is therefore very satisfactory.

Where debts exceed on average one month, it is clear that some debtors must be breaking that rule of good business which says that an honest trader settles his/her debts monthly. The stages for ensuring good control of debtors are as follows:

(i) Appraise the individual debts, and decide which debtors are the problem cases.

(ii) See the debtor personally or write to him/her, pointing out the bad habits that have developed and threatening to cut off credit if the debt is not paid.

(iii) For really bad cases of intentional non-payment you have two courses of action: you can sue the debtor or you can sell the bad debt to a 'debt factor'. If you decide to sell the debt you will receive perhaps 50 per cent of the amount owed—but half a loaf is better than no bread.

(g) Return on Capital Employed

This ratio enables us to compare our business with other businesses as far as the use of the capital employed is concerned. If we work out the return on the capital employed and can see what other businesses are securing from similar investments of capital we can see whether our enterprise is worthwhile.

The formula is:

$$\text{Return on capital employed} = \frac{\text{Total earnings}}{\text{Capital employed}} \times 100$$

Since we count not only our capital invested in the business but also any mortgages and loans from outsiders in the 'capital employed part of the calculation', we must include in the 'returns' the net profit and the interest paid to the outsiders. If we imagine the mortgage rate was 15%, so that on a £15 000 mortgage we paid interest of £2 250 we have total earnings of £2 250 + £7 260 = £9 510.

Taking the capital employed as £61 740 + £15 000, we have:

$$\frac{\text{Total earnings}}{\text{Capital employed}} \times 100$$

$$= \frac{£9\ 510}{£76\ 740} \times 100$$

$$= 12 \cdot 4\%$$

At current rates of interest this is not a very high return on capital employed, but in such situations there may be non-monetary satisfactions to be weighed in the balance (for example do we like being self-employed).

(h) Return on Capital Invested

The last of the important figures used in the appraisal of a Balance Sheet is the *return on capital invested*. It is given by the formula

$$\text{Return on capital invested} = \frac{\text{Net profit}-\text{Opportunity cost}}{\text{Capital invested at start}} \times 100$$

To understand this ratio you will have to think about your business very clearly for a few minutes. You are working in this business to earn a living, and by doing so you surrender the chance of earning money in some other occupation. You could, for example, seek employment as manager in a similar enterprise, working for someone else. You might even take a totally different kind of job, as a clerk, teacher, bus driver, TV personality—the list is endless. By being in business you lose all these opportunities which otherwise would be open to you. The *opportunity cost* of your present business is the best of the lost opportunities you decide not to take up.

Suppose you are making a clear £200 a week out of your present business, but could earn £190 a week as a manager for someone else. All the business is really paying you is £10 a week. Suppose your wife is helping in the business too, and she could earn £150 a week as a copy typist. You are actually worse off by being in business. Of course there is more to job-satisfaction than mere monetary reward, and it may well be that you chose your present occupation because you personally place a high value on the independence, for example, or service to the community which it affords. The 'return on capital invested' is a ratio which enables you to see what extra monetary satisfaction you get from your business. You must add this monetary satisfaction to the non-monetary ones, and then decide whether the whole enterprise is worthwhile.

Let us assume that E. Rawlinson, the proprietor of Sunshine Boutique, could earn £4 500 a year in another employment. We can calculate his return on capital invested as follows:

$$\text{Return on capital invested} = \frac{\text{Net profit}-\text{Opportunity cost}}{\text{Capital invested at start}} \times 100$$

$$= \frac{£7\ 260-£4\ 500}{£58\ 080} \times 100$$

$$= \frac{£2\ 760}{£58\ 080} \times 100$$

$$= \underline{4 \cdot 75\%}$$

Usually a return of about 10 per cent is regarded as a worthwhile figure. A return of 20 per cent is much more satisfactory, and a proprietor only able to earn about 5 per cent could invest his/her capital more fruitfully in a Building Society. However, we should bear in mind the industrialist who, faced with the stricture that he was only in business to make a profit, rebuked his critic with the remark 'Not at all; I am in business to make shoes.' Such a person will not be too worried about a low return on capital investment.

23.7 Exercises in the Control of Business

1. Swish-shops Ltd., has four branches, each selling the same classes of goods in very similar areas. The following results are achieved:

Branch	Quarterly Turnover £	Gross Profit £	Selling Expenses £	Net Profit £
(a) Seatown	42 000	15 000	10 200	?
(b) Riverton	38 000	17 200	8 800	?
(c) Marshville	26 000	8 500	3 250	?
(d) Markton	68 000	19 000	12 000	?

Find the Gross-Profit Percentage for each branch (correct to one decimal place). Find the Net-Profit Percentage for each branch (correct to one decimal place). Hence conclude: (a) which branch is making the best efforts; (b) which branch is making the worst efforts.

Give some reasons why they might be successful or unsuccessful in each case.

2. Newsagents Ltd., has five branches, each selling the same class of goods in very similar areas. The following results are achieved:

Branch	Monthly Turnover £	Gross Profit £	Selling Expenses £	Net Profit £
A	8 250	4 000	1 500	?
B	7 700	3 800	1 850	?
C	9 500	6 200	2 600	?
D	6 500	4 800	1 800	?
E	13 250	4 750	1 350	?

Find the Gross-Profit Percentage for each branch (correct to one decimal place). Find the Net-Profit Percentage for each branch (correct to one decimal place). Hence conclude: (a) which branch is making the best efforts; (b) which branch is making the worst efforts.

Give some reasons why they might be successful or unsuccessful in each case.

3. Fill in the missing parts of the following table.

	Opening Stock	Closing Stock	Average Stock	Mark-up	Rate of Turnover	Sales Figure	Gross Profit
Mr. Smith	£2 000	£3 000	?	10%	20	?	?
Mr. Jones	£4 000	£6 000	?	20%	5	?	?

(Continues overleaf)

Now calculate the Gross-Profit Percentage and the Net-Profit Percentage (correct to one decimal place) bearing in mind that general administration expenses are: Mr. Smith £1 850, Mr. Jones £2 350.

4. Fill in the missing parts of the following table.

	Opening Stock	Closing Stock	Average Stock	Mark-up	Rate of Turnover	Gross Profit	Sales Figure
Mr. Giles	£5 000	£7 000	?	10%	15	?	?
Mr. Slocum	£6 000	£9 000	?	20%	10	?	?

Now calculate the Gross-Profit Percentage and the Net-Profit Percentage (correct to one decimal place) bearing in mind that general administration expenses are: Mr. Giles £3 500, Mr Slocum £4 550.

5. Here is A. Tyler's Balance Sheet. You are to answer the questions below (with calculations if needed).

Balance Sheet
(as at December 31st, 19..)

Capital		£	Fixed Assets		£
At Start		29 000	Goodwill		1 000
add Net Profit	23 300		Premises		28 000
less Drawings	8 600	14 700	Plant and Machinery		12 000
			Motor Vehicles		2 000
		43 700			
					43 000
Long-term Liabilities			Current Assets		
Mortgage		5 000	Stock	4 596	
			Debtors	1 274	
Current Liabilities			Cash at Bank	1 381	
Creditors	1 614		Cash in Hand	72	
Accrued Charges	97		Payments in Advance	88	
		1 711			7 411
		£50 411			£50 411

(a) What is the capital owned by the proprietor?
(b) What is the capital employed in the business?
(c) What is the working capital?
(d) What is the liquid capital?
(e) Work out the acid test ratio (correct to 2 places of decimals).

(Continues overleaf)

(f) Work out the return on capital invested (correct to one decimal place) assuming that Tyler could earn £8 000 a year in an alternative position with none of the responsibilities of a small businessman.

6. Here is R. Montgomery's Balance Sheet. You are to answer the questions below (with calculations if needed).

Balance Sheet
(as at December 31st, 19..)

Capital		£	*Fixed Assets*		£
At Start		42 000	Goodwill		500
add Net Profit	28 750		Premises		46 000
less Drawings	10 250	18 500	Plant and Machinery		18 500
			Motor Vehicles		8 850
		60 500			73 850
Long-term Liabilities			*Current Assets*		
Mortgage		15 000	Stock	7 864	
			Debtors	2 976	
Current Liabilities			Cash at Bank	3 281	
Creditors	12 950		Cash in Hand	475	
Accrued Charges	158		Payments in Advance	162	
		13 108			14 758
		£88 608			£88 608

(a) What is the capital owned by the proprietor?
(b) What is the capital employed in the business?
(c) What is the working capital?
(d) What is the liquid capital?
(e) Work out the acid test ratio (correct to 2 places of decimals).
(f) Work out the return on capital invested, assuming that Montgomery could earn £12 000 a year in an alternative position with none of the responsibilities of a small businessman.

Chapter Twenty-four
Income Tax and the Small Business

24.1 The British Tax System

Taxation is a system adopted by governments to finance their activities. These days, especially in Britain, government agencies perform such a wide variety of activities that enormous sums have to be collected to finance the nation's defence, education, social security and medical services. Whether or not you personally support such programmes, you have to keep within a framework of taxation laws which are imposed by the government and will be enforced against you if you infringe them. This body of rules is being constantly changed and revised, from year to year. Penalties for breaches of the tax laws can be severe, but are usually reduced where full and frank admissions of misconduct are made. The best rule is to keep accurate and honest records, and thus pay your fair contribution to the needs of the nation. Genuine grievances can usually be adequately aired through trade associations, or your Member of Parliament.

The British tax system operates through a series of rules called 'Schedules', each of which deals with a particular type of income. Schedule D is the one that affects most businessmen, and has actually seven 'cases' or subdivisions of income. Case I covers profits which are the result of a trade or business; Case II, covering professional businesses, relates to doctors, accountants, etc.

Taxable Persons. Every person earning income, either from employment or through business activities, is liable to pay tax on that income. Certain 'allowances' may be obtained. For example a 'personal allowance' is given to single people (£2 785) and to married couples (£4 375); these figures vary from year to year. Larger allowances are given for older people and for the blind. Where a firm is operated as a partnership or sole-trading enterprise, the profits of the firm are reduced by the personal allowances mentioned, and tax is only paid on the remaining 'taxable income'.

Limited companies are, however, separate legal personalities, quite independent of the individuals who form the company, and are taxed on the full profits agreed to have been earned. Recently the rate of 'Corporation Tax' (tax on companies) has been reduced and is now 35% for large companies and 25% for small companies.

24.2 Tax Avoidance

While accepting the statutory requirement to keep honest records and pay your fair contribution to the nation's finances, it should be stated that the courts have held that the taxpayer is entitled to take any legal means to avoid paying tax. If the Chancellor imposes a heavy tax on tobacco, I am free to avoid it by giving up smoking. If he taxes certain business activities, it is quite permissible for me to change my arrangements so that I can legally avoid the tax. It is for the Chancellor to devise a tax system which is free of loopholes. What you, as a business proprietor, may not do is to avoid taxation by illegal means, such as making fraudulent declarations.

A word of warning here. It is clearly undesirable for a taxpayer to rewrite his/her whole year's records, since the rewriting of records is usually associated with some sort of fraudulent practice. It might be thought that no one could ever know whether records have been rewritten, but in fact most editions of account books have coded markings which indicate when they were printed. A taxpayer who submits accounts, purporting to start in March, in a book that only rolled off the presses in August, is clearly suspect. He/she may not in fact be guilty of a deceitful practice, having fallen behind with the records through no fault of his/her own. Even so, it will be difficult to establish that records were *efficiently* kept after such a long delay.

24.3 The Adjustment of Profits

Whatever profit you arrive at in your accounts, it is almost certain that the inspector of taxes will adjust it in the light of the tax laws as they stand at the time of assessment. For example, the inspector will add back any expenses which you have deducted if these are disallowed by law. He/she may also deduct any income you have included which is not taxable, such as dividends which have already paid tax at source.

In adjusting your profit the inspector will be guided by certain rules, including those listed below which have been laid down by the courts over the years.

(a) Expenditure which is allowable as a charge against the profits (deductible expenditure) must have been *wholly and necessarily incurred in the earning of the profit*. Thus a telephone call to book accommodation at a trade fair would be deductible, but a call to book your annual holiday would not.

(b) Expenditure which is of a capital nature is not deductible, and depreciation often charged by businessmen in their accounts is not deductible. Instead, capital allowances are deductible, and these vary from year to year as the various Finance Acts of recent years have ordered.

(c) Personal expenditure relating to the proprietor's own pocket, domestic establishment, etc., is to be treated as drawings. It is not allowable as a business expense.

(d) All profits arising from the trade or profession are taxable, including casual earnings and rents receivable. Capital profits may be taxed under the Capital Gains regulations.

24.4 Keeping Up-to-Date on Tax Matters

Unfortunately tax changes occur every year and it is quite impossible for a book of this type to explain the tax system fully or keep its readers up-to-date about changes. There are special publications which cover this ground for the small business. Perhaps the best is *Taxation Simplified*. Subscribers to this publication receive a revised booklet within a few weeks of the Budget, and another later in the year when the Finance Act has been passed by Parliament. Thus the reader is kept aware of the latest changes in taxation and is provided with a mine of information about tax matters. The address of the publishers will be found in the Foreword at the front of this book.

Another useful publication is the 'Money Which' Tax Savings Guide, which is issued annually and has a great deal of useful information on such things as 'How to check an assessment'. 'Money Which' is obtainable from the Consumer Association at the address shown in the front of this book.

24.5 What Happens if you Delay your Tax Return

It is always instructive to spend a few hours in the public gallery of the bankruptcy court. You will soon discover that the Department of Inland Revenue is the chief creditor in many of the cases being heard, and that bankruptcy often results from a procedure which the Department adopts to deal with taxpayers whose returns are late in arrival, or whom they suspect of fraudulent practices.

Let us consider the owner of a small business, perhaps a grocer, who delays sending in his accounts because he is very busy and cannot find the time to complete them. The Inland Revenue authorities have the records of the entire nation to refer to, and consequently know that grocery businesses of this size and situation normally earn between £10 000 and £20 000. They will therefore send him an assessment, without any calculations at all, near the upper end of the scale. They do not expect him to pay it, but they do expect him to wake up and take an interest. If he pays it without a murmur they conclude that they guessed too low, and next year they will send him a much bigger assessment. If he pays that, an even bigger one will follow the next year.

It follows that one should always respond to such an assessment by writing a letter of apology and enclosing one's true profit figures. The inspector of taxes will accept your apology gracefully and establish your true tax assessment without delay. This is payable in two parts for sole traders and partnerships, on January 1st and July 1st of the year following. For companies it is payable as explained on page 83.

Suppose now that his book-keeping records reveal that our grocer is making a net profit of £8 400 per year. According to the statistics available the average business of this type earns much more, says £17 800 a year. Clearly there is something suspicious here, and the inspector of taxes will proceed to investigate the accounts rigorously. You may be called in to discuss the situation. Either the trader can produce some acceptable reason for his/her depressed profit, or he/she may admit that the records are not accurate. Refusal to admit any such thing means a confrontation is inevitable and the trader will be assessed at a much higher figure. If he/she wishes to appeal the trader is going to have to prove the case to the satisfaction of the Commissioners of Inland Revenue.

These examples illustrate that it is highly desirable *(a)* to keep an honest set of accounts in a regular way, week by week throughout the year, and *(b)* to complete and render one's tax returns promptly. Any disagreement should be settled by a visit to the tax office.

The inspector of taxes is always reasonable and always available. Very few tax problems arise in the small business which cannot be solved by keeping accounts systematically with the aid of a Simplex book, a copy of *Income Tax Simplified* and an occasional visit to the tax office.

24.6 Inheritance Tax

When death duties were replaced by Capital Transfer Tax in 1975 considerable apprehension was felt by the owners of small businesses about the new system of taxation. Some of the more worrying aspects were reduced by subsequent legislation and the whole scene is subject to almost annual review. It is also a rather complex and technical body of law which cannot possibly be dealt with fully in the present volume. This tax is now called Inheritance Tax.

As far as small businesses are concerned, from 26.10.1977 only 50% of the value will be charged to the tax when a business passes either by gift or at death. There is a lower limit for individuals of £128 000, so that at present (June 1990) with the 50% rule referred to above a trader whose business is transferred at death or during his/her lifetime would get exemption up to £256 000 in some cases. Once again the rules are complex and cannot be covered in a book of this sort. Inflation means that businesses might come into higher value brackets than £256 000 and consequently be caught by the tax.

It follows that businessmen/women with chargeable property around these figures would do well to look at **inheritance tax mitigation schemes.** These seek to keep the tax as low a level as possible, and to provide, through life assurance policies, sums which will become available in the event of death to meet the Inheritance Tax liability. The subject, like 'Pension Planning' (see below), is one where reliable advice from a consultant is invaluable. Such advice for those interested may be obtained from your local tax consultant, or from one such consultant whose address is given in the foreword of this book.

24.7 Pension Planning

In recent years the extension of earnings related pension schemes to all employees through the National Insurance Scheme has left the self-employed in an anomalous position in that they only qualify for the smaller 'State' pension. This unsatisfactory situation has been resolved by making it possible for self-employed people to provide adequate pensions for themselves if they choose to do so, the premiums payable being subject to tax relief at the highest rate paid by the applicant. If such pensions are provided for controlling directors of private limited companies the rate of relief is the same rate as Corporation Tax.

In order to obtain the tax free concessions the contributions have to be made through an approved body such as a Life Assurance Company. The tax advantages are as follows:

(a) Contributions to the plan are deductible from the earned income of the plan holder for tax purposes. They attract relief at the highest rate of tax paid.

(b) Contributions to such plans accumulate free of all U.K. taxes except Development Land Tax and even this tax is rarely incurred.

(c) Part of the annuity is permitted to be commuted into a tax-free lump on retirement (similar to many pension schemes for employees).

(d) Finally the annuity payable to the insured, or to his/her spouse or dependents, is treated as earned income when it is received.

(e) Death benefits payable to the estates of deceased pensions arising under a Pension Plan can be so arranged as to be free from Capital Transfer Tax.

Of particular interest here is the effect of compound interest on the size of the pension. Never was it truer to say that it pays to start building your pension while you are young. It is almost impossible to catch up later.

Chapter Twenty-five

The Simplex Advice Bureau— Problems Answered

25.1 The Simplex Advice Bureau

In order to help the proprietors of small businesses who have decided to use the Simplex System, George Vyner Ltd. operate an Advice Bureau. The aim is to help those who are having difficulty with their book-keeping—we cannot give financial advice or tax advice since this is the province of the accountant. In order to give financial advice in the United Kingdom it is necessary to register with the Office of Fair Trading. The Director General of Fair Trading has given his opinion that the type of services we are rendering does not call for registration but clearly we must avoid giving advice which should properly come from a professional, and registered, consultant.

Many of the points raised by our correspondents are of general interest, and we intend at each new revision of this book to add any matters whch have been found to give difficulty since the last revision of the book. They are not arranged in any particular order.

25.2 Cash Flow

The new edition of the Simplex D Account Book includes a Cash Flow Forecast. There are several aspects of cash flow which are of interest to the proprietors of small businesses. The term refers in general to the way in which liquid funds (money) move in and out of the business, and the need to keep control of it so that funds are always available to meet requirements. Stocking-up with goods to meet busy periods brings about heavy cash flows out of the business, while at times of heavy selling the buying function may be reduced to a minimum so that cash flows into the business are greater than outlays. Part of this inflow is the profits we are making, but whether these profits are available in cash form depends upon the uses to which the cash flows are put. If we have surplus cash available and decide to use it to purchase motor vehicles we cannot later complain if there are no funds to pay out as profits. It is wise to plan ahead with a Cash Forecast, using two columns for each month, a Budget Column and an 'Actual' Column. An example is shown in Fig. 25.1. The sub-headings under which receipts and payments are listed are linked very closely to the figures which become available in the Simplex system, and it is relatively easy to build up a forecast of cash flow for the month ahead. A full 12 months figures are available although only Month 1 and Month 2 are shown in Fig. 25.1.

Time lags have to be taken into account, especially on such matters as 'Debts Collected' and 'Payments for Business Stock'. It is usual to plan three months ahead, and roll the plan forward every month.

When the actual receipts and payments are made the figures can be inserted in the 'Actual' column. They can they be compared with the budget, and the difference accounted for. An excess payment for business stock might be explained by a favourable opportunity which arose due to the bankruptcy of another trader. It might have to be explained by higher prices, and the budgets in the month ahead might need to be adjusted, and a check made on selling prices to ensure that these higher costs were passed on to consumers wherever possible.

Wherever possible **cash flow smoothing** should be carried out. This means that where we have payments which can be moved to another part of the year when funds are readily available we should do so. Thus annual payments for car tax, car insurance, other types of insurance, pension fund payments etc., can be moved around by agreement with the organisation concerned. To move your motor vehicle insurance to a different part of the year only requires a letter to the insurance company and agreement on an interim payment to provide cover for the few months before the annual payment is paid again on the rearranged date. Similarly new capital expenditure can be put off until the best time for payment.

Notes for completing the cashflow forecast are given in the account book itself and read as follows:

Completing your Cashflow Forecast

A Cashflow Forecast helps you anticipate the amount of cash you will have available at any one time. If you are going to be short of cash (a deficit) you can make arrangements in advance for an overdraft or a loan. If you are going to have a surplus you can make plans to invest, or to buy some asset you know you will need.

The stages in a Cashflow Forecast are as follows:

Budget Figures

1. Whichever month you start to keep your forecast enter its name in the space provided at the top of the month 1 column.

2. Fill in your total balance in hand (cash and bank) at the beginning of the month in line 1.

3. Fill in your 'Receipts' section (lines 2-6) with the money you *hope to take* this month and the debts you *hope to collect this month*. Eg. Invoices issued in January may not be payable until March.

4. The total estimated receipts (line 7) added to line 1 gives the estimated total cash available (line 8).

5. Now fill in the payments you expect to make for the month on lines 9-26. You can move across the page to enter a payment you know to be due in one of the months ahead as soon as you know how much it is (eg. a monthly HP payment could be entered right across the page).

6. When totalled these give the total expected payments to other businesses.

CASHFLOW FORECAST		EXAMPLE JANUARY		MONTH 1		MONTH 2	
		Budget	Actual	Budget	Actual	Budget	Actual
1	Balance in hand (Cash and Bank)	1580	1190				
	RECEIPTS						
2	Daily Takings for month	9625	8925				
3	Debts collected	490	445				
4	Other receipts	180	180				
5	Loans arranged	–					
6	Extra capital contributed	–					
7	Total Receipts (add lines 2 to 6)	10295	9550				
8	Total Cash available (add lines 1 + 7)	11875	10740				
	PAYMENTS						
9	Business stock	6260	6720				
10	Rent & Rates	580	580				
11	Light & Heat	–	–				
12	Carriage & Postages	140	145				
13	Paper	20	20				
14	Motor Expenses	130	137				
15	Travelling	–	62				
16	Cleaning	100	100				
17	Printing & Stationery	55	58				
18	Repairs & Renewals	–	–				
19	Insurance (Business)	100	130				
20	Advertising	60	60				
21	Telephone	–	–				
22	Wages (employees)	1200	1200				
23	Sundries	40	46				
24	Capital Items	240	1100				
25	Loans Repaid	–	–				
26	Other external payments	–	–				
27	Total External Payments (add lines 9 to 26)	8925	10358				
28	Drawings – Proprietor or Partner 1	400	400				
29	,, Partner 2	–					
30	,, Partner 3	–					
31	Total Payments (add lines 27 to 30)	9325	10758				
32	Balance carr. fwd. If line 8 > line 31, balance in Credit → If line 31 > line 8, balance in (Deficit) →	2550 (18)					

Note: The sign > means greater than.

Fig. 25.1 *A Cash flow Forecast*

7. Now enter any drawings and find the total expected payments (line 31).

8. Take line 31 from line 8 to find your estimated cash balance at the end of the month. It it is a deficit (31 bigger than 8) take 8 from 31 and put a bracket round the figure to indicate a negative balance. Now arrange an overdraft to carry you over the bad period.

9. Carry the estimated balance to the start of the new month.

Actual Figures

At the end of the month when you know the actual figures complete the 'actual' column to see how they compare.

Cashflow Smoothing

If at all possible, practice cashflow smoothing. If you have a month where you have a lot to pay out try to rearrange your payments to spread them more evenly. Eg. arrange to pay your rates evenly over the year to avoid a big payment in any one month.

25.3 Break-even Points

It is quite common to see references in business magazines to 'break-even' points, and business persons often write in to the Simplex Advice Bureau asking how they can tell when they have broken even. It is a long story really, but briefly we may say as follows:

(i) We break even when we have covered our total costs, and from that point on everything extra we receive is profit.

(ii) Total costs are made up of 'fixed costs' and 'variable costs'. To explain variable costs first, they are the costs incurred in making our product, and they are called 'variable' because they vary with output. So if I make pizzas with pizza pastry costing ten pence and other items costing 10 pence, and if the labour cost is 5 pence the variable costs of my pizzas are 25 pence each. So long as I sell them for more than 25 pence I shall make a profit on any particular pizza. Let us say I sell them for 50 pence. Then I have covered my variable costs, and have 25 pence left over. This 25 pence is called the 'contribution'.

(iii) To what does it contribute? The answer is it is a contribution towards covering my fixed costs (often called overheads), and once they are covered, and I have broken-even, they are profits of the business. Fixed costs must now be explained. They are the costs that have to be borne whatever the output of the business. Thus I need a factory whether I make 1 000 pizzas or 100 000 pizzas. I need a managing director, a lorry for distribution purposes etc., etc. These are all part of the 'fixed costs', which do not vary directly with output—though I might need a bigger lorry if output grows. Suppose my total fixed costs are £2 000 and I sell 1 pizza. I have a contribution of 25 pence towards my fixed costs and no profit. I shall need to sell 8 000 pizzas to cover my fixed costs, so 8 000 pizzas is my break-even point. After that I shall begin to make a profit.

This can best be followed by looking at the break-even chart in Fig. 25.2.

Dealing with a Loan

present considerable problems to businesses, from a book-keeping
of view, quite apart from the major problem of repaying them. Where a
of money is borrowed over a period of years, and repaid by equal
ents, the repayments in the first year are nearly all interest, and very
epayment of capital. As the years pass the amount of each repayment
interest falls, and the amount that is capital repaid rises.

gine a businessman who borrows £12 000 from a finance company at a
e of interest of 12 per cent per annum, over 7 years. This means that he
pay £12 000 + 84% (7 × 12%) of £12 000 = £22 080. If this is repaid in
thly instalments each instalment will be £262·86. The interest being
will be an expense of the business and deductible on the Profit and Loss
t. The capital repayment will not be deductible as an expense of the
s.

rouble is to know how much of the £262·86 is interest and how much is
being repaid. As with all loans in the early months it is nearly all interest
y little capital repayment. Later—in 6 years time—it will be very little
and nearly all capital. The difficulty arises from the difficulty of not
g the true rate of interest, since a flat rate of interest is usually only
alf the true rate. Fortunately it is now necessary for the finance
y to reveal the true rate of interest on the loan. Let us imagine that this
to be 24 per cent. We can now answer the question 'How much of the
th's instalment is interest'. The answer is

$$
\begin{aligned}
\text{st} &= \text{Original Loan} \times \text{True rate of interest} \div 100 \div 12 \\
&= £12\,000 \times 24 \div 100 \div 12 \\
&= £240 \text{ interest}
\end{aligned}
$$

ve to divide by twelve in the calculation because we only want the
r one month. So of the £262·86 repaid in the first month only £22·86
the other £240 is interest.

second month the amount of the actual capital still on loan is
£22·86 = £11 977·14. This month the interest will be:

$$
\begin{aligned}
&£11\,977\cdot14 \times 24 \div 100 \div 12 \\
&= £239.54
\end{aligned}
$$

re the capital repaid $= £262\cdot86 - £239\cdot54$
$= £23.32$

nth when this calculation has been done you should take the
ount to a special column headed 'Interest' in the Summary of
r expenses.

d of the year there will be over £2 000 to deduct from the profits for
on the loan.

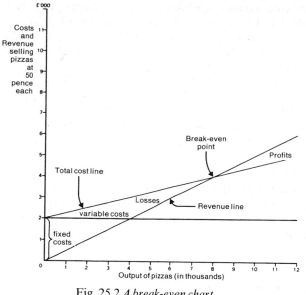

Fig. 25.2 *A break-even chart*

Notes: (i) As the output of pizzas rise from 0-12 000 the variable costs increase
by 25 pence per pizza. As these are incurred over and above the fixed costs we
see the total cost line sloping up towards the £5 000 (£2 000 fixed and £3 000
variable).

(ii) At the same time revenue from the sale of pizzas is rising; £1 000 from
2 000 pizzas, £2 000 from 4 000 pizzas etc.

(iii) Break-even point is at £4 000, where the sale of 8 000 pizzas brings in
£4 000, which exactly covers £2 000 fixed costs and £2 000 variable costs.

(iv) After that point we have profits being made and at 12 000 pizzas we get
profits of £1 000, since revenues are £6 000 and costs £5 000.

25.4 Improving Premises—the Capitalisation of a Revenue Expense

Many small businesses do repair jobs to their own premises, and these are
legitimate expenses of the business and can be deducted from the profits at the
end of year. However, if you finish up by *improving* the premises, or the fixtures
and fittings you have; you cannot count these as business expenses which are
deductible from the profits—you have to take the extra value on as capital
assets of the business (and you may then be entitled to some capital allowance
from the tax inspector).

Let us consider two cases.

(a) You do some repairs, using materials from your ordinary business
stock, and paying your workers some wages. The repairs are just repairs, not
improvements. In this case you need not make any special entries in the

books—all the entries are done already. The materials you used are entered in the Payments for Business Stock and as you cannot sell them now (having used them) this loss will be suffered at the end of the year. The wages you paid will be entered in the wages section of your Payments Other than for Stock and so they need not be entered again. The work done is not a VAT output, so no invoice needs to be issued and no VAT has to be recorded. The business expense has been recorded as extra purchases and extra wages and could be left to go through the books under those headings. If you really want to do so at the end of the year you could reduce the Purchases by the amount of materials used, and reduce the wages by the amount paid to the workers who did the work, and put these amounts in instead as Repairs and Renewals.

(b) In the second case the work done and the materials used result in an improvement to the value of the property. Here you will have to do what is called **'capitalising a revenue expense'**. This means you must make up your mind how much value has been added to the premises as a result of the work. Let us suppose you use £100 materials and £200 labour and it results in a £500 increase in value. You have therefore made a bit of profit on yourself (or really the workers you employ).

The book-keeping entries are as follows:

(a) Deduct £100 from materials—you will have to do this in the Summary of Payments for Business Stock. Make a small entry *in red ink* on the summary—£100 business improvements.

(b) Deduct £200 from wages—you will need to do this in the Summary of Expenses for year—make a small red ink entry in the wages column—£200 business improvements.

(c) The £200 profit presents a little problem. It could be argued that it is not a revenue profit but a capital profit, since it is not a profit in the ordinary way of business. If you decide to treat it as a capital profit do not enter it at the end of the year as a 'miscellaneous receipt' in the Profit and Loss Account (where it will be taxable) but put it in the 'Extra capital contributed' as a capital profit. Tell the Inland Revenue what you have done and hope they will treat you kindly.

(d) Now you only have to enter in the Summary of Capital Expenses in the year £500 as 'Business Improvements £500'. Don't forget to tell the Inland Revenue about this as it will entitle you to a capital allowance.

(e) This is not a VAT output, so no VAT entries are required.

The result is that on one side of the Balance Sheet we have an increase in the value of the premises of £500. On the Capital Account we have an increase of £200—the capital profit and an increase in the net profit of £300 (because the expenses have been reduced in the Trading Account (Purchases £100 less) and in the Profit and Loss Account (Wages £200 less). These expenses have been capitalised.

25.5 Thefts and Burglaries

Thefts and burglaries present a variety of problems to traders, and some of them are raised in this section.

Theft of Stock: Theft of stock by shoplifters and by giving goods to friends—call for action with the police, records are needed. The reason is that the stock losses a for the final accounts of the business when we count the items are not there). We have a smaller stock than we sh the cost of stock sold and lowers the profits. We do no stolen stock, because if we did that we would be taking losses are taken into account when we count the stock.

Theft of Cash: If cash is stolen from the tills it d because it means you are left with a 'Difference on the week. The Simplex Weekly Page on Page 10 shows tha books' differs from 'Cash in hand—as counted' it give Books'. If some sort of difference appears regularly th poor view of it and will almost certainly take the v drawings, and will expect you to treat this as drawing This might seem a bit unfair, but it is up to you to keep theft if it is occurring. You cannot just pretend customers change—staff training is also your respo who are stealing from you get the police in and frigh you can pin down a member of staff charge them admission of the amount embezzled over the past n evidence of a loss explaining a 'difference on book: the end of the year.

Burglaries and Insurance Claims: Burglaries—a fires and floods—require the preparation of inst adopted is to establish what is known and hence amount of the loss. We can usually establish (a) th the financial period and (b) the purchases duri usually calculate the sales during the period. Whe cost price by removing the profit margin we only left (or value it in the case of a fire or flood). Th found by the following formula. Some imaginary

Stock at start—say
Add Purchases during the period

Deduct Sales at cost price

Stock that should be left
Stock actually left

Amount of claim

We may need to add any expenses (such as

Loan point sum instal little that is

Ima flat ra must r 84 mo repaid accoun busines

The capital and ver interest knowin about h compan is stated first mor

Intere

We ha interest f is capital

In the £12 000—

Interest

Therefo

Each m interest an Payments f

By the er interest pai

Recording the loan and the interest

The Simplex D book now includes a special summary at the back for loans made available and their repayments.

The method of recording money borrowed is quite simple. Using the example posed above of a loan from a Finance Co. of £12 000, with interest charged at 12% over 7 years. Immediately we get the Finance Co.'s cheque for £12 000 to pay into our bank account we also become a debtor to the Finance Co. for £22 080, and our standing order for £262·86 will proceed to operate against us each month (and we shall find the payment on our Bank Statement each month). The entries are as follows:

(a) *At the time the loan is arranged*

  (i) Enter the £12 000 as an 'Other Receipt' and put it also in the 'Paid to Bank Section' on the weekly page.

  (ii) Carry the £12 000 to the Loan Summary as shown in Fig. 25.3.

  (iii) Also enter the interest charged £10 080 (making the full debt to the Finance Co. £22 080) on the summary as shown. This £10 080 is a legitimate business expense and should be recorded in the Summary of Expenses using one of the spare columns. However, we shall not be able to charge it all a loss at the end of the financial year—we shall have to do an adjustment to charge only the interest for this year.

  (iv) We haven't imagined an insurance premium for this loan, but if it was insured with a 'one-off' premium this would also be recorded and would again be a legitimate expense of the business.

(b) *At the time a monthly repayment is found on the bank statement*

  (i) Record the standing order on the weekly bank report to recognise that the money has gone out of the Bank Account.

  (ii) Carry the repayment to the Loan Summary as shown in Fig. 25.3. These payments are not deductible business expenses. They are repayments of interest due and the original sum borrowed, but the interest has been already recorded in the Summary of Expenses, and the repayment of the loan borrowed will not have any book-keeping entry until we get to the Balance Sheet—when the sum owing to the Helpful Finance Co. will have been reduced.

(c) *At the end of the financial year*

  (i) At this point, by doing 12 calculations like the one shown above we shall find how much of the 12 monthly payments was interest and how much was repayment of the principal (the sum borrowed).

  (ii) The amount of the interest will be entered in the Profit and Loss Account and the balance as yet unclaimed (i.e. the difference between £10 080 and the year's interest) will be carried to the Balance Sheet as a 'payment in advance.'

25.7 Investments

If a trader buys investments they are frequently part of his/her private transactions and not part of the business activities at all. There are however two reasons why it is sometimes advisable to buy investments for the business.

SUMMARY OF LOAN/MORTGAGE REPAYMENTS

LOAN FROM: **HELPFUL FINANCE CO.**

MORTGAGE FROM:

DATE		MORTGAGE		LOAN	
1ST JAN 19..	TOTAL AMOUNT BORROWED			12,000	00
	INTEREST CHARGED			10,080	00
	INSURANCE PREMIUM CHARGED			—	—

DATE	REPAYMENTS	MORTGAGE		LOAN	
28 JAN 19..	REPAYMENT			262	86
28 FEB 19..	"			262	86
	ETC. ETC.				

Fig. 25.3 *Recording a loan and its Repayments*

These are:

(i) *As a Sinking Fund.* Suppose we depreciate machinery each year by 10 per cent. This reduces the value of the machinery on the books, and also reduces the profits made, so that the owner does not take out more from the business than he/she has really earned. An amount of assets—possibly in money form—is left in the business as a result and it gives the appearance that plenty of money is available. We should really put this money in a safe place so that one fine day, when we need new machinery, it will be available from a source outside the business. We could put it in a deposit account, or in a Building Society, or we could buy investments. Any interest or dividends earned should also be invested. If we do not do this the surplus money may be spent on unnecessary assets—plush furniture for example. Even worse, someone might think he should have a wage increase out of it. If we do not create this sinking fund, to store the money for our new machinery, we shall face problems in the future and may go out of business altogether.

(ii) *To earn income from surplus funds.* Suppose that for some years trade has been brisk, we have ploughed back profits into extra stock etc. and earned good profits from the turnover. A slight 'sneeze' in the economy suggests we cut back on stocks and consolidate our position for a while. Reduced stocks means spare cash is available. We shall now make less profits for turnover is down. The spare cash will not earn money. As a result our total profitability must decline. If this cash is promptly invested as it becomes available instead of merely raising our bank balances we shall get at least some return on it and thus avoid too large a decline in our **Return on Capital Invested.**

25.8 Insurance Claims

When for some reason we suffer a loss, against which we have insured, and make a genuine claim which is conceded by the insurer, book-keeping problems arise. The sum paid as compensation will be an 'Other Receipt' and go into the Daily Page in the 'Other Receipts' section. The problem is to decide how this loss, and the compensation, should be treated in the books. Let us take one or two examples:

(i) *Losses of Business Stock.* Imagine that business stock valued at £500 has been damaged in a fire, and the claim of £500 is paid. The money coming in for the claim will be an 'Other Receipt' as explained above. How shall we write off the damaged stock. The answer is that we don't need to write it off at all. Just put the ashes in the dustbin and forget them. The reason why no action needs to be taken is that Stock is only taken at the end of the year when we do the stock-taking. When we come to 'take stock' at the end of the year, the missing stock will not be there to count, and so the loss will be taken at this point. We cannot count what is not there, and so our Closing Stock figure will be £500 short.

(ii) *Losses of Fixtures and Fittings.* In this case we must make a note of the decline in value due to the fire. The £500 compensation in the Bank account will off-set the reduced Balance Sheet value of the fittings. Write on the

Summary of Capital Expenses 'less losses due to fire £500'. Of course if we spend the money on buying new fittings this will be a Capital Item in the 'Payments other than for Stock' section of the weekly page, and the Fixtures will be increased again by this new Capital Expenditure.

25.9 Searching Questions when Buying a Business

The purchase of a business is one of the most important decisions in a trader's life and it should not be entered into lightly. It may be advisable to take legal advice about it, and to call in a local valuer who will appraise the business, assess the Balance Sheet and accounts of the previous owner and advise about any valuation to be placed on goodwill. It is false economy to save money on a valuer's fee if you do not have sufficient expertise yourself. Never accept things at their face value, and ask plenty of searching questions about the property, the stock, the neighbourhood, the clientèle etc. The law says "Let the buyer beware". Thus if you ask the seller to state in writing that the building is free from woodworm, deliberate failure to declare the worm-eaten nature of the premises constitutes a fraudulent mis-representation, which is actionable. If you don't even ask such a question you have only yourself to blame.

When purchasing a business take the Balance Sheet of the previous owner and consider carefully the assets shown. Using the Balance Sheet in Figure 21.6 as an example (see page 157) the question might be asked 'Are the premises worth £42 000?' If not, why not? A long list of points made in a letter to the seller drawing attention to the state of the roof, the re-pointing necessary, the poor state of the shop-front, the antiquated plumbing, etc., etc., is likely to bring him into a reasonable state of mind about the true value of the property and may save you thousands of pounds. Similarly the fixtures, the motor vehicles (if they are being taken over), the Stock and the Debtors should be closely appraised.

25.10 Some problems arising from the use of Credit Cards, both by traders and customers

(a) *Sales on credit cards.* The weekly page has a special column for recording credit card sales, but note that as far as the till is concerned cash, cheques and credit card vouchers are all regarded as cash for the purpose of counting the contents of the till at the end of the day to work out the 'gross daily takings'.

The entries are as follows:

(i) The actual voucher issued when goods are sold is exactly like a cheque, and should be treated similarly on the Simplex receipts section. Enter the total for credit card vouchers in the column provided and pay them into the bank in the usual way. The full value of these vouchers will be credited to your bank account in about three days (the same time as it takes to clear a cheque).

(ii) Once a month you will receive a statement from the Barclaycard office (or other credit card company) notifying you of the service charge payable, which will be deducted from your account by the direct debit system. You should enter this on one of the lines in your 'Payments other than for Stock' section, and carry it to a column in the Summary of Payments for Expenses. At the end of the year the total of this column will be deducted from the profits in the Profit and Loss Account.

(b) *American Express Vouchers*

American Express use a different system from Barclaycard, Trustcard and Access. They send the trader who has paid in vouchers a cheque for the net value of the vouchers (ie the value of the vouchers less charges). VAT on the original sales is therefore included in the value of the cheque.

It is best not to enter the value of the vouchers at all until you get the credit notification back from AMEX. You then make the following entries.

(i) Enter the *full value of the vouchers* in the Daily Takings (cheques) column, and the words AMEX takings in the particulars column.

(ii) Enter the *full value of the vouchers* in the Paid to Bank column (although you do not have a cheque for that amount, since the cheque you have received is only the net value).

(iii) Enter the AMEX charges in the Payments Other than for Stock section as 'AMEX' commission, in the cheques column. The result is that the sum paid to bank less the commission is the same as the net value of the cheque that has actually reached the bank.

(c) *Items purchased on a business credit card*

Where a business person buys items for business use on Access or Barclaycard a problem arises since the actual payment does not occur until the account is rendered by the Head Office of Access or Barclaycard. You will find the following rules helpful:

(i) When you make a Barclaycard purchase you are given the customer's copy of the slip. (If you eventually register for VAT you may need to ask for a VAT invoice as well—or at least a till receipt which is recognised as valid for VAT purposes). Return to your Simplex D Book and enter this purchase in one of the columns (either Purchases for Business Stock) or Purchases other than for Stock. However, since the money has not gone out yet put brackets round it. i.e. (£45·60) and do not add it in to your total cash payments for that week.

(ii) When you carry the entries to the summaries at the back of the book enter these ones as if they had actually been paid, but put some little sign against it so that you know it has not been paid—the best sign is CR to let you know it is on credit really. This might look like this.

Sundries
CR 45·60

(iii) When you actually receive your monthly account go through it together with your Simplex D Book and tick up the letters CR against all these which are listed on the statement. Thus if the £45·60 shown above was entered on the statement you would tick up the CR on the summary page.

(iv) You may also find some interest entered on the statement. If your card is purely for business use, enter the amount of this interest in the weekly page for the current week, and put brackets round it:

Barclaycard interest (1·62)

When you enter that in the summary page put CR by it but tick it up right away because it is on the statement.

(v) Now you only have to enter the payment you are making on the day you actually make it. This will be a week or two later no doubt. Whether you pay only a part of it or the full amount enter it in the 'Payments other than for Stock' column. This item will not have brackets round it and will be added in to your cash or bank total—because of course it is money going out—but you will not post it to any summary because it has already been entered in little bits in the summary pages as you entered the original slips.

(d) *Purchases on a personal Credit Card*
Many small traders find it convenient to buy items, both capital assets and purchases of business stock, using their personal Barclaycard or other credit card. It presents a little problem, because the business gets the benefit at once but the repayment is made later on. A good solution to this problem is to treat the purchase as a loan made by the proprietor to the business. Suppose we spend £63 on the purchase of business stock and pay on our personal credit card.

(i) Enter the amount of the purchase (£63) in the 'Other Receipts' as 'Loan from proprietor.' Carry this amount to the Loan Summary at the back of the book.

(ii) Enter the amount paid out in 'Payments for Business Stock' as a payment out, in cash. This means that the loan is immediately spent in full.

(iii) When you decide to repay something off the card if the business is in funds enough to do so take the amount (say £25) and enter the payment in the 'Payments other than for stock' section on one of the spare lines (Repayment of loan) and carry it to the loan summary as a repayment. You can then use the £25 to pay off your card, and this will be a purely private transaction and not part of the Simplex D book-keeping.

25.11 Saving Money in a Building Society

Many traders find it helpful to save money in a Building Society rather than a bank. This presents no problem, but we need to consider whether the Deposit Account being used is a 'business only' account or the proprietor's personal account. It is really better to have a separate account for business purposes only, where such items as VAT Output Tax waiting to be paid over to Customs and Excise, or Income Tax waiting to be paid on 1 January or 1 July can be collected. The entries are:
Where the Account is a 'business only' account
(a) Depositing money: enter the item on one of the spare lines in the 'Payments other than for Stock' section—writing 'Transfer to Building Society' in the Nature of Payments column. If you are depositing cash put it in the cash column, if you are making the deposit by cheque enter it in the Bank column. Carry the figure to the Movements in and out of Deposit Account at the back of the book.

(b) Reclaiming Money from the Deposit Account: Withdraw the money from the Deposit Account, and enter it in 'Other receipts', writing 'Withdrawal from Deposit Account' in the 'Particulars' column. Carry this into the Paid to Bank section and pay it in—so that you can write a cheque for the VAT office, Inland Revenue etc. Carry the amount also to the 'Withdrawals' side of the Deposit Account Summary.

(c) Interest earned: Enter this in 'Other Receipts' when you are notified of it, and carry it to the Summary of Other Receipts as a Miscellaneous Receipt—it is a profit of the business. You must also enter the amount as in (a) above as if you were depositing it in cash, to remove the cash received and carry it into the Deposit Account Summary as a further deposit, to record it on your books.

Where the Account is a personal account of the Proprietor

(a) Depositing Money Enter the item as in (a) above, and carry it to the 'Movements in and out of Deposit Account' summary at the back of the book. This will keep a record of how much of the firm's money is in the Deposit Account.

(b) Withdrawing Money. Enter the sum withdrawn as before in 'Other Receipts' and pay it into the bank. Carry the amount to the Deposit Account Summary as before, on the 'Withdrawals' side.

(c) Interest earned. Since some interest will be business interest you must estimate roughly how much this is and enter it as explained in (c) above.

25.12 Receiving money direct to your Bank Account via BACS (the Bankers' Automated Clearing Service)

More and more companies and official bodies are finding it convenient to settle their debts via BACS, the Bankers' Automated Clearing Service. This means that you find the money they have paid you appearing as a credit entry on your Bank Statement when it arrives each month. This is no problem with the Simplex System, indeed it is a very safe way of receiving money, but you do have to make special entries for it. We can best illustrate this by an example. Suppose Opulent Ltd decide to pay you £526 for goods supplied. You find the BACS entry on your statement saying "Opulent Ltd £526" in the credit column and added to your balance in the 'balance' column.

You now:

(a) Enter the £526 in the current week (the week the Bank Statement arrived) in the "By Cheque" column (Col 2) in the Receipts section. It is best to use the line for Sunday if there are no entries on that line. The £526 will then be included in the total of the cheques column and will count as 'takings' and go to the Summary of Takings at the back of the book.

However, if you have already included the £526 in takings at the time you sent the invoice out to Opulent Ltd you would be counting it in the takings twice if you put it in Column 2. In that case put it in Col 4 (Other Receipts) on the Sunday line and it will not be included in your 'takings' summary a second time.

(b) You now enter the £526 in the Paid to Bank summary (because it has already reached the bank) use the Sunday line again, in the cheques column and the total column.

This records the BACS entry fully, but you still have to go to your Debtors Record, whatever it is and make a note that Opulent Ltd have paid. If you keep your copy invoices in a file until paid, remove the copy invoice, mark it paid and refile it in the 'Paid' file. If you use the old 'butcher's book' method (see Fig. 5.3) draw a line through Opulent Ltd's debt to show it is settled.

That concludes the entries necessary.

Note: since the use of BACS is increasing it is possible that you might receive payments that are not for goods or services supplied. Thus you might receive Tax Refunds, Rents or other sums like insurance claims. This makes no difference to the entries except that instead of going in col 2 as Daily Takings cheques, they would go in Col 4 as Other Receipts.

25.13 Repaying a loan at a 'settlement' figure

Many traders who have joined the Enterprise Allowance Scheme have been forced to borrow £1,000 (£2,000 for a partnership) to qualify for the scheme. Once established, if they do not really need the money they feel uncertain how to pay it back. It is very simple. You have the money in your Bank Account and the loan appears in the Loan Summary as one of your liabilities. Possibly interest may have been added already, it depends from whom you borrowed the money. The procedure is:

(a) Ask the lender for a settlement figure. This will usually be less than the outstanding balance if interest has been added already. It will usually be for the amount of the loan, plus interest to date, plus a charge for the lender's trouble and disappointment in having to look for another customer.

(b) Pay the amount by cheque, writing it on one of the spare lines in the current week's 'Payments other than for Stock' section.

(c) Carry this entry to the Loan Summary in the repayments section. This may clear the loan.

(d) If the loan is not cleared it must be because interest has been added to the loan originally (and carried by you to the Summary of Expenses as one of the expenses of the business). They have not asked you to pay the full interest, but have given you a rebate. Write 'Rebate of £......' in the repayments section to clear the loan, and carry this *as a red ink entry* to the Summary of Expenses to reduce the expenses. Write in red ink 'Rebate £......'. When you add up the column at the end of the quarter deduct this figure. You have now repaid the loan and cleared it from your books.

Answers to Exercises

Chapters Two and Three
Numerical answers not required.

Chapter Four
1. Capital £19 608·50. Total of Balance Sheet £46 891·00.
2. Capital £13 017·30. Total of Balance Sheet £17 054·80.
3. Capital £37 720·70. Total of Balance Sheet £81 147·20.
4. Goodwill valued at £1 210. Fixed assets £84 750, current assets £15 250. Capital £100 000.
5. Goodwill valued at £4 250. Fixed assets £77 750; current assets £22 250. Balance Sheet totals £100 000. Capital £70 000. Long-term liabilities £30 000.

Chapter Five
1. Total Takings; cash £1 777·35; cheques £73·65; credit card vouchers £1 038·99; Other Receipts £500; Paid to Bank cash £950; cheques £573·65; credit card vouchers £499·22; toal £2 022·87.
2. Total Takings; cash £1 675·90; cheques £100·00; credit card vouchers £1 267·57; Other Receipts £52·00; Paid to Bank cash £900·00; cheques £100·00. Credit vouchers £1 029·32; total £2 029.32.
3. Total Takings; cash £2 125·25; cheques £317·09; credit card vouchers £1 839·83; Other Receipts £18·25; Paid to Bank cash £1 200, cheques £317·09; credit card vouchers £1 441·57; total £2 958·66.
4. Takings; cash £28·50; cheques £544·00; Other Receipts £57·00; Paid to bank £586·50.

Chapter Six
1. Total payments: cash £31·25, cheques £202·24.
2. Total payments: cash £67·05, cheques £41·05.
3. Total payments: cash £12·81, cheques £291·99.
4. Total payments: cash £51·05, cheques £51·45.

Chapter Seven
1. Total payments: cash £158·90, cheques £138·25.
2. Total payments: cash £203·44, cheques £289·16.
3. Total payments: cash £48·74, cheques £1 099·10.

Chapter Eight
1. Closing Balance in Bank £1 880·01.
2. Closing Balance in Bank £3 207·56.
3. Closing Balance in Bank £3 213·97.
4. Closing Cash Balance £30·27.
5. Closing Cash Balance £53·86. Difference = + £5.
6. Closing Cash Balance £7·00. Difference = − 50 pence.

Chapter Nine
No exercises in this chapter.

Chapter Ten

1. Books of R. Johnson: Daily takings; Cash £1 525·18; cheques £855·96; credit cards £712·60; Bank balance £4 048·42; Cash balance £1 470·21; Difference on books £0·00.
2. Books of Mary Shaw: Daily takings; Cash £2 212·40; cheques £599·49; credit cards £1 565·76; Bank balance £5 318·53; Cash balance £2 457·89; Difference on books − £20·00.

Chapter Eleven

1. Books of R. Coppersmith: Weekly takings £5 203·50; Bank balance £7 037 87; Cash balance £99·45; Difference on books − £5.40.
2. Books of Anne Overton: Weekly takings £6 042·19; Bank balance £5 625·54; Cash balance £437·09; Difference on books £0·00.

Chapter Twelve

1. Books of A. Upson: Daily takings £4 148·90; Bank balance £5 874·36; Cash balance £1 513·78; Difference on books − £5·50.
2. Books of M. Grainger: Daily takings £1 813·21; Bank balance £3 033·91; Cash balance £582·45; Difference on books + £5.

Chapter Thirteen

1. Books of M. Lucas: Daily takings £954·15; Bank balance − £62·27; Cash balance £517·77; Difference on books − £10.
2. Books of R. Tobermory: Daily takings £595·00; Bank balance £1 221·36; Cash Balance £122·50; Difference on books − £1·50.

Chapter Fourteen

1. Books of M. Reagan: Daily takings £1 791·00; Bank balance £5 542·73; Cash balance £377·20; Difference on books £0·00.
2. Books of Pat Sterling: Daily takings £1 288·76; Bank balance £2 173·01; Cash balance £380·95; Difference on books − £10.

Chapter Fifteen

No exercises in this unit.

Chapter Sixteen

The exercises in this unit are self correcting, since the Bank Reconciliation Statement has to come out to the figure given in the exercise.

Chapter Seventeen

1. Net Wages A = £218·68; B = £201·96; C = £156·19.
2. Net Wages G = £217·59; H = £178·18; J = £134·14.
3. Net Wages P = £187·73; Q = £221·27; R = £180·53.

Chapters Eighteen, Nineteen and Twenty

No exercises in these units.

Chapter Twenty-one

1. Books of Tom Price: Gross Profit £16 500·00; Net Profit £9 713·50; Balance Sheet totals £15 994·50.
2. Books of Brian Wood: Gross Profit £11 900·00; Net Profit £5 122·50; Balance Sheet totals £16 260·85.

3. Books of A. Fashionable: Gross Profit £15 425·00; Net Profit £4 216·25; Balance Sheet totals £26 436·87.
4. Books of Julia Browne: Gross Profit £18 955·00; Net Profit £5 451·45; Balance Sheet totals £26 234·40.

Chapter Twenty-two

Section 22.2

1. Books of P. Hawksmoor: Prime Costs £91 382; Cost of Manufactured Goods £128 660; Gross Profit £216 321.
2. Books of T. Jones: Prime Costs £181 751·00; Cost of Manufactured Goods £256 152·50; Gross Profit £99 447·25.

Section 22.5

1. Books of Smith & Jones: Current Accounts, Smith £3 200, Jones £1 400; Balance Sheet totals £24 085·50.
2. Books of Brewer & Stillman: Current Accounts, Brewer £1 450·00, Stillman £100·00; Balance Sheet totals £25 575·75.

Section 22.8

1. Books of A. Limited Co.: Balance on Appropriation Account £13 670; Total of Revenue Reserves £57 170; Ordinary Shareholders' Equity £157 170; Balance Sheet totals £237 170.
2. Books of Robespierre Ltd.: Balance on Appropriation Account £8 145; Total of Revenue Reserves £32 545; Ordinary Shareholders' Equity £114 545; Balance Sheet totals £159 639.

Chapter Twenty-three

1. Net Profits *(a)* £4 800 *(b)* £8 400 *(c)* £5 250 *(d)* £7 000; Gross Profit Percentages *(a)* 35·7% *(b)* 45·3% *(c)* 32·7% *(d)* 27·9%; Net Profit Percentages *(a)* 11·4% *(b)* 22·1% *(c)* 20·2% *(d)* 10·3%.
2. Net Profits *(a)* £2 500 *(b)* £1 950 *(c)* £3 600 *(d)* £3 000 *(e)* £3 400; Gross Profit Percentages *(a)* 48·5% *(b)* 49·4% *(c)* 65·3% *(d)* 73·8% *(e)* 35·8%; Net Profit Percentages *(a)* 30·3% *(b)* 25·3% *(c)* 37·9% *(d)* 46·2% *(e)* 25·7%.
3. Average Stock Smith £2 500, Jones £5 000; Gross Profit, Smith £5 000, Jones £5 000; Sales Figure Smith £55 000, Jones £30 000; Gross Profit Percentages Smith 9·1%, Jones 16·7%; Net Profit Percentages Smith 5·7%, Jones 8·8%.
4. Average Stock Giles £6 000, Slocum £7 500; Gross Profit Giles £9 000, Slocum £15 000; Sales Giles £99 000, Slocum £90 000; Gross Profit Percentage Giles 9·1%, Slocum 16·7%; Net Profit Percentage Giles 5·6%, Slocum 11·6%.
5. Capital owned £43 700; Capital employed £48 700; Working capital £5 700; Liquid capital £1 104; Acid-test ratio = ·65:1; Return on Capital Invested = 52·8%.
6. Capital owned £60 500; Capital employed = £75 500; Working capital £1 650; Liquid capital = − £6 214, Acid test ratio is ·53:1 (Montgomery is in a very illiquid position indeed). Return on Capital Invested = 39·9%.

Chapters Twenty-four and Twenty-five

No exercises in these units.

Index